The Schutzhund Training Manual

The Schutzhund Training Manual

Felix Ho

Photography: Felix Ho, Maggie Ho, Natalie Hill

Matador
9 Priory Business Park,
Wistow Road, Kibworth Beauchamp,
Leicestershire. LE8 0RX
Tel: 0116 279 2299
Email: books@troubador.co.uk
Web: www.troubador.co.uk/matador
Twitter: @matadorbooks

ISBN 978 1788032 513

British Library Cataloguing in Publication Data.
A catalogue record for this book is available from the British Library.

Printed by CPI Ltd, Croyden, UK
Typeset in 11pt Gill Sans (TT) by Troubador Publishing Ltd, Leicester, UK

Matador is an imprint of Troubador Publishing Ltd

*I would like to dedicate this book to my mom, my dad,
and my mentor Julien Steenbeke. This book wouldn't exist without you.*

Foreword
FCI IPO World Championship Judge Mr José Buggenhout, Belgium (Translated from French)

Felix,

First I would like to thank you for entrusting me to write the foreword of your book. I feel very honoured.

I've known Felix for over ten years. I remember we first met in a Malinois breeding kennel. At that time Felix was doing his apprenticeship there. His bitch Eclipse and my dog Esmot were both bred by the Duvetorre kennel. We would often see each other in various competitions and training occasions. I can confirm that Felix is a well-known and successful dog sport competitor.

Because I'm an IPO judge, I've judged Felix in several trials. Without a doubt, he's a competitor with sportsmanship, who respects our sports. At the same time he's a serious competitor.

With his talent and hard work, Felix rose to be a well-known sportsman shortly after his immigration to Belgium. There's no doubt he's a dog handler with finesse. He studied under many top European trainers, and then combined their best systems to develop his own style of training.

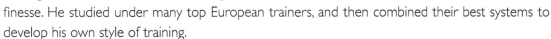

I would like to congratulate Felix. He has put his advanced training systems into a book, demonstrating a modern way for the training of working dog. He explains the Schutzhund program from its beginning, its original function, the introduction of IPO (RCI in French) in the 1950s, European cups, and today's world championships. I started my IPO career in June 1976. Later on I completed my judging certification. As a judge for nearly thirty years, I feel honoured to have been invited to judge ten IPO, FH, and Search and Rescue world championships. Through these years, I've witnessed the evolution in working dog sports.

Several decades ago, working dog competitions were actually trials for practical working dogs. Before my retirement, I was an officer in the Belgian Gendarmerie. My first two sporting trials were with my patrol dogs at that time. This situation is quite rare nowadays. Felix understands the development and changes in working dog sports over the years. He's developed a series of sophisticated systems to train working dogs for the twenty-first century. He spent several hours explaining to me about the contents in his book, so I could understand his work and his intention for this project.

This book focuses on the working abilities, keeping, and training of IPO dogs. It thoroughly explains puppy selection, genetics, behaviour, foundational education, training techniques of each IPO exercise, classical conditioning, operant conditioning, positive reinforcement, negative reinforcement, and the advantages and disadvantages of each training system.

The best dogs are dogs that make their owners happy, and this always goes together with proper training. I strongly believe this book can thoroughly teach you the most sophisticated training systems for competitive working dogs, because this is a text book for our sport. I hope that readers will learn a lot from this manual.

Felix, once again congratulations!
José Buggenhout
FCI IPO World Championship Judge, Belgium

Original Foreword in French

Félix,

En premier je voudrais te remercier pour l'honneur et la confiance que tu m'accordes en me demandant d'écrire ces quelques lignes d'introduction de ton manuel.

Je connais Félix depuis plus de dix ans! En fait, si ma mémoire est bonne, je l'ai rencontré pour la première fois chez un éleveur de malinois où il était stagiaire. Sa chienne de berger belge malinois et mon chien Esmot sont tous deux issus du même élevage "van de Duvetorre". Donc nous nous sommes souvent vus sur les terrains d'entraînement et de concours! Je peux vous confirmer que Félix est un fameux concurrent à vaincre!

J'ai eu l'occasion, comme juge IPO, d'évaluer son travail. Que dire? Un grand sportif qui se conduit comme tel: respectueux des personnes et des règlements! Bref quelqu'un qu'on gagne à connaître!

Félix a très vite appris! De novice, du moins en apparence, il a rapidement grimpé tous les échelons pour devenir un grand compétiteur renommé, un grand technicien du chien! Il a eu l'intelligence de suivre, d'écouter et de tirer profit de l'expérience des grands champions que nous avons ici en Belgique et ailleurs. De ces exemples et de sa propre expérience il a élaboré sa propre technique de travail, très au point il faut le reconnaître.

Je félicite Félix pour ce travail "novateur" dans la présentation du programme IPO actuel. Il relate très bien les origines de cette discipline issue, à la base, du "Schutzhund". L'IPO appelé aussi "RCI" date de 1952, le premier championnat d'Europe eut lieu en Italie en 1954! Depuis beaucoup d'eau a passé sous les ponts! Par expérience personnelle comme conducteur, mon premier concours IPO date de juin 1976, comme juge IPO depuis près de trente ans pendant lesquels j'ai eu l'honneur de juger dix fois des championnats du Monde IPO, FH, Rescue dogs, j'ai pu constater cette évolution!

Du chien d'utilité nous sommes graduellement passés à des chiens de sport et de loisirs! Mes deux premiers de concours étaient mes chiens de service à la Police... Impensable aujourd'hui! Félix a tout compris de cette évolution et des objectifs à atteindre pour former un chien de compétition du 21° siècle. Ma connaissance de la langue chinoise étant plus que limitée... Félix et moi nous nous sommes mis autour d'une table, pendant de nombreuses heures, pendant lesquelles il m'a expliqué, chapitre par chapitre, son travail!

Il a fait sienne la politique que l'entraînement d'un chien sportif dépend tout aussi de la génétique, de son bien-être, que de son milieu de vie, c'est un tout indissociable! Cet ouvrage vous propose une étude profonde du choix du chiot, de la génétique, de l'éthologie du chien, de son éducation de base et de sa formation aux épreuves sportives, fondée sur le conditionnement opérant! Il vous expose différentes façons d'aborder certaines problématiques d'éducation avec, à chaque fois, ses avantages et inconvénients! Il aborde, sans fausse pudeur, les techniques dites à discrimination positive ou négative!

Je crois sincèrement que ce livre peut vous aider, ou vous guider, d'une façon significative dans l'éducation moderne d'un chien de sport! C'est un ouvrage de référence! Maintenant, il faut savoir aussi que le meilleur des chiens est celui qui vous rend heureux!

Félicitations Félix!
Bonne lecture!
José Buggenhout
Juge FCI

CHAPTER ONE

Introduction

Schutzhund/IPO is a programme designed for working dogs, with a long history and deep traditions. It has significant influence on the breeding, selection, and training of utility dogs. It's now an international sport, with tens of thousands of participants around the world. Books about this subject are limited, however. For beginners wishing to start on the right path, it can be a challenging quest.

I began dog training in 1999. Over the years, I've been very fortunate as I received a great deal of help and guidance from some of the most knowledgeable cynologists in the world. Because I majored in biology in my university years, I developed a habit of taking notes and keeping a diary when I was learning how to train dogs. This helped to record my learning, the progress of the dogs, and the effectiveness and limits of different training systems. Since 2005, I've been invited by various cynology organisations to conduct seminars around the world on a yearly basis. In the beginning, I used training notes, diaries, and articles I had written for several dog magazines as my theoretical presentations. The contents expanded as the number of dogs and students I trained increased. It was 2011 when I first started having the notion of developing these materials into a book of Schutzhund training. Due to my busy schedule, and because writing a book is much more demanding than writing a monthly column for magazines, it was sort of an on-and-off project. In the beginning I was writing in both English and Chinese. It was a lot of work and the progress was slow. In autumn 2015, I finally decided I had waited long enough, and it was now or never. Being Chinese myself, and as there was no book in the Chinese language specified in Schutzhund training, I chose to first complete my book in Chinese. I made a commitment and spent two months at home, sitting in front of my computer and doing nothing else but writing for hours every day. Eventually I completed all the written contents of the Chinese version of my book in January 2016.

When I first finished the manuscript in Chinese, I thought I only needed to have it proofread and shoot a few photos and all my work would be done. As I began taking notes for the areas that required photo illustrations, I realised I needed over 700 pictures to meet my standard for publishing. Compared with shooting the photos, writing 140,000 words seemed so easy. Taking the photos for this book was really not a simple assignment. During the shoots, I tried to use dogs of related age and training level to match the topics. I had to find the right locations, the right background, the right weather, and the right time of the day. I had to face the camera at the right angles and memorise what photos were needed for the specific subjects, and the dogs also had to cooperate to produce the right images. There were a lot of obstacles to be overcome. It was spring in Belgium when we began the shoots. The climate of the Belgian spring is unpredictable and polarised. Sometimes it was sunny and fine when we left the house, but as we arrived at the location and took a few shots, thunderstorms could suddenly appear from nowhere. This part of the book was the most time- and energy-consuming. We used my digital reflex camera with sport mode for the photos. Without any formal training in photography, on average we needed to take twenty photos to produce one that was useful for the book. Fortunately, my wife, Maggie, helped me to capture most of the photos. She was very patient with my obsessive way of doing things. Later on by chance, we also met and received help from my friend Natalie Hill, who is a professional photographer from England. After shooting for two months, I finally had all the photos I needed.

The Chinese version of *The Schutzhund Training Manual* was a success as soon as it was published. Many copies were sold and it was positively reviewed by many renowned dog trainers in China. This gave me the confidence and motivation to complete the English version of the manual. In October 2016, again I spent two months at home doing nothing but writing. By 31st December 2016, the English manuscript had been completed, with over 110,000 words.

The Schutzhund Training Manual begins with the brief history and regulations of the sport of Schutzhund/IPO, moving on to working abilities, pack structure, and understanding the basic language of dogs. I then explain puppy selection, training stages and tuning elements, Schutzhund tracking, obedience, then protection learning stage, and the strengthening stage. It's a step-by-step guide from picking the right puppy for the sport to educating him to achieve his IPO3 title. As long as you start with the right dog with sufficient working abilities and follow the instructions in this book, reaching IPO3 isn't a difficult task at all. I've used and tested every system I describe here. With these methods, I've titled seven working dogs in Schutzhund/IPO and Mondio Ring to this date. Every dog I titled was selected at the age of six to seven weeks. The breeds I've trialled with include Malinois, German Shepherd, and Rottweiler. Three of these dogs have competed in a total number of nine IPO world championships with me.

Through reading this manual, I hope you can develop the right understanding of Schutzhund training and the importance of preserving the working breeds. I hope it can help you to successfully train your puppy to IPO3. For the stabilising stage and the perfecting stage of tracking, obedience, and protection, and the system of using the e-collar, I will explain them in detail in my next book, *The Schutzhund Training Manual 2*.

I wish you much fun and success in training your dog.

Felix Ho, 31st December 2016, Belgium

Working Dogs and Doggy Jobs

A working dog is a dog with a specific purpose. This distinguishes him from a pet dog. Working dogs differ from pet dogs in many aspects, including breed, genetic composition, daily management, and training. Usually, a working dog is selected from working breeds. A working breed is a dog breed that was originally bred for a particular function. The breeders selectively bred dogs according to their needs. After many generations, individuals from this group of dogs all share similar characteristics in temperament and looks, forming a standard and becoming a dog breed.

For example, the German Shepherd Dog was first bred for herding sheep. His temperament and physique are suitable for guarding, protection, patrol, and search work, as well as being highly trainable. In the First and Second World Wars, he was largely employed to be a military dog breed. In the modern day, many police forces across the world choose German Shepherds as one of their police dog breeds. Many of them prefer German Shepherds from the working bloodlines and not the beauty bloodlines. The daily management of police dogs is different from the average pet dogs. Some of them live in special police dog kennels looked after by specially trained staff. Some of them live a disciplined lifestyle with their police handlers. Besides the above, working dogs must go through special training in order to be proficient in their jobs. The training module for many police dogs includes a high level of obedience, scent discrimination, and bite work. Therefore, the selective and training criteria of working dogs are much more demanding than the usual family pets.

A doggy job is a specific task the dog owner has appointed for the dog. The most common doggy jobs include but are not limited to:

1. Police, military, and security dogs: patrol, apprehension, crowd control, defence, and guard
2. Scent dog: searching, detecting, and locating people, animals, cadavers, and specific substances such as explosives and narcotics
3. Working sport dog: working dog trials
4. Herding dog: herding sheep and cattle
5. Assistance dog: guiding the blind, disability assistance
6. Hunting dog: hunting, retrieving, catching
7. Sled dog: sled pulling.

In the above seven groups of dog tasks, the selection and training criteria of Groups 1, 2, and 3 share the most similarities. For Group 3, working sport dogs, currently the most internationally recognised dog sports are:

1. Schutzhund/IPO
2. Belgian Ring
3. French Ring

4. Mondio Ring
5. KNPV.

The training system of Schutzhund/IPO is the topic we will focus on in this book.

Brief History and Structure of Schutzhund/IPO

Internationale Prüfungsordnung (IPO) is a German term meaning "International Working Test". It is a century-old programme originating from Western Europe, developed for the evaluation of working dogs. Its evolution was particularly influenced by Germany and Belgium, where many working dog breeds originated. If we want to understand the history of IPO, we must begin with the father of the German Shepherd Dog breed: Captain Max von Stephanitz.

Captain von Stephanitz was born in Dresden, Kingdom of Saxony, into German nobility. He was a career cavalry officer and had served at the veterinary college in Berlin, where he obtained much knowledge about biology, anatomy, and the science of movement, all of which were valuable when he became a dog breeder after his release from his role as captain in the army. He was especially interested in improving the German Shepherd Dogs, as they were the local working dogs of his time. He was an active participant in dog shows and noticed there was a wide range of differences in the shepherd dogs, with no breed standardisation. So he spent much of his time in standardising the breed's appearance and character.

In 1899, the captain founded the Verein für Deutsche Schäferhunde (SV: German Shepherd Club) with several friends and became its first president. Captain von Stephanitz believed the German Shepherd was primarily a working dog, so its working ability must come before its looks. He devoted his life to the breed and developed the Schutzhund programme so the dogs could be tested in tracking, obedience, and protection to evaluate their working instincts for breeding purposes. Schutzhund is a German word meaning "protection dog". The first Schutzhund trial was organised in 1901 in Germany. The first *Bundessiegerprüfung* (national championship) was held on 10th January 1949 in Neu-Isenburg. Twenty-five German Shepherds participated in this championship with their handlers. The winner was Elli Sauermann with her bitch Gerda vom Beckotal, with 97 points in tracking, 95 points in obedience, and 95 points in protection. Schutzhund proved to be an excellent programme to thoroughly assess the working ability of dogs, especially for police and military tasks. Organisations of other German working breeds soon began to introduce Schutzhund into their breeding and training programmes, such as the clubs for Rottweiler, Dobermann, Boxer, Hovawart, and Giant Schnauzer.

According to various sources, Belgium has also been a pioneer in its development of working dog sports. In 1892, Professor Adolphe Reul from the veterinarian faculty of Cureghem had already set the standard of Belgian Shepherd Dogs. In 1899, the police department in Gent founded the first police dog training school in the world. Because of their programme's success, many police forces around the world also followed. The first police dog trial was held in 1903 in the Belgian city of Malines. The exercises in this trial included attack, defending the handler, and object guarding. From then on, Belgium has developed several different working dog sports. The training phases usually include obedience, attack, and scent discrimination. The most recognised Belgian programmes are Ring, Campagne, and RCI.

The full name of RCI is *Règlement de Concours International*. It is in fact IPO in French. As several European countries were developing their national working dog sports after the Second World War, the Fédération Cynologique Internationale (FCI) wanted to structure an international programme for all breeds. In 1950, FCI formulated the foundation of IPO, which was composed of tracking, obedience, and protection.

The golden era of the European working dog world was from the 1950s to the 1990s. Besides the national programmes such as Schutzhund in Germany, Belgian Ring in Belgium, French Ring in France, and KNPV in the Netherlands, since the formation of IPO by FCI, many European working dog breeds gradually joined in. From the 1950s, FCI began organising European Cup yearly, opened to all breeds. IPO's increasing popularity in many countries with many breeds resulted in the organising of many great competitions. In 1990, the first all-breed world championship was organised in Denmark with eighty-one participating dogs. The first world champion in all breeds was Belgian master Jack Schurmann with his German Shepherd Lord with 97, 99, 99 points.

Schutzhund and IPO had a lot in common from the beginning. Coming into the new millennium, SV and FCI reached a mutual agreement; they merged Schutzhund and IPO into one sport, unifying their regulations and titles, and from then on they have settled the name as IPO.

Today, IPO has developed to be an international sporting event, particularly popular in Europe. In Belgium alone, there are several IPO trials every week. Anywhere you go in Belgium, you can drive a car in almost any direction and find an IPO club within an hour or less. As the world's information and transportation technologies advanced, the fascination of Schutzhund hit Asia in the 80s. It first reached Japan, and then Taiwan in the 90s. It was around the turn of the millennium when Schutzhund hit Korea and Mainland China. I have been very fortunate to be invited by various Chinese working dog organisations to conduct seminars and judge over there on a yearly basis since 2005.

Schutzhund has grown to be an important and prestigious sport in the world of dogs because it can meticulously develop and control the instincts, allowing a dog to satisfy his natural impulses through focusing his drives on tasks that are useful for his owner. The tracking phase in Schutzhund can fulfil a dog's hunt drive and exploring drive, while developing his focus and mental clarity and the use of his olfactory system. The obedience phase can fulfil a dog's food drive, pack drive, and freedom drive, while reinforcing his environmental soundness, willingness, agility, and speed. The protection phase can fulfil a dog's hunt drive/prey drive, protection drive, and rank drive while strengthening his competitiveness, courage, power, and physical condition. All these elements are essential for a dog's mental and physical health as well as being practical for his handler. Schutzhund/IPO remains one of the best sports for dogs and their human masters.

Minimum Age for a Dog to Enter IPO Trials

All dogs must reach the minimum age on the day of the trial:

Level	Age
BH	15 months
IPO1	18 months
IPO2	19 months
IPO3	20 months

All dogs, regardless of size, breed, or heritage, may participate at a trial.

BH

Divided into two parts:

Obedience	60 points in total
Temperament test	Pass or fail

BH Obedience Phase		
Exercise 1:	Heeling on leash	15 points
Exercise 2:	Heeling off leash	15 points
Exercise 3:	Sit	10 points
Exercise 4:	Down	10 points
Exercise 5:	Down stay	10 points
Total		60 points
BH Temperament Test		
Exercise 1:	Encounter with a group of people	
Exercise 2:	Encounter with joggers or inline skaters	
Exercise 3:	Encounter with bicyclist	
Exercise 4:	Encounter with cars	
Exercise 5:	Encounter with other dogs	
Exercise 6:	Behaviour of the tethered dog towards other animals when left alone	
Result	Pass or fail	

IPO1

Divided into three phases:

Phase A	100 points
Phase B	100 points
Phase C	100 points
Total	300 points

IPO1 – Phase A – Tracking	
Working out the track: handler track, minimum 300 paces, three legs, two turns	79 points
Locating the articles: two articles (11+10 points)	21 points
Total	100 points

IPO1 – Phase B – Obedience		
Exercise 1:	Heeling off leash	20 points
Exercise 2:	Sit in motion	10 points
Exercise 3:	Down in motion	10 points
Exercise 4:	Retrieve	10 points
Exercise 5:	Retrieve over hurdle	15 points
Exercise 6:	Retrieve over A-frame	15 points
Exercise 7:	Send away	10 points
Exercise 8:	Down stay	10 points
Total		100 points
IPO1 – Phase C – Protection		
Exercise 1:	Search for the decoy	5 points
Exercise 2:	Hold and bark	10 points
Exercise 3:	Prevention of the escape	20 points
Exercise 4:	Re-attack during guarding	35 points
Exercise 5:	Long attack	30 points
Total		100 points

IPO2

Divided into three phases:

Phase A	100 points
Phase B	100 points
Phase C	100 points
Total	300 points

IPO2 – Phase A – Tracking	
Working out the track: stranger track, minimum 400 paces, three legs, two turns	79 points
Locating the articles: two articles (11+10 points)	21 points
Total	100 points

IPO2 – Phase B – Obedience		
Exercise 1:	Heeling off leash	10 points
Exercise 2:	Sit in motion	10 points
Exerci:se 3:	Down in motion	10 points
Exercise 4:	Stand in motion	10 points
Exercise 5:	Retrieve	15 points
Exercise 6:	Retrieve over hurdle	15 points
Exercise 7:	Retrieve over A-frame	10 points
Exercise 8:	Send away	10 points
Exercise 9:	Down stay	10 points
Total		100 points

IPO2 – Phase C – Protection		
Exercise 1:		5 points
Exercise 2:		10 points
Exercise 3:		10 points
Exercise 4:		20 points
Exercise 5:		5 points
Exercise 6:		30 points
Exercise 7:		20 points
Total		100 points

IPO3

Divided into three phases:

Phase A	100 points
Phase B	100 points
Phase C	100 points
Total	300 points

IPO3 – Phase A – Tracking	
Working out the track: stranger track, minimum 600 paces, five legs, four turns	79 points
Locating the articles: three articles (7+7+7 points)	21 points
Total	100 points
IPO3 – Phase B – Obedience		
Exercise 1:	Heeling off leash	10 points
Exercise 2:	Sit in motion	10 points
Exercise 3:	Down in motion (running)	10 points
Exercise 4:	Stand in motion (running)	10 points
Exercise 5:	Retrieve	10 points
Exercise 6:	Retrieve over hurdle	15 points
Exercise 7:	Retrieve over A-frame	15 points
Exercise 8:	Send away	10 points
Exercise 9:	Down stay	10 points
Total		100 points
IPO3 – Phase C – Protection		
Exercise 1:	Search for the decoy	10 points
Exercise 2:	Hold and bark	10 points
Exercise 3:	Prevention of the escape	10 points
Exercise 4:	Re-attack during guarding	20 points
Exercise 5:	Back transport	5 points
Exercise 6:	Attack during back transport	15 points
Exercise 7:	Long attack	10 points
Exercise 8:	Re-attack during guarding	20 points
Total		100 points

Note: The full version of the IPO regulations can be found on my official website, www.FelixHo.be

Working Abilities

Working abilities are genetic criteria essential for working sport dogs, military dogs, police dogs, security dogs, search dogs, and detection dogs. Due to the difficulty and possible danger of the tasks, not just any dog is suitable to be a working animal. All working dogs must go through strict sets of selection criteria before training even begins, just like candidates for military recruits. They can only be accepted when the minimum standards have been met. After the completion of rigorous training programmes, the trainees are examined and selected again. Only the ones that have successfully passed the tests can become certified working dogs. Proficient working dogs typically possess many common genetic characteristics. These traits are working abilities. Working abilities are composed of many different genetic features. According to my past experience in training and breeding, I've categorised a list of twenty essential traits required for a working dog. These standards can be easily and objectively measured:

Working Abilities			
Character	Stability	1.	Self-assurance
		2.	Environmental soundness
	Hardness	3.	Physical robustness
		4.	Emotional resilience
		5.	Mental persistence
	Rank	6.	Dominance/competitiveness
		7.	Focus/presence
		8.	Maturity and composure
Temperament		9.	Drives
		10.	Courage
		11.	Expression and recovery speed
Trainability		12.	Willingness and flexibility
		13.	Problem-solving skill and learning speed
		14.	Mental clarity under excitement and pressure
Physical attributes		15.	Health and longevity
		16.	Functional structure and strength
		17.	Agility and speed
		18.	Endurance and heat tolerance
		19.	Olfaction
Grip		20.	Behaviour in biting

Interpretation of the Twenty Genetic Working Abilities

Because of the possibility of various interpretations by different individuals referring to the table of working abilities, here I shall describe the meaning of my criteria to ensure the clarity of the topics. The twenty genetic components I've set out can be easily measured by observing a dog's behaviour in pre-arranged situations. Some of these components have interlinking relationships with one another. The keyword of my selection is "balance". Every genetic component has to fit well together and complement each other.

Stability

Stability is a dog's tolerance against real or perceived pressure or threat and the threshold for a dog to feel anxious, stressed, or frightened in a given situation. The less easily rattled the dog is, the more stable he is. There are two types of stability: the stability towards living beings and the stability towards environments. If a dog isn't easily startled by various environments, it doesn't necessarily mean he feels as much at ease with people and vice versa.

Self-Assurance

The confidence and sureness of a dog with humans, other dogs, and all other animals.

Environmental Soundness

How comfortable a dog is while exposed to different environments such as places, surfaces, objects, heights, lights, noises, and smells.

Hardness

There are three types of hardness against different types of pressure: physical robustness, emotional resilience, and mental persistence.

Physical Robustness

Hardness against physical force; basically the pain tolerance of a dog.

Emotional Resilience

Thisa is the hardness against negative emotions such as the handler's bad mood and angry voice. I prefer dogs that are carefree and not easily distressed when his handler is angry or raises his voice. However, a degree of sensibility is important for a dog to respond well to his master.

Mental Persistence

Mental persistence is the hardness against mental strain, or determination in a difficult task without wanting to quit. For example, the will to keep going on a very difficult track, drilling on the same obedience routine day after day without a reward, performing the object guarding with a muzzle on as the last exercise of a Belgian Ring trial on a hot summer day. This genetic component is interlinked with temperament but they're not exactly the same. Mental persistence is the dog's sheer pleasure in the work, just for the sake of working. The will to persevere is important for a working dog. A good working dog must have the will to carry on, to come back, even when the odds are against him.

Rank

A dog's sense of self or dignity.

Dominance/Competitiveness

The will to win and to be superior to one's opponent: although a dog in rank drive can also display certain behaviours that resemble signs of dominance, what separates the two is the dog's perception to his own rank. Rank drive is the rank that the dog wants to be, while dominance is the dog's true birth rank. Just because a dog wants to be dominant doesn't mean he's naturally superior in his birth rank. This situation can be encountered all the time with pet dogs that are spoiled by inexperienced owners.

Focus/Presence

The ability to concentrate and the awareness of self and one's surroundings.

Maturity and Composure

Knowing when to act appropriately according to the situation, having self-control, and a serious demeanor. Some people call this trait "being clear in the head". This can be easily observed when two dogs are interacting with each other, especially a grown dog playing with a puppy. Dogs that lack maturity and show a lot of juvenile behaviours usually progress a lot slower in training and have difficulties in taking the protection phase seriously.

Drives

A drive is an instinctual compulsive energy directed towards survival. I've categorised ten primary drives in dogs:

Drive	Behaviour	Goal
Food drive	Eating and drinking	To relieve hunger and thirst for growth, metabolism, and recuperation
Hunt drive/prey drive	Searching, chasing, biting, capturing, killing, holding, and tearing a prey object. There's a slight difference between hunt drive and prey drive. A dog in hunt drive is motivated by the action and excitement of the pursuit. His satisfaction is in the hunting process. A dog in prey drive is motivated by having the prey. His satisfaction is in the fulfilment of his mouth.	To catch food, satisfy hunting instinct, practise hunting skill, possess the prey
Protection drive	Driving out an opponent, protecting oneself, one's possession, territory, offspring, or pack member	To keep safe, expel opponent, and defend resources
Rank drive	To dominate and avoid being dominated	To heighten position in ranking to make decisions, receive better resources, the right to mate, preserve energy

Pack drive	Seeking attention from pack members, socialisation, interaction, play, greeting ritual, cooperation within the pack	To obtain companionship, partnership, and acceptance to increase chances for survival
Exploring drive	To explore one's surroundings with the senses including sight, hearing, touch, olfaction, and taste	To gain information about the environment
Freedom drive	To do as one pleases	To achieve physical and mental liberty
Comfort drive	Avoidance of discomfort, pressure, confrontation, pain, danger, etc. in order to reach comfort and safety. Comfort drive makes learning via negative reinforcement possible. Also known as avoidance drive	To maintain a state of equilibrium and be in peace
Sex drive	Mating	To pass on one's genes
Parental drive	Caring for young	To preserve one's genes

I utilise all of the above primary drives in different areas and stages of my training. Some drives are used in a more specific manner than the others. For example I use rank drive only in bite work towards the decoy and never in tracking and obedience. I use exploring drive only in tracking in combination with food drive. The balance of the above drives is much more important than their quantity. If too much out of proportion, these drives can actually work against training. I prefer a very high level of food drive, hunt drive/prey drive, protection drive, and pack drive, a high level of rank drive, exploring drive, sex drive (for breeding purposes), and parental drive, a medium level of freedom drive, and a low level (but not a lack of) comfort drive to have a dog that can understand negative reinforcement without being too sensitive.

You might ask why I don't have fight drive in my list. This is because, in my opinion, fight drive isn't actually a primary drive but a state of mind and behaviour displaying a flowing fusion of hunt drive/prey drive, protection drive, and rank drive by the dog. Since this is a behaviour that can only be developed through experience by blending the three primary drives, it's not categorised as a primary drive itself.

Another big word that has been a popular topic of discussion among dog trainers is aggression. In my view, aggression is also a behaviour and not a drive, because aggression itself isn't a motive. Think about it; no dog shows aggression for the sake of just being aggressive. There are different motivations behind a particular aggressive behaviour and hence there are different types of aggression. The display of aggression stops when the specific goal is reached. The drives behind aggression are protection drive (showing aggression to drive out an opponent, to protect oneself, one's possession, territory, offspring, or pack member), rank drive (showing aggression to dominate and to avoid being dominated), and comfort drive (showing aggression to stop discomfort, pressure, confrontation, pain, danger, etc. in order to seek comfort and safety). In this case, when the display of aggression fails to stop the pressure, the dog might choose to avoid or simply run away from the source.

Courage

While stability is a dog's tolerance threshold against real or perceived danger, courage is the dog's instinct to go forward when he actually feels threatened. I have seen dogs that are usually stable but when they feel threatened they lack the courage to overcome the threat and go into avoidance. On the other hand, there are dogs that are usually very nervous but when under threat they're willing to go forward to confront the aggressor. Naturally, a very high level of both stability and courage is the most desirable for a working dog.

Expression and Recovery Speed

Looking happy in general and at work, forgiving and forgetting bad experiences quickly.

Willingness and Flexibility

This trait is associated with pack drive. It is the ability to cooperate and work with the handler as a team and this has nothing to do with being submissive. A dog can be willing towards his handler and dominant towards other people at the same time. It simply means the dog can be led. In nature no wolf pack is led by an alpha pup but this same pup grows up to lead the pack after understanding how to be led. Some people justify a dog's inability to be led by associating this inability with dominance. This is something I disagree with. A good leader should be capable of leading and also of being led (by another good leader, of course). Being flexible means having the aptitude to understand compromise within the pack.

Problem-Solving Skill and Learning Speed

Having insight and being a fast learner makes a dog a pleasure to train with.

Mental Clarity under Excitement and Pressure

This is the capacity to stay in the functioning zone (the right balance between motivation and concentration) in tracking, obedience, and protection. A dog has to be able to register his handler's command in order to perform any given task effectively.

Health and Longevity

Long living and free of genetic diseases such as hip dysplasia, elbow dysplasia, arthritis, joint and ligament weakness, epilepsy, pancreas diseases, digestive problems, eye problems, etc.

Functional Structure and Posture

A structure that is built for function and not fashion: a working dog should also have a natural firmness and alertness in his posture and should not sit sloppily or floppily.

Agility and Speed

Coordination, reflex, and the ability to jump high and far the movement of a working dog should be smooth, flexible, and effortless.

Endurance and Heat Tolerance

Being able to work continuously in hot weather is an important factor for a working dog.

Olfaction

A strong sense of smell for tracking and searching.

Grip

The fullness, firmness, calmness, power, attitude, commitment, conviction, and intensity in biting:

although grip is an interlinked component with some of the other criteria such as stability and drives, in my view it is still an independent trait because I've seen many dogs with a lot of character and temperament that naturally bite badly. On the other hand I've also seen many dogs that are nervous and erratic, but with a naturally super grip. The only explanation is that grip is a trait influenced by multiple genetic factors. A full grip provides the most surface area of the bite. It also allows the dog's teeth to distribute the force of the jaws evenly onto the target. Hence it is the most secure. Non-full biting, especially a frontal grip, is dangerous for the dog. A frontal grip means the dog is biting with the front part of his mouth. The teeth that are making contact with the target are mainly the dog's incisors, canines, and pre-molars. The canines would be the teeth that are under particular strain in a frontal grip because they're the longest. Frontal biting in high speed can break the dog's canine teeth as a result. That's why a full grip is so important for a biting dog.

Pack Structure

Understanding Dog Language through the Study of Wolves

At present, one of the most widely accepted scientific theories about the origin of domestic dogs is selective breeding of wolves by humans through many thousands of years. If we want to thoroughly understand the instinct, behaviour, language, and psychology of the domestic dog, one of the most effective ways is through studying his ancestor, the wolf. A wolf is a dog's most natural form. From studying wolves, we can trace many of the original motivations and instincts of canine behaviour. The life of a wolf is inseparable from the pack and hunting. To be capable of training our dogs, we should try to understand their language through thinking and seeing from their perspective.

Wolf Characteristics:

1. Wolves are carnivores.
2. Wolves are predators.
3. Wolves are social animals living in a pack.
4. A wolf pack is a highly organised structure.
5. In the pack, there are different ranks. Each rank has its own status and specific function.

As my work allows me to train and meet with many pioneers in the world of cynology, in 2005 I had the opportunity to interview a renowned wolf behaviourist, Mr Shaun Ellis from England. Shaun has a lot of first-hand experience working with wolves from captive breeding and from the wild. He's also lived among a pack of wild wolves in their natural environment. Some of the information about wolf studies in this chapter was shared with me by Shaun.

The Five Ranks in a Wolf Pack

To thoroughly comprehend canine behaviour, first we have to understand the structure of a pack. Every member of a wolf pack has his own social status, function, responsibilities, skills, and rights. The pack forms an integrated and complex organisation just like a troop of soldiers. Wolves are highly organised animals with a strong sense of teamwork. Everything in their lives revolves around hunting and survival as a pack.

Below are the five ranks in a wolf pack from top to bottom. Every rank has its distinctive role and specialty. Every wolf's rank is mainly decided by genetics, so his ranking is his birthright.

Alpha

In nature, every wolf pack has a pair of alpha wolves. Only the male and female alphas have the right to breed. The male alpha usually makes overall decisions for the pack, while the female alpha dictates what prey items to hunt. The alpha rank is the soul of a wolf pack. His role is to make strategic decisions, distribute food, and pass on his genes. The alpha leads, organises, and protects the pack. His attributes include confidence, composure, astuteness, good judgement, experience, and fairness. If compared with the human world, the position of the alpha wolf is equivalent to the chief executive officer of a company.

Beta

The beta is the right hand of the alpha. He's responsible for the execution of the alpha's plans. He's also the messenger between the alpha and the rest of the pack. He answers directly to the alpha, and has the power to reward, discipline, and educate the other members of the pack. In a large pack, there is usually a male and a female beta; both report to the alpha of their own sex. In a smaller pack, there is usually one, male beta. The beta is typically dominant, bold, proactive, competitive, and cunning. He's comparable with the chief operating officer of a company.

Omega

The omega buffers, dilutes, and mediates hostile situations between pack members. Wolves are social predators. Every wolf is equipped with powerful jaws and sharp teeth for killing large prey. Living in a group, competition and friction are common between individuals. If conflicts are ensued by fighting every time with injuries as a result, the pack would gradually lose its capability to hunt and decrease its chance for survival. When there is a dispute in a pack, the job of the omega is to redirect the attention and aggression onto himself by emitting various sight, sound, tactile, and olfactory signals. There are usually one to two omegas in a pack. They can be either males or females. The omega is slick, sociable, amiable, and efficient. He's a master communicator and he's the personnel manager of the pack. Like the alpha and beta, the omega is a high ranking member of the hierarchy.

Alpha, beta, and omega form the executive management team of a pack. They have a subtle relationship and understanding of each other. In some cases, their positions are interchangeable. For example, when an alpha is injured or killed unexpectedly, the beta or omega might succeed his place, taking up the responsibility of commanding the pack. Another distinctive feature of the relationship between these three ranks is that their communication is primarily by olfactory signals instead of the body language and sound typically utilised by the mid-rank and low rank.

Mid-Rank

The mid-rank is the driving force of a pack. Some experienced mid-rank members are the frontliners in hunts. This is a dangerous position. As prey animals such as deer and wild boar possess sharp horns, hooves, and tusks, frontline hunters could be seriously injured or even killed in action. The mid-rank makes up the majority population of the pack. If there is a loss of one of the frontliners, another one can immediately fill his place. Some of the mid-rank members are nannies. Their responsibility is to help care for the pups. Mid-ranks are characterised by being easy to guide, amenable, and adaptable. They can be compared with the production workers of a company. There is a further seniority order within mid-rankers.

Low Rank

Within the pack, there are usually one or two especially skittish wolves that are hypersensitive to their surroundings, reacting to the slightest noise or change of environment. They're actually very useful members of the pack as they warn other wolves of anything unusual going on in their territory. This information could be associated with prey movement, possible danger, or neighbouring packs' activities. The low-ranker is a suspicious, sensitive, and nervous wolf that is more willing to bark or yelp than to attack. The low-ranker is the meddlesome courier of the pack who is always ready to deliver the latest office gossip.

Ranking by Genetics vs Ranking by Human Influence

In nature, the alpha female wolf has the ability to control the function, number, and sex of the pups in her upcoming litter. Some cynologists believe this unique aptitude is contributed by the alpha female's influence over what prey items for the pack to hunt. Different food sources would directly affect the chemistry in the wolves' bodies, possibly causing their hormonal level to change. A wolf's social status within the pack is largely determined by his genes, and to a small degree on how competitive he is as a pup with his litter siblings in the first few weeks of his life. Very often, the ranking of an eight-week old pup among his litter-mates will remain the same until maturity. Young wolves in the pack would undergo different types of education according to their heritage and functions decided by the alphas. They could remain in the pack or could be dispersed to join or form another pack. Yearling wolves are the apprentices of the pack.

In the human world, many problem dogs are the result of inappropriate management and education by their owners. Some lower ranking dogs become overriding and aggressive to their human families due to a lack of leadership. In such cases the dogs take on the alpha role. The problem is they were not born alphas so they become confused and insecure, just like letting a child run a family. This is not too difficult to solve as long as the owners learn how to properly apply leadership to their dogs. Once this is established, the dogs will be quite happy to fall back into their natural ranks because they were born to follow a leader. Some genetically higher ranking dogs naturally take on the leadership role in their human family when there is a deficiency of firm guidance from the beginning. Such behaviour is of course unacceptable but this is more difficult to fix. As these dogs are dominant by instinct and they have been confirmed as the alphas of the family unknowingly, it will take a lot of time and experience for the owners to re-establish the pack order at home, and sometimes it can be tricky or even dangerous. The best way is to educate dogs about their pack order from puppyhood. Even an alpha puppy can learn to accept his place as a subordinate if his owners are reinforcing their leadership clearly and effectively.

Ranking	Role in the Pack	Characteristics
Alpha	Making strategic decisions, distributing food, and having the right to breed. The alpha leads, organises, and protects the pack	Wise, composed, fair
Beta	The enforcer and representative of the alpha, the beta has the power to reward, discipline, and educate the other members of the pack. He's the communication bridge between the alpha and the rest of the pack	Dominant, courageous, proactive, competitive, cunning
Omega	Mediator of the pack	Slick, sociable, amiable, efficient, a master communicator
Mid-Rank	Driving force of the pack, responsible for hunting and raising young	Easy to guide, amenable, adaptable
Low Rank	Sentry of the pack	Suspicious, sensitive, nervous

If we only focus on the ranking of a dog, alpha, beta, omega, and mid-rank all have the qualities to be prospective working dogs for different tasks but low rank hasn't. The possibility of the above four ranks to make good working dogs also depends on the following elements:

1. The other working abilities besides ranking: a good working dog also needs a suitable temperament, trainability, physical attributes, and grip.
2. The appointed task: working dogs have a wide range of posts and functions, such as patrol, anti-riot, security, searching, and sports. Some jobs demand an independent dog that can think by himself, and some jobs require a compliant dog that is easy to control. Horses for courses; we should find the right job for the right dog and vice versa.
3. The personality, experience, and capacity of the dog handler.

The Role of the Handler in the Pack

Regardless of which rank of dog we select, as an owner or handler, we should always remain in the alpha position (this rule doesn't apply to decoys training a dog in bite work). To be the true alpha of a dog pack, we must train ourselves to demonstrate leadership while interacting with our dogs. A dog will find his position in our world according to his genetic composition and the environment we provide him with. He communicates through body language, sound, and touch, but also a lot with scent, which is very difficult for us to detect. By using a nose that has forty times the olfactory receptors that we have, a dog can communicate with other dogs by releasing and receiving a wide range of scent signals. From one sniff, a dog can distinguish a human's sex, age, mood, health, etc. Therefore, a dog knows straight away if his master is happy, calm, sure, nervous, hesitant, angry, or insecure. You can't hide from his nose. Therefore, the leadership we show must really come from within and not by pretending. Below are five criteria a leader of the pack must possess:

1. A leader is alert and astute. A leader should be aware of every detail within his pack, to maintain structure and order. He must be wise and sharp. A dull and ignorant individual can't make a good leader.
2. A leader is courageous and decisive. Two of the alpha's responsibilities are protecting and making favourable decisions for the pack. There are many similarities between the human world and the animal world. No one likes to be led by a weak and indecisive individual.
3. A leader is calm and confident. Composure, stability, and self-assuredness are qualities essential for leadership. A person that is easily agitated without self-control will never be trusted and respected by his subordinates. This is so simple. How can someone control a team if he can't even control himself?
4. A leader is fair and just. The members of a pack should be rewarded or disciplined according to their merits and faults. A good leader treats his subordinates fairly and honestly.
5. A leader is empathetic and forgiving. On some occasions, members of the pack might make mistakes or even try to challenge the leader's authority. A good leader does what's necessary to maintain his social status and order in the pack. He does so to educate his subordinates so they can cooperate efficiently and serve the pack better, without any bitterness or grudges. The leader's first interest is always for the team as a whole.

The success of a dog handler is strongly influenced by the relationship between himself and his dog. This is called pack management. Good pack management comes from effective communication and mutual understanding between man and dog. There are three main principles:

1. Clear rules and pack structure. To make our dogs obey us, first they must understand what we want. All of our expectations must be explained to our dogs clearly in a way they can

understand. Confusion makes a dog weak and he will lose trust in his handler. For example, once a dog understands the recall exercise, when we call him he must come immediately no matter what distraction he's facing. If the handler always has to call his dog several times before he comes, or the dog doesn't come at all, then the behaviour clearly shows a lack of discipline and structure in the pack.

2. Fairness to the members. Dogs also understand what fair play is – even if they might not always appear to. If the handler is always moody and mean, punishing the dog for what he can't understand, the pack relationship will gradually deteriorate as a result.

3. Earn respect and give respect. Being a creature with a high level of intelligence and capable of expressing a wide range of emotions, a dog makes one of the best companions and colleagues for men. We should treat them with due respect. In contrast, we must also educate our dogs to treat us with respect. For example, behaviour such as biting our hands or clothing and dominant postures must be discouraged.

As every dog has a different birth rank and temperament, a handler must adjust his leadership according to his dog's composition in order to develop his full potential. Here I can give two examples. Please note that, no matter how resilient a dog is, when we're raising puppies we must be patient and tolerant to fully develop their confidence, competitiveness, and drives. For puppies under sixteen weeks, we should give them more freedom and flexibility so they can enjoy a happy and healthy puppyhood. The examples I'm giving now are applicable to dogs over six months old.

Dog 1: A Dominant, Bold, Active, Aggressive, and Cunning Beta

While handling such a dog, I'd first adopt a positive approach (reward-based system) to build a good relationship with him. As a dog of this character is usually headstrong and independent, during the early period in his keeping I won't allow him too much freedom. For example, besides letting him out to go to the toilet, exercising, and training, I shall keep him in a crate indoors, close to me (the crate is big enough for the dog to stand up straight and turn around comfortably). Feeding is limited to the time of training and interacting with me. I want to clearly show this dog that I have complete control over his freedom, food, and exercise without any conflicts. I'm also strict while setting the rules of the pack. For example, I usually let my dogs jump on me while we're playing, but for handling this dog in the early period I wouldn't allow such behaviour. When we have to pass a gate or a corridor, I would teach him to wait until I pass first. The line between our hierarchies has to be very clear. Also, when I handle this dog I shall be more aloof and not give him too much patting or talking in a soft tone. I shall wait until he actively seeks acceptance from me and then I will reward such behaviour.

Dog 2: An Amiable, Compliant, and Friendly Mid-Rank

While interacting with this dog, I'd also start with a positive approach. From the beginning I shall already give him some freedom, such as letting him loose in my house while under supervision. The rules I set for him are more flexible. When he plays with me I allow more affectionate and excitable behaviour to gain his trust and confidence. I want him to feel uninhibited. While passing a gate or corridor I just let him walk. My leadership is clear but I'm much friendlier and more affectionate with this dog, giving more patting and soft praises when he offers any desired behaviour.

Basic Understanding of Dog Language

Just like us, dogs have five senses: sight (eyes), hearing (ears), touch (skin), olfaction (nose), and taste (tongue). Through these senses they receive information from their surrounding environments, and also send out compatible signals to communicate with their pack members. As dog trainers, we must develop our ability to read dogs and speak the language of dogs. The better we can read them, the better we can speak their language, expressing our thoughts in a way they can understand, at the same time knowing their needs. The five senses of dogs are receptors for the following signals:

1. Sight: body language
2. Hearing: sound
3. Touch: touch
4. Smell: scent
5. Taste: body fluid.

Sight

Dogs communicate with each other, humans, and other animals by using different body postures, movements, and facial expressions. If we can understand what their body language means and mimic it back, we can communicate with dogs appropriately and make training much more effective.

While we're studying a dog's body language, we should observe first from large to small, and from wholly to partially. This means when we're trying to read the dog's mind we should initially feel the overall impression of his behaviour before we begin focusing on smaller details. At the same time we should take the current circumstances into consideration, and not judge the dog by a brief Kodak moment. Using human behaviour as an example, laughter usually represents a person's happiness. However, there are many types of laughter. Depending on the person's age, sex, cultural background, social standing, and the situation at the time, a simple laughter can signify many different meanings. It can be a grin, a giggle, a chuckle, a snigger, a sneer, a sad smile, a flirtatious smile, a nervous laugh, or a hysterical laugh. When someone is crying it also doesn't necessarily mean he's sad. Therefore, when we're observing a dog, we have to take the situation and the dog's disposition into account.

Generally speaking, if the dog's posture shows a high stance, head, and tail it usually means he feels good and confident. In contrast, if the dog's posture shows a low stance, head, and tail it usually means he's less sure and not feeling his best. When a dog relaxes his muscles, he usually also relaxes his mind. When his muscles are tense, it could mean he's excited or anxious. There are exceptions to the above observations though. When a wolf or a dog is stalking prey, he often lowers his whole body to make himself as small and close to the ground as possible to avoid being detected by his prey. While two dogs are playing, they often lower their heads and forelegs, demonstrating the "play bow" as an invitation for a game of wrestling.

When a relaxed dog turns his head down or sideways, he usually wants to show friendliness. Because a dog's jaws and teeth are his primary weapons, when he wants to be friendly he often turns his weapons away from the others. To show that he trusts us, a dog might turn his back to us completely so his weapons are facing the furthest from us while he offers his vulnerable side. If the dog is holding something in his mouth while lowering his head, this normally means he wants to protect what he's holding and is not willing to give it up, which is a sign of dominance. A willing dog typically holds up his toy towards us and looks at us eagerly as an invitation to play. When a dog points his head towards us and looks at us with a relaxed posture, it means he's paying attention. When a strange dog looks at us front on with a tense stance, be cautious; a stare like this is a warning and could lead to aggression.

A dog can tell us many different emotions by making his eyes bigger, smaller, harder, softer, blinking, and showing the whites. A dog demonstrating dominance enlarges his eyes while dilating his pupils. His brows are frowning and his glance is hard and challenging. A dog showing friendliness relaxes his eyes while making them smaller. He might blink and his glance is soft and gentle. When a dog fixes his stare on a person or other dog or animal, this could be the prelude of an attack. This differs from an attentive and anticipating look, such as while the dog is begging for food or asking to be taken out for a walk. When there is enough light but the dog's pupils expand, it usually means the dog is anxious. When the dog is really frightened we can also see the whites of his eyes.

When a dog is confident and alert, his ears prick up and forward. When the ears are facing sideways, the dog is normally listening to his surroundings. When the ears point sideways horizontally to the ground, it means he's in doubt. A dog turns his ears back while catching his prey or fighting, in order to protect them. An apprehensive and submissive dog flattens his ears backward as tight as he can to make his head appear smaller (looking like a seal). For dog breeds such as Rottweiler and Boxer with folded ears, we can observe the base of their ears.

When a dog is content and comfortable, his lips are relaxed. His mouth opens slightly and he pants softly like he's smiling. When a dog is trying to obtain more information from an uncertain situation, he closes his mouth and raises his head to sniff the air. An anxious and submissive dog stretches his lips and turns the corners of his mouth downward, like he's making a crying face. If the perceived threat doesn't go away, he might start yawning or even panting heavily. An insecure but submissive dog yawns to show his teeth while looking away. He's saying "I have teeth but I don't want to use them, so please stop bothering me." A dog displaying dominance curls his lips forward while showing his teeth. A dog demonstrating submissive aggression shows his teeth with his tongue stuck out while pulling his ears backward.

The fur of a relaxed dog lies relatively flat and close to the skin. When the dog wants to bluff his opponent by appearing bigger, he fluffs up the hair on his neck, back, and tail (hackling). A curious dog expands his nostrils to investigate. A dog showing compliance and submission raises his paw like he's scratching the air. This behaviour originates from puppyhood, when he used to pump his mother's mammary glands to stimulate lactation. Sometimes a friendly dog hugs his master with his paws (not to be confused with mounting and humping, which is a dominant behaviour). Sometimes when a dog wants to show submission (being scolded by his master or dominated by other dogs), besides raising his paw he might also stick out his tongue while lifting the rear leg so his belly is exposed. A dog lying with his belly shown means he accepts being lower in social status than his opponent. If he trusts the other dog he will relax his tail or might even wag gently. If his tail is tucked firmly against his belly between his legs, he's unsure about the opponent.

The dog's tail is another indicator of his moods. Carrying the tail high normally represents a happy and confident dog. Some dog breeds such as Akita and Husky have tails that naturally curl over their backs. When we're observing them we should take this into consideration and not judge their state of mind depending solely on tail carriage. A horizontally soft carried tail signifies a neutral state of mind. When the tail hangs down with its base lifted up (like a pony tail), the dog is usually uncertain. A tail tucked between the dog's legs means stress, clear submission, or even fear. When a bitch in heat turns her buttocks to a male and lifts her tail to one side showing her vagina, she's ready to accept the male for mating. Different ways of wagging the tail also tell different stories. A stiff raised tail that vibrates quickly indicates alertness and excitement. This is often seen, especially in terrier breeds with their short tails and strong hunting instincts. A gentle wagging tail parallel to the ground usually means neutrality and friendliness. A wagging tail spinning in big circles means friendliness and excitement. A low and slow wagging tail means uncertainty but the dog wishes to be friendly and treated gently.

Many people have seen dogs marking their territories by urinating on objects such as trees and lamp posts. Usually the stronger dominance the dog wants to display, the higher he lifts his leg, spreading his urine high and wide. Bitches that are dominant or during their oestrous cycle can exhibit urine-marking behaviour, too. Some very dominant dogs also defecate on high ground or trees, and kick their dung backward with their hind legs to spread it further while grunting and growling. A dog doing this is imposing his supremacy and saying to the others, "Back off!"

Hearing

Dogs communicate by a range of vocal signals including growls, barks, howls, yelps, whistles, and whimpers. All vocal communication should be observed together with the dog's body language to attain a clear picture of his psychological state. Growling usually indicates dominance and anger. It is a warning prior to a possible bite. There're two main types of growls, one coming from the throat and the other coming from the belly. A belly growl is more serious and powerful and it is difficult to be mistaken for a casual complaint. If the opponent doesn't stop what instigated the belly growl, he might be seriously bitten. There are several types of bark. It could be from playfulness, excitement, warning, aggression, or attention-seeking. A hostile bark can be distinguished by the combination of curled lips, raised hackles, and hardened eyes. A dominant hostile bark is usually mixed with deliberate grunting or snorting sounds. An uncertain hostile bark is usually rapid and unsettled, and could be mixed with a few high-pitched yelps. Playful and excited barking is normally accompanied by eager eyes and by the dog bouncing and spinning around with expectation. Howling originated from wolves for long-distance communication. It serves as a territorial claim, a display of pack unity, recruitment, or a congregation signal. Many dog breeds have lost this form of communication. It is more often displayed by Arctic breeds such as Siberian Husky and Alaskan Malamute. Whistles and whimpers often go together. A dog whistles and whimpers to seek help, attention, or company.

Touch

A puppy already possesses tactile sensation in his mother's uterus. A newborn puppy can't see as his eyes aren't able to open yet. Shortly after birth, he finds his way to his dam's mammary glands by using his senses of touch and smell. At this stage of life, the puppy is kept warm and clean by his mother's licking. In dogs' language, licking one another is a display of care and affection. In nature, wolf pups greet their senior members by licking their lips and throats after the older wolves return from a hunt. The licking stimulates regurgitation from the adults, and the pups feast on the disgorged meat. When our dogs lick our faces and hands, they're trying to ingratiate themselves with us in order to acquire acceptance.

In his daily life, a dog uses different kinds of tactile signals to express different moods and desires. As a general rule, when a dog slightly nudges us with his nose or muzzle with an upward motion, it is a signal of acceptance-seeking. In contrast, if he presses his chin on another dogs especially while standing over his neck or back, this is a clear sign of domination and he's trying to get the other dog to submit. An amplified level of this behaviour is when he puts his paw on the other dog's shoulders or even starts to mount him. If the other dog isn't willing to show submission, the two will start "T'ing up" each other, meaning they will both try to put their heads or paws on the other dog's back, forming a brief "T" shape and going around each other in circles. If this ritual can't settle their dispute in ranking, a fight might ensue. We must never let our dogs mount us, as this is a clear sign of disrespect or challenge.

When puppies from the same litter play, they use their jaws and bodies to wrestle, pounce on, pin down, and bump into each other, to test their siblings' strength, will, reflex, and agility, which are all essential for the lifestyle of a predator. Their play might seem rough but it rarely causes serious harm. Bite inhibition is an important unwritten rule in an established pack. It can be compared to the human world. A family often has disagreements and small quarrels. Family members usually resolve their issues by discussions and compromise. Fighting between grown-up members within the family is a taboo in a civilised society. Similarly, in a wolf pack, fighting is destructive and is usually avoided. Instead, most testing, disputes, and demonstrations of dominance are done through rituals and displays. Real fights within a pack that cause serious injuries don't happen very often. When a mother wolf needs to put one of her unruly pups in line, she first gives a warning by growling. If the pup doesn't stop his mischief, she will grip the pup's muzzle firmly and pin him down onto the ground until he apologises by yelping. The dam does so to educate the pup but not to hurt him.

When I play with my dogs, I encourage them to have body contact with me but I forbid them to grip me or my clothing with their mouths. Under my invitation, they can jump up and put their paws on my torso and give me a hug (a friendly hug without the intention for mounting). They're encouraged to prod their hindquarters and hips to me or nudge me with their heads. In other words, I promote all kinds of active submission behaviour. I reward these actions with food, toys, interaction, and play. This is an effective way for bonding and establishing the appropriate pack relationship, which is vital for training.

Smell

Olfaction is the primary sense of a dog. In many ways it is more important than sight and hearing, as the dog's brain is dominated by a large olfactory cortex. Unfortunately, our sense of smell is much duller. The olfactory signals we can receive from our dogs are very limited. From what we now know, dogs can communicate by scent at least in the following ways:

In a wolf pack, when big prey such as a deer is captured, wolves from different ranking have access to different parts of the carcass. Besides the rule of the alphas being able to eat first, each member also has a particular body part they can eat. The alphas have access of the most nutritious part of the prey such as its heart, liver, and prime meat. The beta has the right to claim a good part of meat, and he also saves a portion of it for the omega. Mid-ranks have the second- or third-class meat and bones depending on the size of the prey, while low-ranks only receive the least nutritious parts such as stomach, intestines, and some bones. As every wolf has a different part of an animal for food, each rank has its own distinctive scent, with the alphas giving the most powerful scent because what they eat is very rich with a strong smell. By eating their appointed parts of the prey, each wolf establishes his social status in the pack with what he eats, and reinforces it by the way he smells.

When a member of the pack wants to heighten his rank or display his dominance, one of his ways is by scent-rolling. Scent-rolling is a behaviour in which a wolf or a dog rolls in a substance with a fecund stench such as the faeces of foxes and fish-eating birds. As the stronger the scent the higher the represented rank, wolves and dogs often scent-roll when they have the opportunity in order to test the reaction of other members of the pack. Consequently, when I see my dog trying to scent-roll during a walk, I will stop him immediately and then make him do a series of obedience exercises to establish my rank over him. If I'm too slow and he's already rolled in the stinky substance, besides stopping him and drilling him with obedience exercises, once we're home I will give him a thorough bath to wash off all that scent. In the following few days, I will give him nothing but cow stomach and fermented grass as food to mimic the diet of a low-rank wolf in the pack. I will also tighten the pack rules in these few days and increase training in obedience to remind him of our pack order.

Dogs can communicate by releasing different pheromones. A dog uses his anal glands to give out olfactory signals. Every time a dog defecates, a portion of the fluid stored in his anal sac is released. By wagging his tail in different ways, a dog displays different visual signals, and at the same time he also releases a cocktail of pheromones to communicate by scent.

A dog's nose can distinguish the age, sex, emotional state, physiological condition, recent meal, and recent visited place of humans, other dogs, and other animals. As our sense of smell is very limited, we still need much more research and development in the studies of the dog's olfaction.

Taste

Some scientific research reported that the sense of taste in dogs is not as keen as in humans. Many animals taste food with a combination of their sense of taste and sense of smell. A dog's nose is much stronger than ours. So how well a dog can taste is difficult to verify. From observation though, we can see that dogs do utilise their taste to receive communication signals from their own kind. For example, dogs often lick other dogs and their secretions such as urine, faeces, and vaginal discharge combined with sniffing to investigate the other dogs' physiological conditions. This is especially obvious during courtship, when the male often tastes the female's vagina to determine if she's ready to conceive. This shows that dogs use their sense of taste to communicate at a certain level.

Effective Communication by Utilising all Five Senses

As dog trainers, we should employ all the above senses to deliver and receive different signals from our dogs. The more effectively we can communicate, the quicker we can read our dogs and send the right messages across, and the easier our training becomes.

Proper Keeping and Kennel Management of Working Dogs

To successfully raise working dogs, the three most essential elements are breeding, keeping, and training. Breeding is the dogs' appropriate genetics, bloodlines, ancestors, and natural working abilities. Keeping is the proper feeding, housing, and daily management of the dogs, which includes kennel construction, food quality, and general operation. Training is the correct education by methodically applying effective systems and sequences so the dogs understand what we want. This needs an experienced trainer and suitable equipment. All the above components are crucial and can't be overlooked.

Kennels

With my own dogs, puppies under six months old and retired dogs are kept inside my house to live with me and my family. For dogs from six months to their retirement from sport, as I spend a lot of time with them in training and exercising every day, I let them live outside in their enclosures so they can enjoy freedom and space.

If you have only one dog, as long as you spend enough time training and exercising him daily, he can happily live inside your house without needing a kennel. If you're a working dog enthusiast and have three dogs or more, kennels will make your life more convenient for sure. If you're a professional trainer or devoted breeder with five dogs or more, then construction of some proper enclosures is a must.

As a general rule, there are two main types of kennels, namely the outdoor kennels and indoor kennels. They both have their advantages and disadvantages. Outdoor kennels allow the dogs to see the view outside and give a better sense of freedom and open space. When the weather is good the dogs can bask in the sun. The downside is, if the dogs staying in the kennels are naturally nervous, every time they see people and animals walking by they will get excited and start to jump around and bark. If this happens many times a day, everybody including you, your dogs, and your neighbours will live in anxiety, which is mentally and physically harmful. When the weather is cold or wet, the outdoor kennels won't make the best living environment. Some dogs are so excitable that they will keep pacing and spinning in the kennels even when rain is pouring outside. This would lower their immunity level, in the short term possibly causing a cold or kennel cough; in the long term this might also lead to rheumatism.

Indoor kennels can separate the dogs from the outside world and block out some of the noise from barking. They also keep the dogs warm and dry from bad weather. The disadvantage is, if you're planning a multiple-dog indoor kennel complex, the barking trapped inside will create serious echoes especially when the dogs can see each other. This is even more stressful for the dogs as the echo inside is much louder than the outside kennels. Dogs living in kennels indoors also can't see the outside world to enjoy the good weather. If the ventilation is not good enough, indoor kennels trap moisture and bacteria, spreading contagious diseases such as kennel cough a lot faster than the outdoor kennels.

You can create the perfect kennels by combining the two designs in one to have indoor/outdoor kennels, with one side of the kennels built inside a roofed building such as a barn, while the other side of the kennels has opened tops. There is a pulley-action sliding trap door between each inside/outside kennel, so you can choose to leave it opened for the dog to access either side, or close it to keep him on a particular side. The dogs run free in the outside kennels during the day while they can also choose to rest inside if they prefer. At night you call them into the inside kennels and close the trap doors so they can sleep in warmth and in peace. The outdoor kennels are made of metal panels, while the indoor kennels can be made of bricks or wood. It is important to insulate the roof for the inside kennels to avoid over- or under-heating in extreme weather. This is for me the best system but it's more expensive and more time-consuming to clean as each dog is taking up two kennels, one for inside and one for outside. The kennels' ground surface needs to be easy to clean with fast drainage. The material must be safe for the dog to walk or lie down on and odour-friendly. Stone gravel about 5 to 10cm thick is the best option. Underneath it, there should be a metal net with suitable hardness or concrete on a sloping angle to prevent digging and promote efficient drainage. Thick timber panels for outdoor use are also a good choice as a kennel floor. Small gaps should be left between the timber panels so water can pass through effectively and there is enough room for thermal expansion and contracting of the wood. The gaps shouldn't be more than 1cm apart or the dogs might accidentally get their toes stuck in between. The timber panels can be rested on bricks or stone gravel for easy drainage. Concrete is used a lot as a surface for kennel flooring but it's usually quite high maintenance. It's not water permeable and needs to be hosed down at least once a day to keep clean if the dog does his toilet business inside. While urine is soaking the concrete, an excited dog often runs in it and bounces the urine back all over his belly and chest. When the urine is mixed with faeces it gets much worse. Dogs that are kept on concrete usually stink as they're covered by their own waste, unless they're showered weekly or trained not to empty themselves in the enclosure. Another disadvantage of concrete for kennel flooring is its stiffness, which is very harsh for the dog's bones, joints, nails, and paws. In winter, concrete stays cold. All these shortcomings can shorten a dog's working life.

A more economical design of the indoor/outdoor kennel system is the partially opened kennel. The dogs get plenty of sun and air while being protected from the wind and the cold. In this construction each kennel is surrounded by wind-proof timber panels with a built-in dog house, so the dog can choose to stay dry and warm when bad weather strikes. This is the system I use:

1. The frame of the kennel complex is made of metal panels. The surrounding walls of the complex are made of thick and heavy timber panels for outdoor use. They cover the north,

east, and west sides of the complex, making its opening south-facing, which is away from direct sunlight, wind, and rain.

2. The back of the complex is facing my training field. As it's blocked by the timber wall, the dogs in the kennels can't see the action on the field. This minimises excitement and barking. There are several well-branched trees in front of the kennels' entries, providing extra coverage from rain and wind.

3. Within the external walls of the complex, there are additional separation walls every two kennels. Each kennel houses one dog (except for puppies). Usually I place a male and a female next to each other's kennel. This way each pair can have a little companionship while preventing the aggression caused by same-sex competitions. For young and friendly puppies from the same litter, sometimes I place two in the same enclosure so they can play and exercise.

4. Each single kennel has the length of 4m and the width of 2m. Inside there's a dog house made of insulated material. The dog is free to go in and out, receiving protection from bad weather.

5. The floor of each kennel is made of the same timber I use for the walls. It gives good insulation and is friendly to the dog's joints and paws. In the middle of the timber floor is a layer of stone gravel for use as a toilet. It is easy to clean and any liquid slides right off.

6. For younger puppies, both sides of the kennel have added walls for extra weather protection. In the middle of the timber floor I put sand instead of stone for use as a toilet.

7. My kennel complex sits at the end of my garden. The entrance faces a neighbouring cattle paddock.

8. Looking out from the kennels, the dogs can relax by watching cows hanging out in the meadow.

For adult dogs (eighteen months old or over), if they have sufficient exercise and freedom daily, at night they can be kept indoors in durable plastic travelling crates so they can stay calm and have

plenty of rest for training the next day (each travelling crate should be big enough for a dog to stand up straight and turn around).

For the housing and upbringing of puppies, I will thoroughly explain it in "The Developing Stage: A Puppy's First Week Home" in Chapter 2. If you wish to keep puppies less than three months old in an indoor kennel at night, the kennel floor should be covered with a layer of wood shavings about 5cm thick instead of gravel to retain warmth and absorb moisture.

Food

For the best health, dogs should be given food that is as natural as possible. In Belgium, we can buy unprocessed dog food quite easily. The primary food source that I feed my dogs is based on raw meat, bones, and offal, mixed with fruit and vegetables. I vary the animal ingredients between lamb, beef, rabbit, duck, chicken, and fish. Natural food promotes health, energy levels, and the dogs' motivation to eat. It's important that we know where the meat is coming from, though. It has to be fresh, clean, and safe to be consumed by dogs. Contaminated food can easily give our dogs illness such as infection of the digestive tract. If you're living in an area where edible raw meat for dogs is unavailable, it's worthwhile to try preparing human-grade lamb meat in thin slices by briefly soaking in almost-boiling water as a supplement to a quality brand of dry dog food. To ensure my dogs can quickly adjust to dry food during travelling for competitions, I use it for training and occasionally as their full meal. International championships can be held anywhere in the world. It's not possible to travel several hundred kilometres with a week's portion of raw meat as it would very quickly decay. My dogs' digestive systems need to be familiar with dry food, so a week before I travel with them I switch to dry food gradually.

Exercises

Puppies and grown dogs all need a certain amount of exercise and freedom including walks, socialisation, training, interaction, and physical conditioning. The quantity of activity for every dog is different. We should consider this based on their age, health, fitness, and disposition.

Medical Attention

Working dogs are athletes that go through vigorous exercise daily. Small injuries such as muscle strains, sprains, and bruises often occur. As dog owners, we should have a family veterinarian who specialises in treating dogs. Vaccinations and deworming should be performed as scheduled to ensure our dogs' general health. There should be a first-aid kit in the kennel with disinfectant, bandages, medical cotton, nail clippers, brush, and frequently used medicine for dogs such as deworming tablets, flea and tick repellent, ear wash, eye disinfecting cream, and antibiotics.

Recording

When necessary, we should take notes of certain events such as vaccination and deworming dates, medication period and doses, recovery progress, bitches' oestrous cycles, mating dates, mating partners, litter due dates, birth dates, etc. Every important detail should be clear and traceable.

Training Equipment

There are various systems and methods we can employ while training dogs. The proper use of associated equipment can increase the effectiveness of our training. In the list below, you can see the most frequently used apparatus while training dogs for Schutzhund/IPO. The utilisation of each tool will be explained in its related chapter.

Equipment	Use
Flat collar	The collar worn by the dog daily for walks, tracking, obedience, and bite work; it can be made of nylon or leather
Wide flat collar	A wider version of the flat collar used by young dogs during bite work. An increased width allows the dog to pull into the collar during bite work without choking
Waist band	For training the stand exercise
Slip chain	The only collar allowed during IPO trials
Plastic pinch collar	For introducing the early steps of negative reinforcement by blocking and leading
Pinch collar	For negative reinforcement by blocking and leading
Constricting collar	For negative reinforcement by blocking and leading. It is used to reduce excitement
Electric collar	Works as an invisible leash, allowing the handler to "touch" his dog from a long distance. Also known as *teletact* in Belgium. Tele = distant and tact = contact; distant contact
Electric tail band	Works as an invisible whip like a jockey's riding crop in accelerating his racehorse. It allows the handler to "tap" his dog on the tail from a long distance. Used mainly for speed and direction in going forward

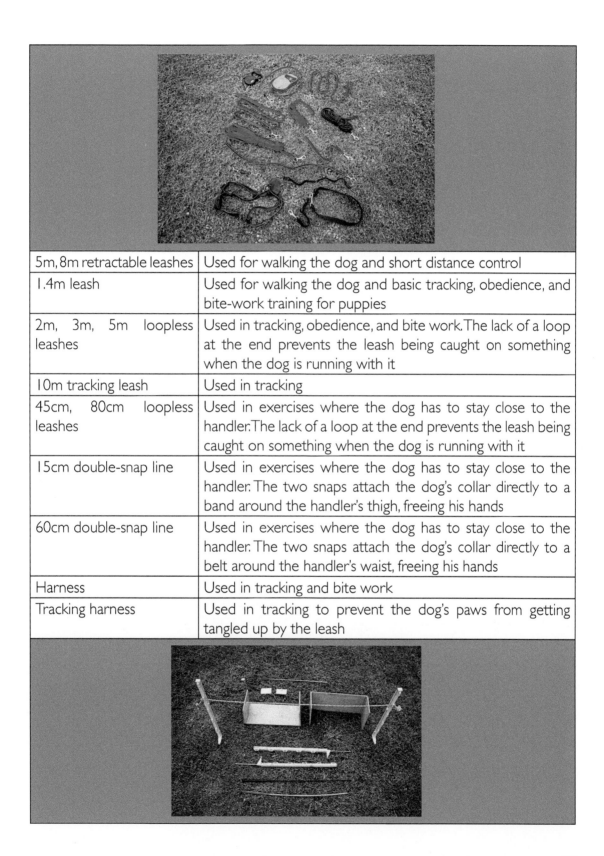

5m, 8m retractable leashes	Used for walking the dog and short distance control
1.4m leash	Used for walking the dog and basic tracking, obedience, and bite-work training for puppies
2m, 3m, 5m loopless leashes	Used in tracking, obedience, and bite work. The lack of a loop at the end prevents the leash being caught on something when the dog is running with it
10m tracking leash	Used in tracking
45cm, 80cm loopless leashes	Used in exercises where the dog has to stay close to the handler. The lack of a loop at the end prevents the leash being caught on something when the dog is running with it
15cm double-snap line	Used in exercises where the dog has to stay close to the handler. The two snaps attach the dog's collar directly to a band around the handler's thigh, freeing his hands
60cm double-snap line	Used in exercises where the dog has to stay close to the handler. The two snaps attach the dog's collar directly to a belt around the handler's waist, freeing his hands
Harness	Used in tracking and bite work
Tracking harness	Used in tracking to prevent the dog's paws from getting tangled up by the leash

Clicker	A tool to confirm a desired behaviour during positive reinforcement
Target stick	A tool for targeting
Target tag	A tool for targeting
Target plates	A pair of flat panels for the dog to lie on
Portable fence	A temporary barrier formed by driving a group of portable sticks into the ground. Used to limit a dog's movement to improve precision
Portable stick	Plastic sticks that can be thrust into the ground. Used to limit a dog's movement to improve precision
Riding whip, rattan stick	Tool for reversed targeting

1m hurdle	Used for jumping in obedience training
1.8m A-frame	Used for climbing in obedience training
Article indication box	A wooden box used to increase the focus and precision of the article indication of tracking

650g wooden dumbbell	The appointed retrieval object in the obedience phase of IPO1 trials
1000g wooden dumbbell	The appointed retrieval object in the obedience phase of IPO2 trials

2000g wooden dumbbell	The appointed retrieval object in the obedience phase of IPO3 trials
Fluffy ball	A toy to encourage puppies to bite and push
Fluffy bite roll	A toy to encourage puppies to bite and hold
Rubber ball	A toy for the dog to bite and play fetch with
Rubber ball with rope	A toy for the dog to bite, play fetch, and tug-of-war with
Floating ball	A toy for the dog to play fetch with while swimming
Floating dummy	A toy for the dog to play fetch and tug-of-war with while swimming
Jute bite roll	A toy to encourage puppies to bite and hold
Ball stand	A stick with a ring on top for holding a ball. Can be pushed into the ground. For teaching the hide search and the back transport

Retrieving table	A metal frame for teaching the dog to hold the dumbbell securely

Puppy bite tug	A target for teaching puppies how to bite and hold
Puppy sleeve	A target for teaching puppies how to bite and hold. Can be worn on the arm by the decoy

Young dog sleeve	A sleeve for young dogs to bite. Harder and bulkier than the puppy sleeve
Leg sleeve	A sleeve for teaching dogs to bite the bad guy's leg. Can be worn on the leg by the decoy
Hard bite cushion	A target for teaching young dogs how to tackle during an off leash attack. Same hardness as the trial sleeve but smaller in size. Can be worn on the decoy's arm or held at different angles to encourage the dog to leap into the bite
Trial sleeve	The appointed protective sleeve worn by the decoy in all IPO trials.
Scratch pants	A pair of overalls made of scratch-proof fabric. Worn by the decoy for protection from scratching during bite work

Padded stick	A leather and foam padded stick used to condition the dogs in bite work to desensitise them to being hit by the bad guy
Clatter stick	A bamboo stick split into quarters. When rattled it produces a loud clapping noise. Used in bite work to desensitise dogs to noises
Whip	A whip that makes a loud pop when cracked by the decoy. Used for increasing various drives in bite work
Starter pistol	A tool to desensitise dogs to gunshot noise
Tracking flag	A flag to mark the start of a track
Small food box	Used for teaching puppies to indicate articles on the track
Tracking articles	To be placed on the track for the dogs to search and indicate
Handler leg band	To be fastened to the handler's thigh. Used together with the double snap line to teach heeling
Handler waist band	To be fastened to the handler's waist. Used together with the double snap line to teach the "Here" (front position)
Training vest	A multiple-pocketed vest for the handler to carry many different tools for his training

CHAPTER TWO

Common Working Dog Breeds

The following dog breeds are the most popular among Schutzhund/IPO, police, military, and security patrol work:

Dog Breed	Land of Origin	Approx. Weight	Popularity in Schutzhund/IPO
Malinois	Belgium	30–40kg	★★★★★
Tervuren	Belgium	30–40kg	★★★½☆
Groenendael	Belgium	30–40kg	★½☆☆☆
Laekenois	Belgium	30–40kg	★★☆☆☆
German Shepherd Dog	Germany	35–45kg	★★★★★
Dutch Shepherd Dog	Netherlands	30–40kg	★★☆☆☆
Border Collie	United Kingdom	15–25kg	★☆☆☆☆
Beauceron	France	35–45kg	★★☆☆☆
Briard	France	30–40kg	★☆☆☆☆
Bouvier des Flandres	Belgium	40–50kg	★★☆☆☆
Rottweiler	Germany	40–50kg	★★★★½
Dobermann	Germany	35–45kg	★★★☆☆
Boxer	Germany	35–45kg	★★☆☆☆
Giant Schnauzer	Germany	40–50kg	★★☆☆☆
Hovawart	Germany	30–40kg	★☆☆☆☆
Airedale Terrier	United Kingdom	25–35kg	★☆☆☆☆

Note: The star rating is only a general indication of the breeds' popularity in the world of Schutzhund/IPO. The fewer number of stars only means that the breeds are less often seen in our sport, but could excel in other disciplines.

Malinois

Tervuren

Groenendael

Laekenois

German Shepherd Dog

Dutch Shepherd Dog

Border Collie

Beauceron

Briard

Bouvier des Flandres

Rottweiler

Dobermann

Boxer

Giant Schnauzer

Hovawart

Airedale Terrier

The Above Photos Were Provided by the Following Owners:

- BR.001: Eclipse van de Duvetorre IPO3, Felix Ho, Belgium
- BR.002: Drakar du Clos d'Ypsi MR3, Jeannine Coupe, Belgium
- BR.003: Garry du Jardin du Malézy IPO3, Ellen Bronsema, Netherlands
- BR.004: From Laeken Paradis Kalé BH, Brigitte Broekx, Belgium
- BR.005: Quint vom Fuchsgraben2000 IPO3, Peter Diedrichkeit, Germany
- BR.006: Grog von Carolus Magnus IPO3, Karin Weishäupl, Germany
- BR.007: Lillifee in blue-sable IV.Queen of Eskalony, Mario Diederley, Germany
- BR.008: Honil des Marais de Saint Gratien FR2, Aurélie Mechin, France
- BR.009: Kyos du Pont de L'Escaut IPO2, Luc Flamand, Belgium
- BR.010: Waldo BH, Eric De Gendt, Belgium
- BR.011: Badboy vom Checkpoint Charlie IPO1, Felix Ho, Belgium
- BR.012: Rico vom Grenzturm, Roman Rauner, Austria
- BR.013: Heloise van't Duyverlohof, Isabel Duyck, Belgium
- BR.014: Raptor von Elberfeld IPO3, Jennifer Hüffer, Germany
- BR.015: Ajushi vom Drei Ruten Berg IPO3, Georg Weber, Germany
- BR.016: Moneypenny von der Weiler Burg, Philip Mauch, Germany

Puppy Selection

When I decide to start a new dog for IPO competitions, I normally choose a puppy between the ages of seven and eight weeks old. The reasons are:

1. A puppy of this age has just completed the basic development of his senses. He's fully aware of his environment. At the same time he's like a blank piece of paper and will absorb information like a sponge. This is the most mouldable age. I can teach many of the foundation training techniques to this puppy by imprinting.
2. This is the best age for a puppy to leave his mother and nest. If he leaves his dam and siblings too early, he will miss adequate education in the canine language such as social skills, pack order, and parental care. If he leaves too late it will be more difficult for him to bond with the new handler. The age between seven to eight weeks is just right. I only need one week to develop a strong bond and pack order with this puppy.
3. As the puppy is raised by me from a very young age, I will know his whole history from the beginning. If any health problems or behavioural issues arise in the future, it will be easier for me to trace back their origin and solve them accordingly.
4. All of the competitive accomplishments the dog achieves will be a direct result of the hard work of my teammates and me, and not because of someone else's training from before. It's like a sculptor who selects the right piece of marble, carefully roughs it out, meticulously carves it, finely polishes it, and eventually produces his masterpiece. For me, this is the greatest satisfaction of dog training.

Breeds and Bloodlines

Although the most common dog breeds seen in IPO today are the sixteen breeds I've mentioned above, in fact only two of these breeds really excel at the highest level in the sport. Their success is way beyond the rest in the all-breed world championship. They're the Belgian Malinois and the German Shepherd. As for the other fourteen breeds, there are some great dogs for working, but it is relatively more difficult to find individuals that can match the working abilities for the Malinois and the Shepherd, especially in the department of trainability.

Practically, selecting a working dog is not as simple as just picking up a puppy from a working breed. Before we take on a new puppy, we should first at least have some basic understanding of his breed's original purpose and its general temperament and speak to as many people as possible that have owned, trained, and competed with this breed to know what we're getting into. Personally, I've owned and titled three different working breeds including Malinois, German Shepherd, and Rottweiler. I like to work with many different dog breeds, as each time I start with a new breed I learn a lot from their characteristics, which are less often seen in other breeds. Once I've decided which breed I'll start with as my next new project, I'll do some research on which kennels of this breed are the most successful in working trials. I'll contact these breeders and explain to them what my intention is and what I expect from the puppy. I like to spend some time with the breeders so I can listen to their views and visions of the breed and their preferred bloodlines. Usually, the best working breeders are private kennels owned by diehard working dogs enthusiasts. Most of the outstanding kennels share the features below:

1. There is a clean, tranquil, and orderly environment for the dogs to live in.
2. The dogs are healthy, lively, confident, and happy.
3. The breeder is an experienced trainer himself. He's passionate about cynology and has many likeminded friends that respect him.
4. The breeder can demonstrate the actual working quality of his dogs, such as tracking, obedience, and bite work, instead of running or posing for the show ring.
5. The breeder is knowledgeable about the ancestors of his dogs and how their qualities influence his current breeding, and he can tell me their strengths and weaknesses without bias. Most successful working dog breeders have bred dogs that do well in working trials or are active in service work such as police and military. It's worthwhile looking up these dogs to see their working qualities.

I'll observe the breeder's dogs in training and in a natural environment such as walking in a forest. If he agrees, I'll put on a protection sleeve and work some of his dogs in bite work. If I feel the breeder's vision is compatible with mine, I'll order a puppy from one of his upcoming litters that suits me most. I'll discuss with him about what age I shall pick up the puppy and how I prefer to test him in my selection process. The breeder will let me know which pick of the litter I have. For example, the first pick means I'll be the first person to select my puppy from the litter. The second pick means there'll be one person making his selection before me, and so on. The higher the pick, the better chance I'll have to select the puppy I prefer most. However, not every dog handler looks for the same thing. One dog trainer's first pick could be another's second, third, or fourth preference. In some exceptional occasions, when the whole litter has supreme working qualities, any random choice is a super puppy, but this is very rare.

I like both male and female dogs and have competed with both. If I'm to select a puppy for breeding purposes, usually I'll take a female, because it's the bitch that gives birth to puppies. When I have a good female and I want to have a litter, all I need to do is to find her a suitable male, pay his owner a stud fee, and do a mating. Then I'll have a whole litter that belongs to me under my kennel name. I can take my time and choose my next puppy from this and continue with the bloodline. If I'm to select a puppy mainly for competition purposes, usually I'll take a male, because generally male dogs are more resilient and tolerant. They're also less prone to psychological and physiological fluctuations due to hormonal changes such as estrous cycles, pregnancy, and lactation. Some males do get a little crazy when there are females in heat in his kennel, however, especially stud dogs that have experience in mating.

Age of Puppy Selection

If the puppies are bred by me and born in my kennels, quite often I can already see which one would suit me most by the time they reach six weeks old. If the puppies are born with another breeder, usually I'll select them between the ages of seven and eight weeks (forty-nine to fifty-six days old). At this age the puppies have just completed the basic development of their senses but they haven't had too much formal training. It's easier to see their natural reaction during the observation based on their instincts and not artificial conditioning.

Campbell Puppy Evaluation

The Campbell puppy evaluation was developed by the late American cynologist Mr William E. Campbell (1929–2014) in the 1960s. It's used to assess the temperament of puppies between the ages of forty-nine and fifty-six days. This test helps to give a prediction of how confident, sociable, flexible, dominant, and independent the puppy will become as he matures, so each puppy can have a better chance of matching the right owner. The evaluation must conform to the following rules:

1. The evaluated puppies should be from forty-nine to fifty-six days old. Carrying out the test before or after this period can lose its accuracy, as the puppies could be premature or over-conditioned.
2. The evaluator should be a total stranger to the puppies without any previous encounter. If I'm the breeder, I'd invite an experienced friend over who is unknown to the puppies to perform the test.
3. The place for the evaluation should be completely unknown to the puppies without any previous contact. There should be no distractions involving sight, sound, or smell (an enclosure that many dogs have used as a toilet or a paddock littered with cow dung is not suitable). The breeder or anyone known by the puppies should stay out of sight. It can be outdoors or indoors, such as a football field or a basketball court.
4. The Campbell puppy evaluation can only be carried out once for each puppy. We want to see the instinctual reaction of the puppy when he first comes across the given situations in the test.
5. The puppies shouldn't be fed or played with for a minimum of four hours before the test to preserve their energy, interest, and alertness. They should not be dewormed or vaccinated within twenty-four hours prior the test to ensure they're at their best condition.
6. All puppies should be tested equally and consistently. The evaluation should be carried out as objectively and scientifically as possible.
7. The puppies are tested separately and one by one. Their reactions are recorded by pen

and paper, rated from high to low as A, B, C D, and E accordingly.

Since the development of this test by Mr Campbell, there have been several different versions and scoring methods. I've modified this into the system below for clearer results, better calculations, and easier comparison between the puppies.

Social Interaction	
Procedure: The evaluator carries one puppy and places him in the centre of the testing ground. He walks about 10m away, then turns around, crouches down invitingly while clapping, and calls the puppy to him. The intention of this assessment is to observe the confidence and interest of the puppy towards a total stranger in a strange place	
Rating of the puppy's possible reactions:	
Comes immediately and quickly or never leaves the evaluator while he walks away, tail up, likes to make body contact such as climbing up onto the evaluator, bites the evaluator or his clothing confidently	A
Comes immediately and quickly or never leaves the evaluator while he walks away, tail up, likes to make body contact such as climbing up onto the evaluator	B
Takes a little time before approaching, comes easily, tail carried horizontally or slightly lower	C
Takes quite a while before coming hesitantly, tail down	D
Doesn't come at all, freezes worriedly, or runs away in panic	E

Interest in Following	
Procedure: The evaluator stands up and walks away from the puppy slowly for about 10m. The intention of this assessment is to observe the puppy's confidence, interest, and competitiveness. While still in the litter, puppies often follow their mother between her legs in order to suckle. To fight for the best milk they often try to hold on to her mammary glands determinedly while pushing out their siblings. After the first encounter, a resilient puppy often does the same to his newly met "friend"	
Rating of the puppy's possible reactions:	
Follows immediately and quickly, tail up, likes to walk between the evaluator's legs and make body contact, bites the evaluator or his clothing confidently	A
Follows immediately and quickly, tail up, likes to walk between the evaluator's legs and make body contact	B
Takes a little time before following, tail carried horizontally or slightly lower, walks behind or next to the evaluator	C
Takes quite a while before following hesitantly, hangs around loosely without much focus, tail down	D
Doesn't follow at all, freezes worriedly, or runs away in panic	E

Response to Domination	
Procedure: The evaluator flips the puppy upside down and pins him onto the ground firmly with one hand, so that the puppy's belly is facing up. He looks directly in the puppy's eyes and prevents him from getting up for about thirty seconds. The intention of this assessment is to observe the puppy's behaviour while being dominated by a stranger. This is called the "alpha roll" and a dominant puppy usually protests vigorously once realising the evaluator's meaning	
Rating of the puppy's possible reactions	
Resists strongly and confidently by scratching, kicking, and growling, tail out, heart not beating especially fast, bites	A
Resists strongly and confidently by scratching, kicking, and growling, tail out, heart not beating especially fast	B
Takes a little time before resisting, the protest goes on and off, tail out	C
Doesn't resist but relaxed	D
Freezes completely, increased heart rate, tail tucked between legs, panic	E

Response to Challenge

Procedure: The evaluator releases the puppy from the previous test and lets him get back up onto his feet. He now crouches in front of the puppy and strokes him firmly, slowly, and deliberately on his back for thirty seconds. The intention of this assessment is to observe two things. First is the puppy's recovery ability straight after the previous domination. A good working puppy should be directly active, while a lesser one might stay on the ground passively or goes away trying to avoid further confrontation. Second is the puppy's response to being "T'ed up", which is a direct challenge from the evaluator (please refer to Chapter 1, Part 6, "Basic Understanding of Dog Language, Touch")

Rating of the puppy's possible reactions:

Directly makes contact with the evaluator by climbing up confidently, seeks eye contact, bites	A
Directly makes contact with the evaluator by climbing up confidently, seeks eye contact	B
Likes to make contact with the evaluator without climbing up	C
Doesn't accept being "T'ed up", walks away but not afraid	D
Freezes worriedly, tail tucked between legs, clearly stressed, or runs away in panic	E

Acceptance of Being Lifted	
Procedure: The evaluator stands and picks up the puppy by holding his belly off the ground for thirty seconds. This behaviour mimics a large predator such as an eagle snatching up its prey in the air. The intention of this assessment is to observe the puppy's reaction when confronted by predatory behaviour	
Rating of the puppy's possible reactions:	
Resists strongly and confidently by scratching, kicking, and growling, tail out, heart not beating especially fast, bites	A
Resists strongly and confidently by scratching, kicking, and growling, tail out, heart not beating especially fast	B
Takes a little time before resisting, the protest goes on and off, tail out	C
Doesn't resist but relaxed	D
Freezes completely, increased heart rate, tail tucked between legs, panic	E

In the Campbell puppy evaluation, the main elements we can observe are the puppy's self-assurance, environmental soundness, mental persistence, dominance/competitiveness, focus/presence, maturity and composure, courage, expression and recovery speed, willingness and flexibility, mental clarity under excitement and pressure, protection drive, rank drive, and pack drive.

The evaluator writes down every rating of every test. To make it convenient for comparison, we translate all the ratings to scores, A = 4 points, B = 3 points, C = 2 points, D = 1 point, E = 0 points. If a puppy receives all As in the five tests (which is extremely rare), then the total score would be 4 x 5 = 20 points. The higher the score means the higher the above working qualities shown in the evaluation, and the more potential the puppy has as a working dog. We can divide the tested puppies into five classes, combining with the environmental evaluation and the bite evaluation as further references for the final selection.

Campbell Evaluation Scoring	Class
20–17 points	High
16–13 points	Mid-high
12–9 points	Medium (passing score = 10 points)
8–5 points	Mid-low (fail)
4–0 points	Low (fail)

Environmental Evaluation

After all the puppies in the whole nest have been tested, we can take them to another place for the environmental evaluation. The appraisal should be set up as follows:

1. The environmental evaluation begins after the Campbell puppy evaluation.
2. The evaluator is still the same person.
3. The place of this observation has to be another location where the puppies have never been. The criteria are opposite from before, though. This time we choose a place with slight visual, audio, and olfactory distractions, such as a low-traffic park or a university campus. The breeder can watch from a distance if he likes. To prevent the puppies running into hazards, we let them wear a collar and a 5m retractable leash.
4. The evaluator prepares a fluffy ball or a fluffy bite roll and puts it in his pocket for the ensuing bite evaluation.
5. All puppies should be tested equally and consistently. The evaluation should be carried out as objectively and scientifically as possible.
6. The puppies are tested separately one by one. Their reactions are recorded by pen and paper, rated from high to low as A, B, C, D, and E accordingly.
7. Right after each puppy's completion of this test, the bite evaluation begins.

Environmental Evaluation	
Procedure: The evaluator takes the puppy for a three- to five-minute walk in the middle of the park. He calls the puppy occasionally to keep him following. He observes the puppy's reaction towards the surrounding environment, people, and noises	
Rating of the puppy's possible reactions:	
Walks happily and confidently, tail up, curious and outgoing to his surroundings, no hesitation or reservation at all	A

Walks happily and confidently, tail up, curious and outgoing to his surroundings, a little hesitant to sudden movements or noises made by nearby people but recovers straight away	B
Walks slowly with care or pauses often, tail carried horizontally or slightly lower, curious to his surroundings but a little hesitant	C
Walks very slowly with doubt and pauses all the time, tail down, uncertain gaze and facial expression, prepared to flee at any time	D
Doesn't want to walk, tail tucked between legs, cringes, freezes, shakes, or runs away in panic and looks for places to hide	E

In the environmental evaluation, the working abilities we observe are the puppy's self-assurance, environmental soundness, dominance/competitiveness, focus/presence, courage, expression and recovery speed, willingness and flexibility, and pack drive.

For convenience, we translate all the ratings to scores, A = 20 points, B = 15 points, C = 10 points, D = 5 points, E = 0 points. The evaluator can choose to further distinguish the differences within a rating by numbers. For example, he can differentiate the "A" rating into 20 points, 19 points, 18 points, 17 points, and 16 points. This way he can compare two or more puppies within the same rating in finer detail.

Environmental Evaluation Rating	Scoring
A	20
B	15
C	10
D	5
E	0

Bite Evaluation

Right after the previous assessment and before moving on to the next puppy, the evaluator takes the puppy to a quiet quarter of the park, unclips the leash, and directly begins the bite evaluation. In the bite evaluation, we mainly test the puppy's self-assurance, mental persistence, agility and speed, hunt drive/prey drive, protection drive, rank drive, and grip.

Like the other two assessments, we translate all the ratings to scores, A = 20 points, B = 15 points, C = 10 points, D = 5 points, E = 0 points. Once again, the evaluator can choose to further distinguish a rating by numbers. He can differentiate the "A" rating into 20 points, 19 points, 18 points, 17 points, and 16 points to compare two or more puppies within the same rating.

Bite Evaluation

Procedure: The evaluator crouches in front of the puppy and shows him the fluffy bite roll. He moves the bite roll on the ground in a jerky, quivering motion, mimicking the movement of prey, just like he's teasing a cat to chase a toy mouse attached to a string..

If the puppy bites the toy, the evaluator shakes it gently and weakly to simulate a struggling mouse, while patting the puppy's back or pushing his chest with another hand to see if he gets distracted by the contact and lets go of the toy.

Sometimes he holds the puppy gently by the muzzle to pretend he wants to take the toy away by jerking the bite roll downward.

The aim of this whole exercise is to imitate a hunting session and observe the puppy's hunting instincts and determination to keep his prey from a bigger and stronger opponent (the evaluator)

Rating of the puppy's possible reactions:	
Shows direct interest by chasing and biting the toy, well calculated strike, tries to fill his mouth once he has a hold, bites harder when pushed, clearly wants to display dominance to the evaluator by protecting the toy	A
Shows direct interest by chasing and biting the toy, tries to fill his mouth once he has a hold, bites harder when pushed	B
Shows interest in biting but takes a few test strikes before holding onto the toy, a little hesitant when touched or pushed, grip not full or not very strong	C
Shows little interest in biting but not stressed	D
Shows no interest in biting at all, behaves nervously by cringing or trying to flee	E

Scoring of the Three Evaluations

The Campbell puppy evaluation, environmental evaluation, and bite evaluation each has a maximum score of 20 points. Together they make 60 points in total. Below we can categorise the tested puppies into five classes to help the selection process.

The Total Scores of Campbell, Environmental, and Bite Evaluation	Class	Characteristics
60–49 points	High	Dominant, courageous, active, bold, tenacious, competitive, extremely difficult to tame. Suitable for tasks that need a high level of independence and a veteran handler with a lot of experience with dogs of high caliber. If in the wrong hands, this puppy can grow up to be a very dangerous dog. He has many qualities of the alpha. If he can pass on his qualities to his offspring, he has the potential to be a super producer of brilliant working dogs
48–37 points	Mid-high	Dominant, courageous, active, and bold, while flexible and forgiving at the same time. With an experienced handler, this puppy has a strong possibility of being an outstanding working dog. He has many qualities of the beta

36–25 points	Medium (passing score = 30 points)	Although mild-tempered, a puppy scoring 30 to 36 points has a good balance between wildness and tameness. He has enough determination to overcome difficult challenges in a task while being relatively easy to control. A typical worker, he has many qualities of the mid-rank. With patience and encouragement, even a green handler has the potential to make this puppy a fine working animal. A puppy scoring 25 to 29 points is slightly below the passing line. Sometimes he has the potential of coming out of his shell when given the chance
24–13 points	Mid-low (fail)	Slightly hesitant, passive, and reserved, this puppy needs a very gentle and patient handler to build his confidence. It will be a time-consuming job and the result is often mediocre at best. He has qualities of a mid-low ranking dog. Not high enough to be a mid-rank, yet not low enough to be a low-ranker
12–0 points	Low (fail)	Submissive, timid, passive, and nervous. Unfortunately, this puppy isn't suitable for being a working dog. He has many qualities of the low rank
If I get an "E" rating in any test, the puppy fails immediately as a working prospect regardless of his total score. This puppy needs a good family that's willing to accept the way he is. In Europe, we have a lot of fine working dog breeders. There's no need to place my bet on a dog that I feel doubtful about.		

Considerable Factors after the Evaluations

After the three evaluations, I already have a clear idea about the working quality of the whole litter. Now I will select my puppy using an elimination system by filtering out all the puppies that didn't pass so that I can focus on the rest. Any puppy with a total score of less than 25/60 points, or receiving any E rating, will not be considered. In my experience, a puppy that shows an E rating behaviour (extremely shy) in any assessment usually can't pass in the overall picture. Even if he can, his performance is usually very unpredictable as he matures.

A high passing percentage for the whole litter is very important. If there's a 70% failure rate (seven out ten puppies fail in the evaluations), even if the other three are top scoring puppies, usually I won't consider them. My experience tells me that in this scenario, no matter how good these three puppies are at this moment, when they become adults they usually can't keep up the early promise they've shown. The inconsistency in the test results of the litter as a whole normally indicates a lack of genetic potency.

From the many puppies I've evaluated, potent working litters all share the features below:

1. The working abilities of the puppies in the whole litter are consistent with very little difference.
2. The size and physical structure of all the puppies are uniform.
3. The puppies in such a litter are highly competitive. They fight frequently and vigorously, and most of the time they're evenly matched. Very often the breeder has to separate them as early as six weeks to avoid serious injuries.
4. The mother of the puppies is usually quite gentle with strong maternal instincts.

Handler for dog, dog for handler

Puppies that have obtained a minimum score of 30/60 from the three evaluations have passed the first round of selection. As long as they're provided with proper care and methodical training and grow up healthily, they have a good possibility of being capable working dogs. Each handler should choose a puppy according the following factors:

1. The handler's personality
2. The handler's ability
3. The handler's living environment and the people he lives with
4. The experience of the handler's support team (e.g. coach and decoy)
5. The primary purpose of the puppy.

Sports cars are owned by a lot of people, but how many of them can bring out the full power of their cars? Tenacious dogs are revered by a lot of working dog fans, but how many of them can handle such dogs? A sports car driven incorrectly can cause a crash or even a fatality. A tenacious dog handled improperly can cause a serious accident or even death. The best dog for a handler isn't necessary the strongest dog, but a dog that suits him most. As a general rule, a placid and mellow handler is more suitable for a medium puppy, and an assertive and intense handler is more suitable for a mid-high to high puppy. The power of the dog should be proportional to his handler's capability and understanding. If the dog is particularly dominant, the handler must ensure the presence of such an animal will not disturb the peace and safety of his family, housemates, and neighbours. The handler's teammates such as his coach and decoy should have adequate experience with a dog of this category. If the sole purpose of the new prospect is for working trials or breeding and the handler has adequate competence, the powerful mid-high or high puppy is often the ideal choice. If the primary intention of the puppy is for family companionship that can enjoy the sport of Schutzhund/IPO as a leisure-time hobby, the easier-going medium puppy is probably the most suitable preference.

My Personal Choice

When I take on a new puppy, usually it is for one or more of the following reasons:

1. Breeding: producing working offspring of my preference
2. Working trials: competition in Schutzhund/IPO or other working dog sports
3. Research: taking on a new dog breed that I haven't trained before, in order to broaden my knowledge as a dog handler.

For my selection, I typically focus on puppies with a score of 36/60 and above. To save time and for more precise judgments, I immediately start the elimination process from the Campbell puppy evaluation. I adopt a "Three Passes In" system. For example, I'm testing a litter of seven puppies. In the Campbell puppy evaluation, six of the seven puppies obtain 12/20 points or over, and one of them receives 8/20. I'd already give this puppy back to the breeder and not assess him further in the other two evaluations (unless the breeder requests me to continue testing the puppy for his interest). In the environmental evaluation, five puppies out of the six remaining ones obtain a score of 20/20 and one of them obtains 10/20. If I see that the 10/20 puppy is also mediocre in the bite evaluation, I'll also give him back to the breeder directly. So now I have five puppies to focus on. I'll observe how they bite and record who the best biter is. This way in a short time I already have a picture of who the strongest puppy is today. When there are no more puppies I can eliminate and the difference in their working abilities is very small, I'll base the selection on my gut feeling or pick up the one that has clicked with me. The physical beauty of the puppy is usually the last aspect I consider when they're all very even in working qualities. From the moment I say this is my new puppy, the training begins.

Early Talents vs Late Bloomers

There are two types of great working dogs; the early talent and the late bloomer. The early talent is the puppy that passes the three evaluations with flying colours and maintains his outstanding working qualities as he matures. He's easy to spot and is always the star throughout his entire career. A late bloomer is the puppy that passes the three evaluations unassumingly with a medium score but turns out to be an extraordinary individual when he reaches adulthood. Such a dog goes under the radar as a puppy but then unexpectedly sheds his sluggishness after adolescence and transforms into a magnificent specimen. Unfortunately, sometimes substandard working dogs can emerge in just the same way, too. I've seen mediocre puppies growing up to be inadequate working dogs as predicted, but I've also seen promising puppies turning out to be underachievers dramatically when they're adults. The timing of the gene expression of every dog varies. Be it in sport dogs, performance horses, or racing pigeons, one of the most challenging tasks is the selection of the young prospect.

Effectiveness of the Evaluations, Changes that May Occur as the Puppy Grows, Environmental Influences, Instincts vs Moldability

The Campbell puppy evaluation, environmental evaluation, and bite evaluation show us each puppy's starting point. They allow us to discover the best-performing puppy on the day of the tests. Nevertheless, these evaluations still have their limits. The factors include:

1. The evaluations can only tell us the puppies' performances on the day. How they develop in the future can change drastically. For example, two twin brothers in a human family could vary in height at different times of their lives. The older brother could be taller when they are children, and then the younger brother could be the taller of the two by the time they're adults.
2. If a puppy is sick, for example having an upset stomach on the day of the test, this could affect his evaluation results in a negative way, making him look weaker than he really is.
3. Although the genes of the puppies inherited from their parents remain unchanged, what their genes express can vary at different rates as the puppies grow. As I've mentioned before, the most promising puppy in the evaluation can turn out to be mediocre as an adult, and the inconspicuous puppy that was sleeping in the corner when his siblings were actively biting the evaluator could turn out to be the best dog of a generation. There is also a third type of puppy with an extraordinary trainability that can absorb information like a sponge. Their mouldability is so high that their finishing line seems to be unlimited. This kind of puppy usually has the characteristics of being highly adaptive, highly flexible, with a superb recovery rate.
4. Last but not least, there is also the environmental factor. The same puppy going to two different handlers can become two completely different dogs. As the personality, skill, understanding, intention, training team, and lifestyle of each handler is different from another, the same dog raised by different handlers would most probably develop in different ways.

What's more important – an instinctual behaviour or a learned behaviour, a high starting point or a far finishing line? This is a popular debate among dog trainers and breeders. The end result is of course what counts, but early signs of aptitude are valuable to increase our odds for success as well. For me, the trainability of a dog is one of his most powerful instincts as it can be developed with almost no limits, allowing the dog to perform spectacular feats. Under the nurture of a skilled handler, a dog with high mouldability can become a super-impressive working animal.

Modern puppy evaluations in different forms do have their limits, but using a set of objective, consistent, and systematic measurements would still give us much better chances to select the right puppy compared with making a random pick without any fundamental supports. From my experience, puppies that pass the three evaluations above with a minimum score of 30/60 have a 70% to 80% success rate of being certified Schutzhund/IPO dogs.

Training Stages and Elements for Tuning

When we're training a dog, we need to progressively shape his behaviour, working on different elements at different times. The learning attitude and the vitality in an exercise are two of the most important elements in an IPO dog. If seriously damaged, they will take a long time to repair before the dog looks happy and confident in his work again. Therefore, the motivation of learning is the first element we develop, and then we raise the other criteria step by step as training advances. We can take the heeling exercise in the obedience phase for example. As I prefer to begin teaching a dog with positive approaches, first I have to figure out what he likes, such as food, then use this as his motivation to reinforce the desired behaviour. To teach the dog to walk by my side, first he has to focus on me. I keep on rewarding him so he's encouraged to keep watching me while heeling by my side. I then teach him to lift his head high and stretch his paws out as he's marching, and teach him the "Heel" command once he understands the exercise. When he's clear of the command, I show him how to park himself beside me from a distance away as quickly as possible. Subsequently I train him under different levels of distractions to increase his reliability so his heeling becomes consistent in a wide range of situations. Any time when I give the command "Heel", he will slide next to me with full attention and strides next to me gleefully as I begin to walk. Finally I fine-tune his precision, so once I've given the command he will walk as I walk, and stop as I stop, willingly, unfailingly, and accurately. This element takes a lot of repetitions and drilling, so that the dog can have the behaviour imprinted into his mind by muscle memory. Precision is usually the last criterion of an exercise. As it demands the dog to be absolutely correct down to the last centimetre, it requires a lot of mental power.

Elements for Tuning

1. Learning attitude: to develop the puppy's curiosity, trust in his handler, and the motivation to learn new things.
2. Focus: to be attentive in learning. In tracking the puppy should pay attention to the targeted scent on the ground; in heeling he should pay attention to the handler's eyes and body; in bite work he should pay attention to the decoy and the sleeve.
3. Drive: the willingness to work.
4. Vitality: the joyful expression while working.
5. Clarity: direct execution of an exercise under all circumstances as soon as the dog hears the command.
6. Speed: the dog should adapt to whatever tempo the exercise requires.
7. Reliability: unaffected by any disruption and continues to work.
8. Precision: bite means bite, out means out, absolute focus and accuracy.

Training Stages

Training stages mean the essential phases a dog must go through, from totally untrained to being able to complete a given task reliably. As I usually start with puppies from the age of seven weeks, I will give an approximate age of reference for each stage, but because not every handler begins with a puppy, and each dog has different working abilities, the most important aspect of consideration is the observation of the dog's progress in training in order to decide when to advance to the next stage.

Furthermore, the training progress of tracking, obedience, and protection doesn't necessarily develop at the same rate. It's possible the dog can proceed to the strengthening stage in tracking and obedience while he still has to remain in the learning stage in protection. Sometimes, even in the same discipline (tracking, obedience, and protection are the three disciplines in IPO), different exercises can progress at different rates, too. Consequently, the most significant factor of consideration is not the age of the dog, but his pace of learning. This is the same as children learning in schools. A child's learning in different subjects often evolves at different rates. He might progress faster in some subjects while progressing slower in others. In the mid-term examinations, he could obtain an A in English, a B in Science, and a C in Mathematics. If we're to provide him extra tutorials, the module should be set according his development in these subjects accordingly.

1. Developing stage (approximate age of reference: six to nine weeks): Main goal is to develop the dog's interest in learning and motivation to earn his reward

The developing stage can be described as the kindergarten of puppies. This is the stage when a seven- to nine-week old puppy first arrives in the new handler's home. In a period of one to two weeks, we develop all the fundamental working drives, pack management, basic discipline, socialisation and habituation, clicker introduction, positive reinforcement, basic scent discrimination, and bite work foundation. All these elements support the puppy's learning attitude, thinking, and proactiveness. This stage prepares the dog to learn.

2. Learning stage (approximate age of reference: two to four months): Main goal is to let the dog understand our request through positive reinforcement and develop his motivation for training, making subconscious behaviour become conscious

This is the primary stage of training. The handler employs positive reinforcement after discovering what motivates the puppy. For example, if we're to use food as a training reward, the first thing is to make the dog understand he can get the food when he does what we want. Most of the actions we want our dogs to perform are parts of their natural behaviour. Our intention is to bring consciousness into a once subconscious behaviour, so it can eventually be a conscious behaviour that's under stimulus control. Let's take the heeling exercise for example. A puppy naturally knows how to follow his mother. My first step in teaching heeling is to lure the puppy with food so he can follow me on my left side as I'm walking. When he can follow my food-holding hand consistently, I progress to the next step with targeting, and then introduce the "Heel" command. In time, I fade out targeting, so the dog can heel next to me reliably without the help of food or a target.

3. Strengthening stage (approximate age of reference: four to eighteen months): Main goal is to solidify a behaviour through negative reinforcement, so the dog understands, even when there is no instant reward, he still has to comply and complete a given task

In the learning stage, the dog has associated a positive feeling towards the exercise. He's learned that by performing a behaviour desired by the handler he can get a reward. His primary motivation for performing the action is to obtain food. The more he's rewarded, the more he wants to offer the behaviour. In the strengthening stage, we give the dog a secondary motivation to perform the action. We show him that by coordinating with us, besides getting a reward, he can also avoid pressure. For example, when the dog has gone through the learning stage of heeling, we can combine the use of negative reinforcement by blocking and leading, bringing him to my left side. I show him that next to my left leg is his comfort zone as once he goes there after I've given the "Heel" command the pressure will end instantly, and the food reward is also delivered as before. Later in this stage, I'll add distraction during training to teach the dog to always comply to me even when there are other interruptions. In order to raise the dog's energy after the pressure, I'll also insert other drives such as hunt drive/prey drive, so he becomes more and more resilient as training advances.

4. Stabilising stage (approximate age of reference: eighteen to thirty months): Main goal is to make the learned behaviour a reflex when the command is given

The dog has gone through both positive and negative reinforcement in the previous stages. Now we get him used to performing the behaviour in a wide range of environments and situations to strengthen his clarity to the verbal command, speed, and reliability. The distraction level is also increased. This stage requires a lot of repetition to develop muscle memory so that the behaviour becomes a reflex.

5. Perfecting stage (approximate age of reference: thirty months and above): Main goal is to develop each exercise to the dog's fullest potential

This is the last stage of training. Its function is to refine, polish, and maintain the previously learned exercises, so their vitality, focus, speed, reliability, and precision are all in the best balance. This is the championship competition level.

First Three Days for a Puppy to Settle in with His New Handler: Pack Management, Basic Rules, Exposure, Drive Building, Introduction of the Clicker

First Day

A puppy's first week home is a very important period. In this entire week, I try to spend as much time with my new puppy as possible, especially in the first three days. This is the turning point where the puppy leaves his mother and siblings and goes to live with his new handler. The experience of this time, good and bad, can have imprinting effects on the puppy and directly influences his behaviour in the future. Correct handling of the puppy during this time is particularly crucial. A skilled handler can take full advantage of this one week and show many essential training elements to the seven-week-old puppy. My goal for the first three days is to build the puppy's confidence, develop his drive for food and toys, and introduce positive reinforcement with a clicker.

When I've selected the right puppy, his training begins as soon as I carry him to my car. If I have a family member or friend with me for the trip home, I'll let him drive and I'll carry the puppy in my lap, or vice versa. If I'm driving alone, I'll put the puppy in an earlier-prepared crate. Inside the crate there's an old towel to keep the puppy warm and dry. If the drive is more than three hours, I'll make stops on the way to give him a chance to go to the toilet.

When we arrive home, the first thing I do is to let the puppy out and give him some water to drink. I'll let him run and stretch in my garden and empty himself in a specific corner on the lawn. As he's urinating or defecating, I'll link the cue "Peepee" or "Caca". By associating these words with the behaviour frequently enough over a period of time, we can eventually make our dogs go to the toilet on command. If the weather is good and I see that the puppy is still energetic after the trip, I'll prepare some food that I've obtained from the breeder for the puppy, let him wear a collar and a retractable leash, and take him for a walk around my neighbourhood for ten to fifteen minutes.

Goal:

1. To allow the puppy a way to expend any excess energy so he can calm down more easily and have some rest at home (if the puppy is already tired or car sick, I won't take him for the walk and will directly let him rest).

2. To familiarise the puppy with the environment he's living in and to begin socialisation

and habituation. In the first few days I'll take him to the relatively quiet areas around my neighbourhood so he can gradually adapt to the new surroundings.

3. To start building a pack relationship with the puppy, teaching him his name, and get him used to wearing a collar and leash. If the puppy tends to walk behind me (which is often the case in the first week), I'll call his name and run away from him. As he's wearing a retractable leash, even when I run away he's still attached, but because the leash is extendable the puppy won't have an unpleasant feeling of being dragged along and he'll usually start to run after me. When he comes to me, I'll praise him cheerfully with my voice and feed him a little bit of food to reinforce him for the recall.

Feeding

When we get home, I'll feed the puppy. For youngsters between the ages of seven and twelve weeks, I usually feed them three times a day: once in the morning, once around noon, and once in the evening. I combine feeding with training and interaction to develop their motivation for work. In the first three days I'll feed my new puppy the same food from the breeder, and gradually change it to raw meat over a week to avoid upsetting his digestive system.

In Belgium, I primarily feed my dogs a combination of naturally prepared food including raw meat, bones, offal, vegetables, and fruits. There are several companies in Western Europe that make quality raw food so it's quite convenient for me to get it.

Besides being healthier and closer to what wild canines eat in nature, raw animal products can also directly increase the dog's food drive, which is very useful for training. For the development of an adaptable digestive system, I also give my dogs dry food in training and occasionally as full meals (please refer to Chapter 1, "Proper Keeping and Kennel Management of Working Dogs – Food").

In some parts of the world, where suitable raw meat for direct consumption is difficult to acquire, thinly sliced lamb meat soaked in boiling water for one to two seconds can be used as an alternative to develop the food drive for puppies.

When working with food drive, the most obvious criterion is of course having a hungry puppy. There's no point trying to encourage a dog to eat when he's already full. Sometimes the most effective way to enhance a dog's motivation for food is by keeping him a little hungry, or letting him only get about 70% to 80% full during most of his meals while ensuring he's strong and healthy. This rule applies to all of the training mentioned below involving the use of food. To further amplify food drive for young puppies, I use the three methods below:

1. Hand snatch: I take a handful of raw meat and let the puppy smell it. As long as he's hungry he'll show interest in my hand. At the beginning, as soon as his nose touches my hand I'll give him a little bite of the meat. Most healthy puppies are crazy about raw meat. Even if they've never eaten raw meat before, once given a taste many of them will start fighting your hand to get to it. When I feel the puppy wants the meat badly enough, I'll squeeze my fist so he has to fight my hand to try snatching the meat out of it; the moment I feel him trying to take the meat by force, I reward him by opening my hand a little bit so he can snatch a small bite of it from my hand before I quickly close it again. I repeat this procedure and feed him every time he snatches while moving my hand around so he has to follow it in order to snatch the food. This technique greatly boosts the puppy's obsession and ruthlessness for food as what's fought over and won by force is usually much more interesting and valuable than just receiving it open-handedly. This mindset is very useful and powerful for our future training (sometimes when the puppy gets too crazy in feeding, it is best to wear gloves so your hands won't be wounded by his bite).

2. Food bowl competition: I place the raw meat in a bowl and let the puppy eat it while holding him by his chest and belly from behind. As he's eating, I slightly pull him away from the bowl or try to gently push his head to the side, stimulating him to guard his food. When he starts guarding the meat by growling or snarling, I let him go so he can take a few gulps again. I repeat this exercise until he's about halfway through and let him finish the rest undisturbed. My goal is to develop the intensity of the puppy's food drive by keeping him focused on the meat, but not being aggressive to me. That's why I stay behind him and not in front of him. If your puppy turns around and shows aggression to you instead of the food, it means you're over-stimulating him and his focus isn't on the food anymore.

3. Food box scratching: I place the meat in a plastic container with the lid on, and let the puppy sniff it by slightly opening the lid and then letting it close. Because the puppy wants the meat, he'll try different ways to open the container, and naturally starts to scratch it with his paws. At this moment I open the top of the container and let him have a few bites, then close it again and repeat the procedure.

Note: Some puppies show a decrease of food motivation during their first week home. It could be due to stress from the change of environment and handler. If your new puppy is not very interested in eating, it's best to first give him some time to settle before moving directly into drive development. At this stage, your first priority should be building the puppy's confidence and trust in you. Animal training doesn't always go how we plan it. When in doubt, sometimes it's better to take our time rather than rushing into things impulsively.

As long as our puppy is happy and hungry, the above techniques can be done individually or alternatively in one meal. The purpose of this training is to develop the puppy's natural food drive to its fullest potential and use it for our training, especially in tracking and in obedience. Its objective is to bring out the dog's maximum motivation for food, and the spirit of overcoming all obstacles in order to obtain his goal. These methods must be applied correctly, so that when the puppy is disturbed while eating, he will channel his frustration into the food by eating faster and more intensely. The puppy's target of aggression must be the food and not his handler. When I do this exercise with my puppies, I can put my hands in their bowls while they're eating without them showing any hostility to my hands. This training doesn't contradict my leadership in the pack. In nature, the rules of a wolf pack will be gradually applied as the pups mature. Young wolves under the age of four months receive a great deal of education in hunting and intra-pack competition. Pups at this age run around the pack openly with their "puppy licenses". During this period, senior wolves of the pack would tolerate or even encourage the pups to be bold and uninhibited in order to develop their survival mentality and abilities.

In the wild, wolves have to strive and scheme everyday, depending on their resilience and cunning to survive. To successfully train a working dog is to continuously maintain the balance of his wildness and tameness. It's the same as our use of fire. Used properly, fire can keep us warm and cook our food. Used wrongly, fire can destroy our homes and take our lives. Handling a working dog perfectly is the same as using fire flawlessly. From observing wolf behaviour in nature, we can employ many of their natural ways of living in training our working dogs. Fire is easier to manipulate when a little spark becomes a flame. If hampered too early, the spark will extinguish completely and I'll have to start all over again. I've adopted the exact analogy to bringing up my puppies, fanning the spark to create a flame and then controlling the fire to suit my needs. For effective management and maintaining my leadership, the above feeding techniques are suitable for puppies under sixteen weeks old. Once I've developed enough fire in them, I won't need to continue with these methods of feeding anymore. The same principle goes with the bite development below.

A word of caution for green handlers and dog owners with children: be sensible while developing your dog. You can bring up your puppy as wild as you want but you need to be 100% capable of controlling him at all times. Don't create a monster that becomes a menace to society and be on the news because of a tragic accident. Be a responsible dog owner and only apply the techniques I show you in the book when you fully understand them and feel comfortable in their application. It took me many years to develop these skills and sometimes I learned my lessons by making mistakes.

After I've fed my puppy, I'll play with him briefly by interacting with him, making body contact, patting him, hugging him, and letting him jump into my lap, but I never allow him to bite me. This is to mimic the puppy's mother (alpha female) reinforcing her rank after feeding. If the puppy starts to bite me or my clothes, I'll disapprove of his behaviour by giving a low grunt (or just a simple "No" in a low and firm tone) while looking at him squarely, and then take him by the collar and slowly and deliberately pull him away. My aim is to show him my strength and self-control as his leader while stopping an undesired behaviour. If he bites me again for the second time, I'll warn him in the exact same way. If it still doesn't stop his biting, after I grunt for the third time I'll hold his muzzle firmly until he gives a whine to apologise for his unruliness. This is a simulation of the mother dog disciplining her disorderly puppies by holding them by the muzzles and pinning them down. As soon as he stops biting me, I praise him and pat him gently to show him that I don't hold a grudge against his mistakes (a leader is empathetic and forgiving). I employ this three-strike policy when dealing with unruly behaviour.

Now the puppy has a full belly, I'll take him to the appointed location in my garden and wait for him to empty himself. Just like before I'll link the verbal signals as he's urinating and defecating. After all the activities, the puppy should now feel quite tired. I'll take him into my house and let him rest in a quarter especially prepared for him. Usually I use a cage or a puppy pen in an area of the house where I sit around most. There should be an old towel or blanket in the cage to keep the puppy warm and dry. I put the puppy in the cage and let him sleep right next to me to prevent stress due to his feeling of isolation and abandonment. The size of the cage should allow the puppy to stand, turn around, and lie down comfortably, but it shouldn't be so big that he can urinate in one corner and sleep in another. When the dimension of the resting area is just right, the puppy usually learns to hold on from urinating to avoid soiling his cage. During the day, I take him out around every two hours so he has a chance to go to the toilet. Water should be offered frequently but in small amounts, as a large consumption of water at one time usually makes the puppy want to urinate several times in the next few hours without much control of his bladder. During every outing, I spend some time playing with him or go out for a walk. I let him explore around the house under supervision so he can learn what he can do and can't do, such as not jumping on the sofa, not biting electric cables, not chasing the cat, etc. A working dog needs to learn when to work, when to play, and when to rest. In a wolf pack, it's the alpha that decides most of the group activities, such as when to wake up, when to hunt, when to eat, and when to sleep. Sufficient rest is just as important as adequate exercise.

To reduce the puppy's need to go to the toilet at night, I limit his water intake from 19:00 and also feed him his third meal of the day during this hour. I let him out one last time right before I go to sleep and then I place his cage on the floor next to my bed so he's always by my side. If necessary I put my hand or fingers in his cage to maintain contact at the beginning of the night in order to keep him calm. If he protests in the cage by making noises, I first ignore him for five minutes. If he still doesn't stop after that I give a low grunt and then tap the cage a few times to make him stop. Normally, after all the travelling and changing of environment in the first day, the puppy is very tired, and he should fall asleep quite soon after settling by my bed. Most puppies of this age need to go to the toilet at least once in the middle of the night. As they usually avoid dirtying the cage, they're very likely to let you know when they need to go by whining or knocking at the cage. After this they can usually sleep until the morning. To effectively and efficiently toilet-train them, during my puppies' first week home I usually sleep lightly so I can pay attention to their needs to prevent them urinating in the cage, because once a puppy has done this several times it can quickly become a habit and it's not nice to have to get up in the middle of every night to spend half an hour washing his cage and cleaning up after him. When toilet-trained properly this way, most puppies can sleep through the whole night by the time they're nine to ten weeks old.

Wolfish Dog, Sheepish Dog, Piggish Dog. The Fairy vs the Devil

At the initial stage of puppy training, shall we raise the drive to the maximum or shall we keep it to just the sufficient level in order to develop his motivation for working?

The temperament of a dog is a combination of his genetics, his mother's upbringing, and his handler's education.

A wolfish dog is a highly driven, persevering, and tenacious animal that would stop at nothing to reach his goal. When prohibited from getting what he wants, this dog won't hesitate to break the rules and take it by force. As he's extremely greedy, once we can explain to him that he can get what he wants by doing what we want he's willing to commit himself fully and to conquer all obstructions to accomplish the task. The one thing we have to be cautious about is as this dog is very headstrong, he's only suitable for a handler with a lot of experience training aggressive dogs, otherwise it can be very dangerous.

A sheepish dog is a dog with adequate drive and a high level of compliance and flexibility. He prefers to play by the rules and use his imagination to figure out what his handler wants. In comparison with the wolfish dog, the sheepish dog is more respectful and polite. When prohibited from getting what he wants, this dog would try to be diplomatic and creative in order to impress his handler. He's rarely forceful in his persuasion. He has very high trainability and usually doesn't need hard corrections to be put in line.

A piggish dog is a lazy animal with no interest in food, in play, in biting, or in action. It's very difficult to train this dog with positive reinforcement as he doesn't want anything badly enough to be motivated. If you use negative reinforcement, he'll do just enough to avoid the pressure and nothing more. Such a dog is not suitable to be a working dog, as he can find no enjoyment in the work and his handler can also find no pleasure in training him. Time is better spent on a dog that naturally loves action.

A good working dog should possess the wolfish characteristics and the sheepish characteristics in one. The balance of his disposition should depend on the preference of the handler, and a suitable puppy should be selected accordingly.

The fairy and the devil are two analogies which describe the wildness and tameness of dogs. A dog's temperament is influenced by his genes and environment. The devil is the wild, reckless, and self-governing brute of a dog. Sometimes it's caused by the lack of management by his handler, and sometimes it can be a mixture of the dog's heritage and environment. A bit of a devil in a growing puppy is not a bad idea as long as the handler knows when to tighten his reins. A dog must not be more dominant than his master.

The fairy is the sweet, pleasing, and amiable dog without a bit of badness in him. He's often a natural omega or mid-rank with a high level of willingness. The fairy is a super family dog or companion dog. He usually excels in obedience. The handler only has to be careful that his dog is not too submissive in bite work, acting the same way towards the decoy (the bad guy).

The training of working dogs is much different from the training of pet dogs. The function of a pet dog is to be a good companion at home. He only needs to know basic obedience and be manageable in day-to-day situations. The tamer he is the better. In contrast, a working dog not only has to be compliant in his daily life; he also needs to work independently in scent discrimination and confront aggressive intruders in certain situations, biting when he needs to bite and coming back when he needs to come back. For that reason, we have to always maintain a working dog's wildness and tameness in order to fully utilise his potential.

Regarding whether to raise a puppy with maximum drive or just develop enough of it for him to do his job, it's really up to the individual dog and what you can handle. There's a significant difference in driving a little family car in town and driving a big sports car on a racetrack. The more powerful the car, the finer your handling has to be. All the development of drives is beneficial only when they're working in your favour. As you're developing the drives of your dog, you should also establish the matching level of control. The fastest sports car performs at its best when driven by the right driver.

Second Day

On the second day, the first thing I do when I wake up is to take out my puppy so he can go to the toilet. After I get changed and have breakfast, I prepare his food in a plastic container and take him for a fifteen-minute walk around my neighbourhood. I walk him with the same retractable leash as yesterday. During the walk, I observe and adjust the following elements according to the puppy's behaviour:

1. Pack management
2. Basic discipline
3. Socialisation and habituation
4. Physiological status
5. Physical conditioning.

I prefer my puppy to walk easily in front of me with the leash slightly taut while he's exploring his surroundings. If he walks behind me or doesn't follow at all, I'd always have to turn around to look at him and this is very tiring. If he circles around me, I'd always have to switch hands holding the leash and this is very inconvenient. It's also dangerous for the puppy as I might accidentally step on him. If he walks in front of me but keeps pulling excitedly, when he's older and bigger it'll be very exhausting for both me and him. Dog training is about making your life easier and making the dog work for you. The first way is the best way. This will also be beneficial in the tracking and bite work training later on.

The first step is to teach him not to walk behind me by using the same method as yesterday. Every time the puppy is behind me, I call his name and run away. Once he's by my side, I reward him with my praise, a pat, and some meat. In these three rewards, the meat is usually the most attractive payment for the puppy. The praising and patting are the prelude to the meat. Repeated enough, he will have a positive feeling towards the praising and patting because the meat always comes afterwards (classical conditioning). The puppy will very quickly learn it is more beneficial walking next to me than behind me. From then on I can reduce rewarding him while he's next to me. Usually his curiosity about his surroundings will cause him to walk in front of me very soon. I also observe his food motivation during the walk to decide if it's a good time to introduce clicker training when we get home, or whether I should wait until he's more motivated.

During our daily walk, I decide in which direction we go, where we go, and how fast we go. I use my puppy's name every time I want him to come, change directions, or distract him from an undesired behaviour such as biting or eating rubbish from the ground. I combine calling his name with running away, and reinforce him coming to me by praising, patting, and feeding. Very soon I can have a balance. My puppy will walk in front of me at the end of the leash happily, and comes to me directly when I call his name.

My intention is to give my puppy a positive feeling every time I take him for a walk. In the first few days I usually take him to more tranquil places with quiet streets and low traffic, letting him adapt to different environments and people gradually. I encourage all friendly strangers to play with him under my supervision. In the first one year of my puppy's life, I do a lot of socialisation and habituation with people of different ages, sexes, races, and cultures. As long as they interact with him in a positive way, I welcome them all. As with other dogs, because I can't be sure where strange dogs have been and if they're carrying any diseases such as kennel cough, usually I only let my puppy play with dogs that I know well such as my other dogs or puppies from my colleagues. With other domestic animals such as cows, horses, sheep, pigs, cats, chickens, ducks, etc., as long as they're not dangerous, I'd let them interact with my puppy in a friendly way. If my puppy is too dominant or aggressive to other animals, I'd recall him and direct his attention onto me to prevent him fixating on the animals (a predatory behaviour). Sometimes puppies show hesitation or anxiety to animals or objects they haven't encountered before (seeing a bull or a fire hydrant for the first time). On such occasions, I'll approach that animal or object confidently and calmly with my puppy and show him that we're in no danger (a leader is bold and decisive; a leader is calm and confident). If it's an object like a fire hydrant, I'll sit on it so the puppy sees that there's no threat. I'll do this briefly and not make a big deal out of it, as if I try too hard to convince the puppy he might think the object is something he should worry about and becomes more concerned. Usually after seeing the same object for a few days the puppy won't think any more of it. I try to expose him to different people, objects, environment, and noises daily, so he can adapt to a wide range of scenarios.

Besides formal training, I walk my dogs for a minimum of fifteen minutes daily, sometimes once in the morning and once in the evening. In addition to the benefits of exercise during a walk, a dog can also explore his environment with his senses. Every dog has his habits. We observe these habits every day in order to assess our dogs' physiological and psychological condition. For example, I always observe my dogs' stool to check for any signs of intestinal upsets or the need of deworming. If my dog normally walks easily and happily but today he's walking slower and the tail is carried lower than usual, I'll pay closer attention to see if he's injured or fatigued, or if I need to ease the intensity of our training for a few days. If my bitch starts urinating with a high leg against a tree for the first time in months, I'd check if she's coming into heat soon. From observing our dogs closely, we can find many answers to our questions.

Introducing the Clicker

When we're home from our walk, if my puppy is still hungry, I introduce the clicker with the rest of the meat from the plastic container. A clicker is a training tool made of a supple piece of metal sheet fitted in a small plastic box, the size of a matchbox. When the metal sheet is pressed by the trainer's thumb, the device makes a metallic clicking sound, hence the name "clicker". The clicker is used together with positive reinforcement as a marker of desired behaviour. The basic principle of the clicker system is to link the "click" sound with a reward such as a piece of food to confirm a desired behaviour from the dog. The "click" becomes an important communication bridge between the trainer and the dog as it's clear, precise, and effective. The advantages of clicker training include:

1. The "click" sound produced by the clicker is distinctive, clear, concise, and consistent. It won't change as a result of the emotional fluctuation of the trainer.
2. It works like a camera that's able to capture the exact moment of a behaviour.
3. Because of its conciseness, the dog can understand quicker and easier which exact behaviour got him the reward.
4. By using a marking sound as the communication bridge with food, it's more accurate and effective than just using food alone. The trainer can also delay the time of food presentation and he can work with the dog from a distance away.

The introduction of the clicker is pretty simple. I take a handful of raw meat with my left hand while holding the clicker with my right. I run backwards and call my puppy's name. As soon as he runs up to me I press the clicker to make a "click" sound, followed by feeding him a bite of fresh meat. I repeat this step, running away while calling his name, then click and feed. I'd like to emphasise at this stage that every time after I click, I feed my puppy a good bite of meat. This is different from the traditional "click and treat" method, which encourages giving the dog a small piece of food (just big enough to keep his motivation) instead of a large chunk, so that the dog doesn't get full so quickly, his drive is maintained at a moderate level, and you can have a lot more repetitions. This technique is fine to produce a fairy of a dog, being amiable and living by the rules, a mindset that I employ at a later stage when the dog is older. Right now I want to create a devil out of my puppy, so the technique I utilise is the "click and feast" method, letting the puppy snatch a good gulp of meat out of my hand after every click. At this age, I first develop the "wolf" in my puppy, creating a mentality of stopping at nothing

in order to reach his goal. To do this, the reward has to be high enough so he will forget about the obstacles along the way. The greater the reward, and higher the motivation, and the more hardship the dog is willing to conquer to achieve his aim. Introducing this technique at an early age will imprint the mindset into the puppy's head. This will raise his drive, hardness, and competitiveness, which are all very important elements for future training. I want my puppy to have a strong positive association every time he hears the click at the moment, and be willing to do anything to cause me to click. With the "click and feast" method, a handful of meat is enough for around three to five bites. Every time a handful runs out, I take another handful and repeat the process. I continue until the puppy finishes a whole meal. After using this technique for a few days at every meal, the puppy would have made an extremely powerful association with the click. From then on I can stop the "click and feast" method and adopt the "click and treat". The puppy will have a "wolf" mentality already.

The introduction of the clicker can also be used when the puppy is eating out of his bowl. First I put the meat into his food bowl. As he's eating, I pull him away from the bowl from behind (just like yesterday). When the puppy protects his food by growling or snarling, I click and let him eat again. I repeat this a few times until there's about half of the food left and let him finish the rest undisturbed.

We call the meat the "primary reinforcer" and the clicking sound the "conditioned reinforcer". The meat is a natural attraction to the puppy, something he wants by instinct and something he needs for survival. The sound of the clicker didn't mean anything at the beginning. We made it mean something by linking it with the primary reinforcer (the meat). After many repetitions the puppy has made an association with the two. Every time he hears the click he expects food. This is called "classical conditioning". In the developing stage, I link the click with the meat with the above technique in every meal.

After the puppy's eaten, I play with him briefly like yesterday. After he goes to the toilet, I put him into his cage and get on with my other work, but I'm always around.

Bite Development

Around midday, after letting my puppy out for a few minutes, I take out a toy to do some bite training with him. My preferred toys for a puppy's bite development include a towel, a fluffy ball, a puppy bite tug, and a puppy sleeve.

The toys for bite exercise at this stage should have the following criteria:

1. Plump, fulfilling for the puppy's mouth when bitten
2. Soft, comfortable for the puppy to bite
3. Suitable in size for handling and moving around by me; it should also be easy for the puppy to pick up.

The goal for bite development:

1. Developing the puppy's hunting instinct
2. Developing the puppy's hunt drive/prey drive, protection drive, and rank drive
3. Developing a full, firm, and calm grip
4. Teaching the puppy to compose himself and stay near me after winning the sleeve, and not running around without control.

I take my puppy to a quiet quarter in my garden (never on the spot where he goes to the toilet). I show him the toy and move it in a jerky way on the ground, simulating the movement of prey to stimulate his hunt drive/prey drive, encouraging him to chase and bite it. In simple words, simulating the movement of prey is to move the toy in a way similar to when a mouse sees a cat. A mouse usually tries to escape by running away from the cat or running across in front of the cat. The mouse wouldn't run directly at the cat. I crouch on the ground and move the toy around, sometimes changing the direction of the movement, so the puppy also has to change direction in pursuit of the toy trying to catch it. When I see the puppy is highly interested, I slow down the movement of the toy so he can bite it successfully and fully. Once he has a hold of the toy, my job is to keep his grip full, firm, and calm, to let him feel strong and victorious. To achieve this, I need to maintain his drive by imitating the movements of the prey with the four techniques below:

1. I shake the toy weakly like a mouse struggling to free himself while captured by a cat. Because the puppy doesn't want to lose his toy, usually he bites harder.

2. I press down on the toy and the puppy's muzzle at the same time with one hand to make him feel I'm trying to snatch the toy out of his mouth. He has to bite with more force to prevent me from stealing his toy. This is also the first step to developing his protection drive (the puppy is protecting his prey).

3. I can turn the puppy around so his hindquarters are facing me and his head is facing out, with my two hands, one on top and one at the bottom, I pretend to pry open his mouth to steal his toy, but act like he's too strong when I feel he increases the force of his grip. This makes him feel powerful and confident.

4. I take a hold of his toy when he still has it in his mouth and push it onto the ground so he also has to bite down to hold it. By doing so, not only does the puppy bite harder, but also he naturally bites deeper in a downward motion to fill his mouth. This stimulates his rank drive. When his grip is full, firm, and calm, I let him win the toy as a reward for the good biting. The winning of the prey item satisfies his prey drive.

Some puppies like to run away after winning the toy. In this situation, I'll use one of the following methods to keep him:

1. Attach the toy to a rope: as long as the puppy is interested in the toy, he won't let go of it. I can attach a rope to it so I can control the puppy like I'm fishing. Every time he runs too far with the toy, all I need to do is to pull the rope back in.
2. Limit the puppy's freedom with my hands: I can control the puppy's freedom by blocking or holding him with my hands when he wants to run away with the toy.
3. Limit the puppy's freedom in a playpen: I can do the bite training with the puppy in a small pen or a small room. The surface of the place should provide a good footing for the puppy. A slippery floor, such as tile floor, is not suitable as it's easy to make the puppy slip and hurt himself, undermining his confidence. I also avoid doing this kind of training in his kennel run, as the enclosure should be a place for relaxation and not for excitement. If the dog is used to being excited in his kennel run, he might begin a barking or pacing problem when put in there in the future.

After the puppy has won the toy, if we just let him be, most likely he'll drop the toy after a while, put his paw on it, and start tearing it apart, just like a wolf would do after catching and killing a rabbit. Of course, we can't allow such behaviour unless we want him to develop a very bad habit of biting and buy a new toy after every bite session. Instead, we teach the puppy behaviour that is favourable to our training. We teach him that after he's won the prey, even when it's dead (not moving), very soon it'll come back to life again (moving), or someone (me) will try to steal it away from him. As the puppy wants to keep his prey, he'll start to realise the best way to keep it is to hold it firmly regardless if it's moving or still. From here I can develop his proactiveness in biting, meaning he'll bite no matter if the target is moving or still.

Out

In the terminology of the training of working dogs, to "out" means to release the bite. The technique of pretending to pry open the puppy's mouth is excellent to strengthen the grip but it's also very good for teaching the out. While applying this technique for the out, I hold the puppy with his hindquarters facing me, and his head facing forward. With my two hands, one on top and one at the bottom, I pry open his mouth as a puppy of this age is not strong enough to resist this, he has no choice but to release the toy. As the toy drops out of his mouth, I link the behaviour with the "Out" command. When the toy is on the ground, I hold my puppy by his chest or collar with one hand, and move the toy around with another to stimulate his hunt drive/prey drive again. Once the puppy is focused and driven, I release him and let him bite the toy as I link the behaviour with the command "Fetch", repeating the whole biting exercise again.

I play with the puppy using the above biting and outing techniques. After the second or third time he outs, as I'm holding his collar and teasing him with the toy, all of a sudden I stand up and end the game. For puppy training, the most essential focal point is its quality and not its quantity. It is very important to stop the lesson on a high note when the puppy is still motivated. He must be left with a feeling of not having enough, so in the next session he'll start with a high level of motivation.

At the beginning stage of bite development, I usually continue the training for three to five days consecutively. Once the behaviour has been established, I can do this every second day. In Belgium, I have an excellent support team, so my puppies normally start bite work with my decoy from eight weeks old (sometimes even earlier). If a handler doesn't have a suitable decoy but he has experience in bite work himself, he can teach his own puppy most of the basic biting techniques, but there should be an assistant to hold the leash for the puppy.

After I finish the bite training session, I prepare my puppy's noon meal in a plastic container with a lid. I take a clicker and place the container in front of the puppy. I open the container a little so he can smell the raw meat in it, while holding him from behind to prevent him from stealing the meat. When I see he's very enthusiastic to get to the food by pulling forward or scratching the food box, I click and release him so he can take one or two bites of the meat. I then close the box again and repeat the same procedure. Every time the puppy shows a high level of motivation by pulling and scratching, I click and release him so he can take a few mouthfuls of food. I continue until there's about one-third of the meat left in the box and let him finish it with one last click.

Adapting to the Outdoor Kennel

During the day, I usually place my dogs in the outside kennel enclosures so they can enjoy the freedom and fresh air while they're not busy with training. The dimensions of each of my outdoor kennels are 4m long, 2m wide, and 1.8m high, with a dog house inside to protect the dog from rain and wind. The kennel floor is made of thick pieces of timber for dryness and insulation, with stone gravel in the middle of the kennel for use as a toilet and for drainage. From a young age, I begin accustoming my puppies to relax in the outdoor enclosures. In the beginning, I choose to place them in the enclosures when they're calm and relaxed, such as after a meal. I go into one of the kennels with my puppy and stay there with him for about five minutes so he has time to explore it before taking him out again. We go through this process every day, staying in the kennel together for a few minutes and then going out. Once my puppy is used to this, I put him in the kennel alone for a few minutes before letting him out again. Gradually I increase his alone time in the outdoor enclosure to one hour. By the time he's three months old he's happy to stay in the kennel during the day without protest. I then have the option to decide whether to raise him as an inside dog or an outside dog.

Travelling in the Car

After lunch and accustoming to the outside kennel, I let my puppy go to the toilet and then rest in his crate in the house for about two hours. If the weather is good in the afternoon, I take him for a drive and to a new location for his socialisation and habituation. I prepare his third meal of the day in a plastic box and then put him in a crate in the back of my car. During the journey the puppy might whine or cry in the crate. I ignore this. Usually after a few trips he'll understand there's no big deal and will stop this behaviour by himself. I drive to a more bustling place such as a small town, then put on the retractable leash and take my puppy for a walk. I observe the puppy's behaviour during the walk. If he's confident and happy, I'll continue to walk in areas with a good amount of people and traffic. If he's a bit hesitant, I wouldn't force him, and will choose to walk in an area that's calmer. Occasionally I call my puppy to me and reward him with some meat.

After a stroll of fifteen to thirty minutes (the length of the walk depends on the puppy's confidence and liveliness), I take him to a quiet area and offer him the box of food. If his motivation for food decreases (some puppies temporarily lose their appetite during travelling), I'd wait until we're home before offering food again. If his desire for food is just the same as at home, I'd let him take a few mouthfuls before pulling him away like yesterday to increase his enthusiasm. When he growls or snarls at the food box to protect it, I click and reward him by letting him eat again. I repeat this a few times and let him finish the rest. When we get home, the arrangement is the same as last night.

Third Day

The arrangement on the third day since my puppy came home is pretty much the same as the second day. After these initial three days, the puppy should have established the following notions:

1. I'm his leader and teacher. I decide pack activities such as when to eat, sleep, play, and explore. I treat him kindly and fairly. I provide him with food, shelter, company, and protection.
2. He knows when and where to go to the toilet.
3. He knows his crate in the house is for resting. There are some rules to follow inside the house such as not jumping on the sofa and not biting electric cables. The outdoor enclosure is another place for relaxation where he enjoys more space and freedom.
4. He's developed a lot of interest in me, his food, and his toys.
5. When he hears the sound of the clicker, he'll expect food.
6. He likes going out for a wander with me because it's fun and he can explore different environments.
7. He gradually becomes more and more confident with strangers, other dogs, and other animals.

The Fourth to the Seventh Day for a Puppy to Settle In with His New Handler: Learning to Learn (Free Shaping, Luring, Targeting), Scent Pad

After spending three days with me, my puppy should be very confident and familiar with my role, the new environments, the basic discipline, the sound of the clicker, and his bite toys. In the second half of the week, in addition to the training of the first three days, I'll also start to teach him several learning systems based on positive reinforcement with the aid of a clicker. They include free shaping, luring, and targeting.

For the systems that involve negative reinforcement, I'll wait until the puppy is about nine to ten weeks old before introducing some parts of its techniques, and then gradually advance the progress as the puppy matures. Regarding the use of the electric collar (teletact), as electricity itself can't give the dog clear directions, before the introduction of this device the dog must have a strong foundation of training with leading, pressing, and reverse targeting. Once he's about ten to eighteen months and with a good understanding of the above systems of negative reinforcement, we can then consider introducing the teletact at a very low stimulation level. The exact timing of bringing in the teletact depends mainly on the training level and hardness of the dog. The electric collar is never intended to hurt the dog but it serves as an extension of a skilful dog trainer's hands, leash, and whip, all of which can be used to praise the dog, guide the dog, and correct the dog. There's nothing magical or evil about the scientific use of the e-collar. Do not be misled by prejudice based on ignorance and stories. Every tool is only as good as its owner and there's no difference with the teletact. Perhaps its critics need to find out more about how it works before they try to ban it. To help you understand the characteristics of both positive and negative reinforcement and their advantages and disadvantages, I'll explain them in detail in this chapter. For the more advanced and sophisticated systems of using the teletact, I'll talk about them in depth in *The Schutzhund Training Manual 2*.

Positive Reinforcement, Negative Reinforcement

Animal training systems can be grouped into two main categories, which are positive reinforcement and negative reinforcement. In simple words, positive reinforcement is the use of reward to increase the frequency of a desired behaviour. For example, if I want my dog to sit, I encourage him to sit by giving him food. After a certain amount of repetition, the dog is willing to sit because he knows this can earn him food.

Negative reinforcement is the use of pressure to increase the frequency of a desired behaviour. If I want my dog to sit, I encourage him to sit by tightening his leash upward to make him uncomfortable. As soon as he sits, I end the pressure of the leash. After a certain amount of repetition, the dog is willing to sit because he wants to avoid the tension of the leash.

Reinforcer

The effectiveness of positive reinforcement is based on the dog's aspiration for a good feeling; and the effectiveness of negative reinforcement is based on the dog's avoidance of an uncomfortable feeling. In the two examples above, the food brings a good feeling to the dog, while the tension of the leash brings an uncomfortable feeling to the dog. They're known as reinforcers in training. As food can directly increase a dog's chance of survival, and pressure can directly decrease a dog's chance of survival, they're known as "primary reinforcers".

A conditioned reinforcer is a signal that doesn't have any meaning to a dog at the beginning. We link it with a primary reinforcer using classical conditioning to give it a meaning to the dog. When I press the clicker just before every time I feed my dog, after some repetition he will associate the "click" sound with food. For the dog, the "click" is positive. If I make a grunt every time just before I give the leash a tug, after some repetitions the dog will associate my grunt with the unpleasant feeling. For the dog, my grunt is negative. The "click" and the grunt didn't mean anything to the dog originally. After I link them with primary reinforcers (offering food or tugging at the leash), they become signals with valuable information. They're conditioned reinforcers.

Positive Reinforcement	
Advantages	Disadvantages
• The dog becomes proactive • Develops a happy working attitude and liveliness • Promotes a good relationship between the dog and his handler • Increases the dog's trust in his handler • Enhances focus	• Difficult to achieve a high level of reliability by using positive reinforcement alone • When the dog's motivation changes, he might temporarily or permanently lose interest in the reward • Difficult to establish a sense of seriousness in the work with some dogs • Difficult to apply to dogs that are lazy with no motivation

Negative Reinforcement	
Advantages	Disadvantages
• Can achieve a high level of reliability • Even when the dog's motivation changes, negative reinforcement can still convince him to continue his task • Can establish a sense of seriousness • Can be applied to dogs that are lazy with no motivation, because we can motivate them to avoid the pressure	• Difficult to achieve a happy working attitude and liveliness by using negative reinforcement alone • Can sabotage the relationship between the dog and his handler as incorrect application can diminish the dog's trust in his handler

The best training arrangement is combining positive reinforcement and negative reinforcement effectively. By blending the soft way and the hard way together, the two systems complement each other, possessing all of the above advantages and eliminating all the disadvantages.

Eight Types of Positive and Negative Reinforcing Techniques

1. Free shaping (positive)
2. Luring (positive)
3. Targeting (positive)
4. Blocking (negative)
5. Leading (negative)
6. Pressing (negative)
7. Reverse targeting (negative)
8. Electric stimulation (negative).

Working to Achieve, Working to Avoid

Free Shaping

Free shaping is a training method of rewarding the dog's spontaneous behaviour with a marker (clicker) and reward (food). It has the following unique attributes:

1. It is the best way to stimulate a dog's imagination.
2. It develops a highly proactive dog.
3. As the dog must guess what the handler wants during free shaping, paying attention to which behaviour gets rewarded, the dog will develop a strong sense of self-awareness.
4. The handler can train the dog without any hints of body language and physical contact. He can just sit back with the clicker and let the dog work by himself to develop a wide range of behaviours.
5. As the dog is always the initiator of the free shaping game and the handler is always the reactor, this encourages active submission from the dog and directly strengthens the handler's leadership.

First Step of Free Shaping

After two to three days of clicker introduction in every meal, the puppy should have made a link between the "click" and the food. I can do a simple test to see if he has made the association by just pressing the clicker in front of him. If he responds by directly paying attention to me with an anticipating expression (demanding me to "pay him" with food), I know he understands what the "click" means. Now he can start the free shaping game.

In the past few days, the puppy has learned that, when I run away and call his name, as soon as he catches up with me I'll click and feed him. I'll now free shape him to look at me first. This should happen without much effort as the puppy is quite used to paying attention to me by now. I prepare a clicker and his usual meal of raw meat, and bring him to an outdoor or indoor environment without any distractions. I walk around slowly and randomly without saying a word while paying attention to my puppy's behaviour without looking directly at him. He's allowed to hang around me freely without a leash. As soon as he looks at me by chance, I click and give him a bite of meat. I continue to walk around. Every time my puppy looks at me, I click and feed. After several repetitions, the length and frequency of his attention should increase significantly. At the beginning he might look at me once briefly every several seconds. Now he's more likely to keep his attention for longer and doesn't look away so much. I immediately increase my demand according to his advancement, now waiting for him to look at me for longer (three to five seconds) before I click and reward. I keep the session for one to three minutes, ending it when the puppy is the most concentrated by clicking one last time and let him have the rest of his meal. This is known as the jackpot reward, when a large reward is given to reinforce a major breakthrough in training or to end a successful session on a high note.

A Passive Handler

Free shaping is the best way to develop a dog's proactiveness and imagination. In the last lesson, I've established the puppy looking at me by free shaping, but as I was walking around in the session I was still influencing him somehow with my body language. In this lesson, I want my puppy to be completely proactive while I am completely passive. I'll click and offer him food while sitting in a chair without any extra movement. The clicker will be the only communication bridge we have in this session, so the puppy has to rely solely on self-discovery to figure out what I want him to do.

In the past few days, I've rewarded the puppy's attention to me many times, including calling him over, letting him snatch the meat from my hands, and looking at me. If I ask for a similar behaviour again in this session, the puppy won't have a significant breakthrough in his understanding. For that reason, I'll ask for a completely different behaviour: he has to go away from me and focus on something else. In addition, with all the food motivation enhancing training we've done in the first half of the week, the puppy would've developed the "wolf" in him and has become extremely driven for food. I can now reward him with dry dog food instead of raw meat in training, going to click and treat from the click and feast before. The toned-down version of the food will keep the puppy calmer and more concentrated on his own behaviour, thus enabling him to think better in training. The size of the dry kibble should be easy for me to handle and easy for the puppy to swallow. If it's too small, it can accidentally drop out of my hands. If this happens too many times, the puppy will start to pay more attention to the ground searching for the dropped food instead of what he's supposed to do. If the dry kibble is too big, the puppy will spend too much time chewing and swallowing it. By the time he's finished eating the food, he's already forgotten what he's supposed to do. Round kibble around the size of $1cm^3$ to $2.25cm^3$ is usually what I use. The puppy can quickly swallow it and directly focus back onto his task. Each time I hold about three to eight kibbles in my hand for easy manoeuvring. I can also use cooked beef heart cut into the same dimensions if the puppy is not especially keen on dry food.

Preparation

1. A clicker
2. Sufficient amount of dry dog food
3. A place without distractions
4. A basket big enough for the puppy to stand in
5. A chair.

In a quiet area, I place the basket onto the ground and put the chair about 2m in front of it. I sit in the chair and let the puppy run around freely. All I do is to observe his behaviour and click at the right moments. In this session, I aim to make the puppy understand that standing in the basket will get him the reward through "successive approximations". Basically, successive approximation is a sequence of rewards that offers positive reinforcement for behaviour changes that are consecutive steps towards the final desired behaviour. In the beginning, every time the puppy turns his head in the direction of the basket, I click and let him come to me for a kibble. The reinforcement increases the frequency of such behaviour. After a few times, I refrain from reinforcing until he takes one step towards the basket. My intention is to build progress of the behaviour towards my final goal (puppy standing in the basket) without rewarding any unrelated behaviour. I continue to reward the puppy for moving towards the basket. By reinforcing a sequence of successive approximations, I increase the chances of an unlikely action in a short time. The successive approximations reinforced are gradually more precise approximations of my end goal. As training progresses I stop reinforcing the less precise approximations. This free shaping lesson can be summarised as the following steps:

1. I reinforce the puppy when he slightly turns towards the basket
2. I reinforce the puppy when he takes a step towards the basket
3. I reinforce the puppy when he's within a certain distance of the basket
4. I reinforce the puppy when he touches the basket with any part of his body
5. I reinforce the puppy when he enters the basket with any one of his paws
6. I reinforce the puppy when all four of his paws are in the basket
7. I reinforce the puppy when he's standing with all four of his paws in the basket.

In this lesson, every time I click, the puppy learns he's getting closer to the end goal. By varying the amount of dog kibbles I reward him after the click, I can also give him information about how close he is. I give him one kibble for a small progress, and three to five kibbles for a major progression. For example, when he first looks at the basket, I offer him one kibble after the click. When he touches the basket with his paw for the first time, I offer him five kibbles after the click, extra for excellence. The jackpot comes when he's standing in the basket. I give a verbal signal "Yes" as an indication of the end of the behaviour and let him have the rest of his meal.

Please take note that every dog learns differently. Even the same dog trained by different handlers will respond in a different way. Although we have a set goal for every training session, the progress doesn't always necessarily go according to our plans. In the first few lessons of free shaping, if the puppy can't reach the end behaviour after five minutes we should end the session while he's ahead without giving him the final jackpot (the big meal). We should spend some time to figure out why the puppy couldn't achieve the goal in the previous session and then start over again when it's time to feed him his next meal. We can also lower the criteria so the puppy can have a quick success next time to develop his confidence and motivation for the game. With some patience and careful observations, it won't be long before our puppies understand what we want.

One of the reasons that free shaping is very effective in developing a dog's proactiveness and imagination is because it makes the dog believe he's actually controlling us. The dog thinks he's manipulating us into clicking and feeding him food by changing his behaviour. Every time he correctly guesses what we want, he gets to eat. This is a very powerful mindset for the training of a working dog because the dog is always eager to learn.

Shaping a Wide Range of Behaviours

In the initial lessons of free shaping, our main goal is to develop the puppy's creativity. We should encourage him to try on a different type of behaviour in each free shaping session. Behaviours for training can be categorised into several types according to their characteristics. Some behaviours are static, some are active, some are vocal, some are silent, some are related to a target, etc. We can select a different type of behaviour for the puppy to work out in every lesson, shaping his behaviour towards the end picture gradually to stimulate his mind. This way, his behavioural repertoire will be multidimensional and not fixed in one or two forms.

Types of Shapeable Behaviours

1. Movement (walking forward, walking backwards, walking sideways, bobbing the head, raising the paw)
2. Position (sit, down, stand)
3. Locating (front position, basic position, article indication)
4. Going somewhere (send away, hide search, target plates)
5. Jumping (bouncing, jumping up, jumping ahead, climbing)
6. Holding something (biting, retrieving)
7. Looking (looking at the handler, decoy, article)
8. Targeting (following the hand, target tag, target stick, ball)

9. Vocalisation (barking)
10. Pawing (pawing at the food box)
11. Semi-autonomous behaviour (sneezing, yawning, hiccuping, fur-shaking, stretching).

Diversifying the Behaviours

In comparing free shaping, luring, and targeting for training the same simple behaviour such as making a dog sit, free shaping is usually the slowest method. Unlike luring and targeting, which can offer the dog clear visual or olfactory directions, free shaping doesn't have such advantages. Consequently, I use luring and targeting to teach most of the IPO trial exercises to my dogs instead. However, as the effectiveness of free shaping in expanding the dog's proactiveness, creativity, self-discovery, and self-awareness is second to none, I use this system a lot with young puppies and dogs that are having a spell away from formal competition training. Free shaping remains a valuable system and has an important role in animal training. In the early stages of free shaping, we should follow the rules below:

1. Be Diverse Instead of Specific

Free shaping works on the principle of successive approximations, so throughout a training session a dog's behaviour is extended and funnelled into our final picture without broadening and derailing into other unrelated behaviours. This is the advantage and disadvantage of the system at the same time. As dogs are creatures of habit, too many sessions in one single direction will very quickly kill off the repertoire of the dog's behaviours and make him one-dimensional. For example, if I free shape a dog to pay attention to me over many sessions, it'll be very difficult to free shape him to look at something else in the next session. Instead, if I'm to use free shaping, I change the type of behaviour in every session so my dog will establish a wide range of behaviours to prevent him from being set in a rigid form. If I've reinforced him to look at me in the last lesson, I'll reinforce him to look at something else away from me in the next lesson (looking at his food bowl). If he knows walking forwards, next he should learn walking backwards. If he knows barking, next he should learn spinning. To utilise free shaping to its full potential, the behaviour portfolio we build should be fluid, flexible, and multi-dimensional. The dog should be able to quickly adapt in free shaping sessions.

2. Go Dynamic Instead of Static

Still positions such as sit, down, stand, etc. will quickly fix the dog into one motionless behaviour and prevent him from offering other actions. At the beginning stage of free shaping I usually avoid them. Instead, I prefer movements such as jumping, spinning, barking, etc. to keep the dog busy.

3. Keep the Sessions Short and Frequent Instead of Long and Irregular

I feed my puppies three times a day. Usually I use one or two meals in a day for free shaping, leaving the rest for other training or just letting the puppy eat in peace (their brains need to rest, too). As he has plenty of opportunities for practice during puppyhood, free shaping sessions should be short and constructive, usually not exceeding five minutes. As soon as the puppy advances or reaches my goal, I end the session on a good note and give him his jackpot by letting him finish the rest of his meal. This way he's always interested to learn and never gets bored.

After a few days of free shaping practice, the puppy should be very responsive to me and the sound of the clicker. I'll start delaying the food delivery after the click. First I click and feed right away. Then I click and wait one second before I feed, then two seconds, three seconds, four seconds, five seconds, and so on. I further extend this step, clicking when the puppy is offering a correct behaviour without immediately offering him food, and click again when he continues the correct behaviour when he maintains the desired action, I then say "Yes" and feed him a kibble. By doing this, I'm teaching the puppy two very clear and informative signals, the "click" and the "Yes". The "click" doesn't mean the end of a behaviour anymore; instead, it means "what you're doing is correct, keep going". The "Yes" means "what you're doing is correct, you can now end the behaviour".

When the training progresses to a certain level, I want the dog to only finish the correct behaviour when I say "Yes". I decide when an exercise ends and not the dog. For example, once the dog understands what "Sit" means, a single command "Sit" means "sit and stay until I release you or tell you to do something else". This is very important for achieving stimulus control later on. We don't use the "click" as an ending signal because it is risky. In a trial or in practical street work, someone on the sideline can press a clicker or a metal container to sabotage your work. If your dog is used to hearing the "click" as a signal of good behaviour and dismissal, you run the risk of him leaving the exercise in a critical situation.

Through the practice of free shaping, we're able to obtain valuable information about our dogs' minds, understanding how each of them learns. I'll continue to employ free shaping extensively until my puppy is about four months, then I'll gradually emphasise the training more on luring and targeting to develop the basic components of all the IPO trial exercises. This is because, although free shaping has many unique benefits, it also has some limits that need to be compensated with the aid of other training systems. Its limits include:

1. Free shaping doesn't offer the dog any physical directions.
2. The dog always has to guess what the handler wants. He might not guess correctly every time.
3. When the dog keeps guessing wrongly and gets stuck in his progress, both the dog and the handler get very frustrated.
4. When training reaches a certain stage, we want every command to be a reflex without any thinking. Too much thinking at this level is not good. Everything has to be an automatic response to achieve speed and precision. It has to be a muscle memory.

5. If we teach all the exercises with free shaping, the more exercises we teach, the higher the risk the dog will mix up the commands and become confused.
6. If we use free shaping only and a problem arises, there's no base to step back on, because the base of free shaping is guessing.
7. Compared with luring and targeting, free shaping is much slower in teaching a new exercise.

Luring

Luring has the following characteristics:

1. It is direct
2. The handler can easily offer visual and olfactory directions to the dog with the food he's holding and the way he moves the food.
3. The handler can get the dog doing the desired behaviour very quickly.

Application

I hold some dry dog kibbles with my left hand and a clicker with my right. I let the puppy smell my left hand so he knows I'm holding the food. When he shows interest, I move my hand away. As soon as he chases after my hand and makes contact, I click and reward him with a kibble. At this point, my main focus is to reinforce the puppy when he follows my food hand like a magnet. He should be very keen to maintain contact with my food hand. After a few repetitions, I switch hands

so now I'm holding the kibbles with my right hand and the clicker with my left. I manipulate the puppy's movements by moving my food hand in different directions, such as moving it upwards, downwards, left, right, fast, slow, straight, and in circles. I can also manoeuvre him to jump over and go under obstacles.

Targeting

Targeting has the following characteristics:

1. The dog no longer follows my hand solely because I'm holding food. He follows it because we've established trust.
2. The handler can easily offer visual direction to the dog with the way he moves his hand or target.
3. The handler can employ a target stick to extend the length of his arm and increase the distance between him and the dog. He can also utilise a target tag to free up his hands.

Application

I hold the clicker in my left hand while my right hand remains empty. I show the palm of my right hand to the puppy. As we already have a very good relationship and my puppy is used to interacting with me and taking food out of my hands, he will naturally come to touch my palm with his nose even if I'm not holding any food. However, if he doesn't come to touch my palm willingly, I'll touch his nose with my right hand. As soon as his nose makes contact with my palm, I click to mark this behaviour, and then my right hand reaches into my pocket and I offer him a kibble. I then move

my palm away from him and invite him to touch it with his nose again. The technique is pretty much the same as luring. The only difference is now I don't "bribe" the puppy by holding food in my hand anymore. He must offer me the correct behaviour first (touching my palm with his nose) before I pay him. Targeting combines some of the distinctive advantages of both free shaping and luring, including the "work before pay" of free shaping and the offering of physical direction in luring. Besides using my hand as a target, I can also employ anything that is clearly visible for the dog for the same function. A target stick can become an extension of my arm, while a target tag can be attached to my clothing, allowing the dog to focus on any object I choose.

Avoidance Training: Blocking, Leading, Pressing, and Reverse Targeting

Blocking, leading, pressing, and reverse targeting have the following characteristics:

1. The handler can easily offer physical direction to the dog by touch.
2. The handler can increase the speed of a behaviour in a short time.
3. When the foundation of these four techniques has been established, the introduction of the electric collar is simple and easy.

The base of negative reinforcement is avoidance training. It includes blocking, leading, pressing, reverse targeting, and electric stimulation. Electric stimulation is not to be mislabelled as shock training. We're dog trainers, not butchers slaughtering cattle in an abattoir (no disrespect to butchers). Shocking a dog with electricity cannot achieve anything more than, well, giving him a shock. However, when applied in a low level just enough to make a dog uncomfortable and combine this with a substantial reward when he's reached the desired behaviour, we can significantly intensify his focus as well as boosting his drive for working. Avoidance training is the use of a dog's comfort drive as his motivation in completing a task. Comfort drive is a dog's desire to stop an uncomfortable feeling. In equestrian, a large degree of avoidance training is employed. As the rider is always in contact with the horse by sitting on his back, he can constantly communicate with the animal positively or negatively through the sense of touch. Below I'll use several examples in the application of negative reinforcement in equestrian to explain the concepts in avoidance training.

Blocking: An Example of the Halter's Application in Equestrian

A halter is a headgear used to lead or tie up a horse. It fits behind the horse's ears and around his muzzle. A rider or stable hand uses a halter and a lead to attach a horse onto a wall or a stake to limit his activities and keep him secure. If the horse moves around too much, he'll give himself a tug when reaching the end of the lead, causing discomfort. After several times of this unpleasant feeling, he learns to stand calmly while being tied up.

We can use the same principle to maintain the stability when our dogs are sitting, standing, and lying down.

Leading: An Example of the Reins' Application in Equestrian

A rider uses the reins to control his horse. Working together with the bridle and bit, the reins are tightened or loosened independently or together to control the direction and the speed of the horse. When the rider puts tension on one of the reins, the horse feels a discomfort on his mouth where the bit is. Because the horse wants to find a way to end the uncomfortable feeling, the rider is able to control his movements with the reins. When the rider tightens the left rein as the horse is moving forward, the horse will feel pressure on the left side of his mouth. To avoid this, the horse naturally turns his head to the left, and his body follows. When the rider sees the horse has made the turn, he loosens the rein and there's no more pressure on the bit. When the rider wants the horse to turn right, he tightens the right rein. For slowing down, he puts tension on both reins. When he keeps the tension even when the horse has slowed down, the animal will come to a stop.

This technique is called leading, as we use the reins to lead the horse, giving him directions by the sense of touch. We can apply the same method to train a dog by tightening and loosening his collar and leash.

Pressing: An Example of the Spurs' Application in Equestrian

A spur is a blunt piece of metal worn in pairs on the heels of a rider's boots. Its function is to direct a horse to move forward or sideways while riding. When a rider wants his horse to move to the right laterally, he pushes the left side of the horse's abdomen with the spur on his left heel. To avoid the pressure, the horse steps sideways to the right and the pressure stops. To make the horse accelerate, the rider squeezes the horse's belly with both heels. This is called pressing.

By pressing different parts of a dog's body, we can also get him to change his behaviour.

Reverse Targeting: An Example of the Whip's Application in Equestrian

When a trainer first teaches his horse to jump over an obstacle, he simply places a pole on the ground in front of the animal and leads him over it. The horse instinctively avoids slipping on the pole by hopping over it. Once he's confident in hopping over a pole on the ground, the trainer gradually increases its height so that he's able to jump over the full height eventually. This is called reverse targeting because we teach the animal to avoid the target instead of seeking contact with it. The pole is a visual target for the horse to avoid. He jumps over it to avoid making contact.

In a horse race, jockeys use their whips (riding crops) to strike the horses' buttocks for additional acceleration during the finishing sprint. While being struck from behind, a horse instinctively bolts to escape from the pressure. The target of avoidance is the whip. In training and in a race, a jockey usually gives a visual cue to the horse by showing him the whip before the strike. Through classical conditioning, most horses learn that the display of the whip is the presage of the strike, thus they already start to sprint when they see the swing of the whip before the actual strike. The swing of the whip is a "conditioned aversive signal", just like the principle of the clicker but used in a negative sense.

In dog training, we can also apply the two reverse targeting techniques above to enhance the speed and precision of our dogs.

Electric Stimulation

The correct introduction of the teletact requires a solid foundation of blocking, leading, pressing, and reverse targeting. This book is intended to lay the base for you through the combination of positive and negative reinforcement. When you've gained the finesse from practising the techniques explained in this book, you should be ready to learn the system of using electricity in *The Schutzhund Training Manual 2*.

Things to Remember while Employing Avoidance Training:

1. The pressure must be applied with direction so the dog knows how to switch it off by offering the desired behaviour.
2. The lighter the pressure the better: we want to achieve the desired behaviour by minimum discomfort.
3. The quicker the dog realises how to end the pressure the better.
4. The pressure ends immediately when the desired behaviour is achieved. If the pressure doesn't stop, the dog won't be able to learn through negative reinforcement.
5. Negative reinforcement is best combined with positive reinforcement so the dog can rebound after pressure, making him more resilient (rapid recovery after pressure and coming up in drive). The old German trainers came up with the perfect phrase in expressing this: *Trieb – Zwang – Trieb* (Drive – Compulsion – Drive).
6. Never apply the kind of pressure that the dog can't tolerate; if the pressure is too overwhelming, you run the risk of permanently destroying the dog's confidence, or a hard one will bite you.
7. One tactile signal for one behaviour to ensure clarity. A pull on the horse's reins cannot mean stop and go all at once.

Six Steps to Introducing Negative Reinforcement:

Pressure with Direction → Discomfort → Change of Behaviour →
Pressure Ends → Comfort → Reward

When we first introduce avoidance training, our goal is to apply very slight discomfort to the dog via the sense of touch. To offer the dog a quick way out of the pressure, I also use luring as an aid. As soon as the slight pressure comes, my luring hand (hand holding food) quickly guides the dog into the desired behaviour and then the pressure stops. As the dog already understands luring before we introduce negative reinforcement, he understands how to escape the pressure very quickly and willingly. He'll learn that, by complying with me, not only can he earn a reward; he can also avoid the pressure.

A Comprehensive System

All of the eight techniques above have their strengths and weaknesses in animal training. I employ every one of them according to my dogs' temperaments, their training levels, and the exercises they're learning. By mixing and matching these training methods in various degrees and orders, I can construct a custom-made training program for each of my dogs. The more tools I have in my head, the more effectively I can apply them and the easier and quicker I can work out the best way to achieve a particular behaviour. We have to thoroughly understand the application of each method, so we can develop a system that is both soft and hard, just like the Ying and the Yang in Chinese philosophy. By successfully communicating with our dogs with visual, audio, tactile, olfactory, and taste signals, we can competently apply both positive and negative methods.

Cross-Training

The term cross-training is widely used in modern sports. It means an athlete training in activities other than his usual sport. Its purpose is to improve general performance. Cross-training takes advantage of the particular benefits of one training method to complement the inadequacy of another, developing an all-round competitor and increasing his chances of winning.

For example, in boxing, besides the traditional training in the gym such as shadow boxing, hitting the bags, hitting the target mitts, and free sparring, the fighters also utilise other exercises such as running, skipping, and weight training. The supplementary exercises offer benefits that are difficult to achieve from traditional training alone. All these activities are valuable in contributing to the boxers' endurance, speed, power, balance, and cardiovascular fitness function.

Another example is the sport of mixed martial arts (MMA). Besides practising in their original fighting style, fighters also learn other fighting systems to expand their skills. A Muay Thai fighter who is proficient in stand-up striking might participate in wrestling to make up for deficiencies of striking alone. Then he might also take up Brazilian jujitsu to employ submission techniques such as joint locks and chokes. MMA fighters usually train in several different fighting styles to be all-rounders in their sport.

The main topic of this book is about Schutzhund/IPO. In practice, when I'm training my own IPO dogs I infuse a lot of elements from other dog sports and dog training disciplines. Cross-training especially in puppyhood can bring many advantages in a dog's sporting career which include:

1. It develops the puppy's mind, broadens his experience, improves his ability to learn.
2. It aids the dog to learn the IPO exercises better and quicker. Many training techniques of other styles offer more effective ways to teach a behaviour than the orthodox IPO methods.
3. A wider range of exercises increases a puppy's interest in learning. It will be less likely for him to be easily bored by repeating the same exercises all the time.
4. It makes the dog more versatile with more functions. There are multi-tasking dual purpose (sport/police) or dual titled (IPO/Ring) dogs that are excellent examples of the success of cross-training.
5. It increases the dog's practicality. Besides making an excellent sport dog, an IPO dog should also be a good canine citizen that fits well in his master's daily life.
6. It develops the dog's practicality for personal protection in actual combat. The original function of a Schutzhund focuses on his ability to protect his master. We must remember the roots of our sport and its function is not solely for performing on the competition field. Guarding, security, and protection of his master are all essential functions of a Schutzhund. Once the dog is up to a certain training level, he can benefit greatly from exercises that include the full-body bite suit, hidden sleeve, and boxing with a muzzle on.

Scent Pad

The scent pad is the foundation training for scent discrimination. As I allow my puppy to eat the food I put down on the ground during this training, I need to first teach him when he can eat from the ground and when he can't to prevent him eating animal faeces and rubbish on the paddocks. This is quite simple. When I take my puppy for a walk in the fields, I prepare some food and keep him on a retractable leash. I deliberately walk him on a paddock with abundant cow or horse dung. Most dogs like to eat dung because there are a lot of beneficial bacteria for their digestive system. I can't allow this however, as a dog eating indiscriminately off the ground can be easily poisoned. When my puppy is about to eat the dung, I give a low grunt and give his leash a slight tug to stop the behaviour. If he tries again I'll correct him again. How hard I have to tug depends on the most effective level to stop the puppy from eating dung. When he stops trying, I call him over and reward him with praising and a kibble. After a few repetitions, my grunt will be known as a conditioned aversive signal. From then on I can use this before a correction to give the puppy a chance to stop an undesired behaviour and avoid a tug on the leash. I walk him for about fifteen minutes on the paddock. When I see he ignores the manure, I'll call him and reinforce the good behaviour with praising and food again. When I see he understands the rule, the next day I'll take him to a field without any livestock manure to start the scent pad training.

Training Goal

1. Allow the puppy to learn through self-discovery by letting him realise there's food where there's my scent
2. Encourage him to track down my scent with his nose
3. Let him concentrate on the scent and be reinforced by the food I've laid down, allow him to search until he's eaten 70% to 100% of the food.

Preparation

1. Boiled beef heart or beef liver, cut into cubes of around 0.5cm, thirty to forty pieces.
2. An indication flag to mark the location of the scent pad.
3. A green piece of grassland, the more lush the grass the better; the height of the grass should be about 5cm to 10cm and there should be no visual, audio, or olfactory distraction for the puppy.
4. The person who lays his scent on a field for the dog to search is known as the track layer. When training a puppy or a young dog, for convenience the handler usually takes up the role of the track layer himself.

The best condition to teach foundation tracking is a cool morning with plenty of moisture on the ground, without any wind or rain. I come to the grassland, take a spot with a high density of grass, and insert the flag into the ground on my left (this is where the starting flag is set in an IPO trial). I then walk clockwise (to the right), forming a circle with a diameter of 60 to 100cm. The size of the circle depends on the size of the puppy. The bigger he is, the wider the circle. The diameter of the circle should be roughly equal to the puppy's length from his nose to the tip of his tail. When I make the steps, I do so lightly. It's not necessary and not recommended to stomp the steps or rub the feet heavily onto the ground, as a person's weight alone is enough to leave plenty of scent on the grass. In contrast, I want to do this as lightly as possible. By leaving just enough of my scent on the ground, I sharpen my puppy's sense of smell. After forming a circle, I step further inward spirally, gradually approaching the centre of the circle, so that my footsteps fill up every inch of the circle. This is known as the scent pad because it is full of my scent.

5. I put thirty to forty pieces of the beef heart in the circle. The meat should be placed at the roots of the grass and not the top, to prevent the puppy from seeing it. If the puppy can see the food, he'll start searching with his eyes instead of his nose. Don't bury the food into the ground though. This will cause the puppy to dig instead of to track. There's only food where I've stepped. I don't put any beef heart outside of the scent pad.

Scent Pad

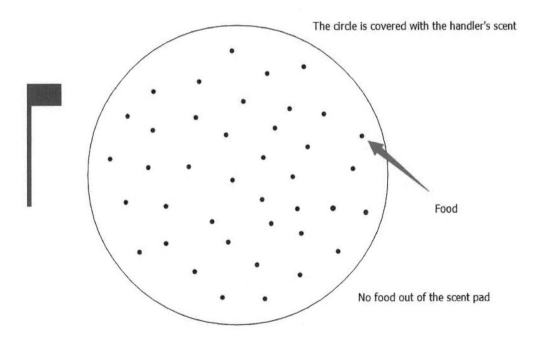

The circle is covered with the handler's scent

Food

No food out of the scent pad

6. When we first start to teach a puppy scent discrimination, the temperature should be cool (no more than 25°C). The grass should be moist and there should be minimum wind in the area. These are the optimum conditions for a dog to use his nose. Hot, dry, and windy conditions make it difficult for a dog to search. We should leave this kind of weather for later when the dog already has a very solid foundation in tracking.

The puppy must be hungry for tracking. Before we start, I first walk my puppy on a 1.4m leash for several minutes around the training field so he can empty himself and get accustomed to the environment. I then walk him towards the scent pad. When he's about 2m from the circle, I pick him up and slowly place him into scent pad head-first, so he can pick up the scent. When I see he starts sniffing, I put him to the ground so he can start working his nose. The puppy can now smell there's food where there's my scent. This gets him interested and he'll follow my scent in order to eat the beef heart. I let him search on his own with the leash held loosely. When he's fully concentrated, I should be able to hear obvious sniffing noises from him breathing through his nose intensely. This is an indicator of him working his sense of smell. I'd occasionally stroke him slightly on his back to desensitise him to my touch while he's tracking, so he won't be distracted if I have to touch him to guide his searching in the future. If he goes out of the circle, I'll give him the distance of the leash and about ten seconds. Usually when he realises there's no food where there's no scent, he'll come back into the scent pad on his own. If he's out of the circle for more than ten seconds and stops searching, I'll gently pull him back into the circle. When I see he keeps sniffing with good focus and he's eaten most of the food, I'll say "Yes" to tell him "good job, you can end the search", and pick him up to finish the session.

Scent pad training is an interesting game for puppies. As long as a puppy is motivated with food, I can do this almost every day until it's time to proceed to the next level. Normally, after five to ten consecutive days of scent pad training, the puppy will make great progress. When he shows the following behaviours, I can consider advancing the training to the straight track:

1. The puppy gets excited when he sees the starting flag and immediately begins searching on the scent pad.
2. Once he's entered the scent pad, he searches diligently with great focus without lifting his head or looking around.
3. I can hear clear sniffing sounds as he tracks.
4. If he happens to step out of the scent pad, he'll immediately return to the circle to continue the search.
5. He can keep tracking for three minutes or finish all the food in the scent pad.

Training Cycle

Training cycle is the usual routine I follow every time I interact with my dogs. When we're training animals, we should form good habits. Adequate planning and preparation increase our chances of success:

1. Having the necessities before training (e.g. before we start scent pad training the puppy must be hungry)
2. Training goal (e.g. puppy searching the scent pad with focus)
3. Preparation (e.g. cutting enough beef heart, having a starting flag, finding a suitable tracking field)
4. Planning the steps (e.g. lay down the scent pad, put down food, walk the puppy before the track, place him onto the scent pad)
5. Execution and observation (e.g. carry out the plan and see what the dog does)
6. After training, analysis and review (e.g. how did the puppy perform, did he work according to the plan?)
7. Points for attention (e.g. did the puppy work according to the plan, are there things I can do better next time?)
8. Next step (e.g. continuing scent pad training or advancing to straight track).

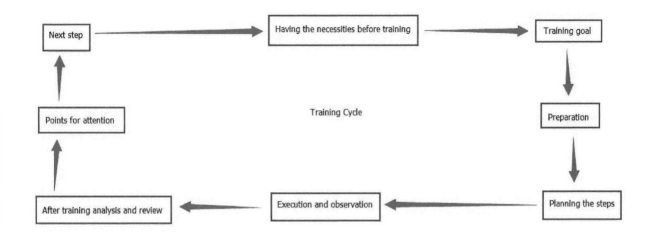

Timetable of a Puppy's First Week Home: Example

	1st Day	2nd Day	3rd Day	4th Day	5th Day	6th Day	7th Day
Morning	Puppy selection	Walk CI Rest	Walk CI Rest	Walk FS OE Rest	CR Walk LU Rest	Walk SP LU Rest	Walk SP TG Rest
Noon	Journey home	BD CI OE Rest	BD CI OE Rest	CR Walk LU Rest	BD OE Rest	BD TG OE Rest	FS OE Rest
Evening	Walk Feed Rest	CR Walk CI Rest	CR Walk CI Rest	BD OE Rest	Walk FS OE Rest	FS OE Rest	BD LU OE Rest

CR = Car ride

OE = Outdoor enclosure

CI = Clicker introduction

FS = Free shaping

LU = Luring

TG = Targeting

BD = Bite development

SP = Scent pad

IPO Commands in English, German, and Dutch

Below are the most common IPO commands in several languages, including English, German, and Dutch. Handlers are allowed to use any language they prefer in a trial as long as it's consistent (you can't use English for one command and use German for another).

Behaviour	English Command	German Command	Dutch Command
Commands for Tracking			
Track	Seek	Such	Zoek
Article indication	Show me	Object	Object
Slow down	Slow	Langsam	Langzaam
Commands for Obedience			
Basic position	Return	Fuss	Voet
Heel	Heel	Fuss	Volg
Sit	Sit	Sitz	Zit
Down	Down	Platz	Af
Stand	Stand	Steh	Sta
Front position	Here	Hier	Hier
Retrieve	Bring	Bring	Breng
Release dumbbell	Give	Aus	Los
Over hurdle	Jump	Hopp	Spring
Over wall	Over	Uber	Over
Send away	Go	Voraus	Vooruit
Attention to handler	Look	Sehen	Kijk
Attention forward	Watch	Sehen	Waak
Heel right	Right	Recht	Rechts
To target plate	Target	Platz	Plaats
Touch	Touch	Anfassen	Tegen
Commands for Protection			
Running around hide	Search	Vorang	Revier
Bite	Take him	Packen	Stellen
Release the bite	Out	Aus	Los
Back transport	Transport	Transport	Transport
Side transport	Side transport	Transport	Zij transport
Bark	Bark	Gib laut	Blaf
Alert	Watch him	Pass auf	Let op
Walk backwards	Back	Zurück	Achteruit

Signals for Confirmation and Disapproval			
Clicker sound	"Click"	"Click"	"Click"
Praise	Good	Brav	Prima
Finish	Yes	Ja	Ja
Fetch	Fetch	Pack	Pak het
No	No	Nein	Nee
Grunt	Oi	Pfui	Foei

CHAPTER THREE

Tracking Learning Stage

Winning Criteria in IPO Tracking

1. The dog has to be highly focused in following the track layer's scent with his sense of smell.
2. The dog has to follow the track layer's scent from footstep to footstep.
3. The dog has to track with a deep nose (nose close to the ground).
4. He should display confidence and decisiveness while finding the scent.
5. His tracking speed should be consistent from the beginning to the end of the track.
6. He should be precise in following the straight legs and corners.
7. He should indicate the articles accurately (small objects left on the track by the track layer).

Tracking Training Components Table

The sport of IPO includes three disciplines: tracking, obedience, and protection. The purpose of this book is to explain the progression of the making of an IPO3 dog from puppyhood in detail. The training systems I present here are intended to develop a dog's full genetic potential so he can reach the highest points possible in an IPO trial. To make it easy for puppies to learn the required exercises, I've broken them down to single independent foundation components. All you need to do is to first teach your puppy these building blocks following my guidance, and then put them together to develop each exercise. As each basic component is very easy to teach, training a puppy this way is fast and clear. When necessary, the components can be taken apart at any time, so you can improve certain elements of an exercise (such as speed, style, precision, etc.) once the dog has reached a higher level.

	IPO3 Tracking Exercises	
Basic components	Tracking	Article indication
Scent discrimination	✓	
Pointing forward		✓
Down		✓

Scent

When the track layer walks on a field, he alters the scents of the area in the following ways:

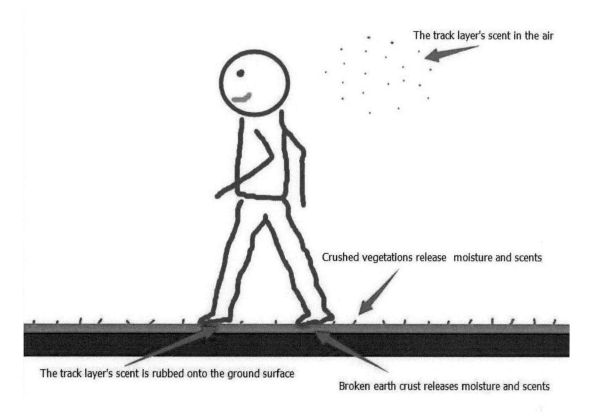

The track layer's scent in the air

Crushed vegetations release moisture and scents

The track layer's scent is rubbed onto the ground surface

Broken earth crust releases moisture and scents

1. He leaves his scent in the air.
2. The plants he's stepped on are crushed. Crushed vegetation releases moisture and scents.
3. The earth crust he's stepped on is broken. Broken earth crust releases moisture and scents.
4. By walking on the field, his scent is rubbed onto its surface.

We teach our IPO dogs to track the scent of the track layer left on the surface of the field, because:

1. If we teach our dogs to follow the track layer's scent in the air, they'll form a habit of lifting their heads, which contradicts the IPO trial rules for tracking with a deep nose. Air scents can also be easily moved by wind.
2. If we teach our dogs to follow the scent of crushed vegetation, they might wrongly follow the crushed vegetation scent caused by other people or animals that have walked on the field.
3. Just like crushed vegetation, the scent released by broken earth crust can also be caused by other people or animals.

4. We teach our dogs to follow the scent rubbed off onto the ground by the track layer. The scent particles contain the skin scraps, hair, sweat, and garment fragments of the track layer. Our dogs learn that all they have to do is to use the person's scent from the start of the track (where he put down the flag) as his target and follow this to the end. This ensures clarity, precision, and a deep nose for IPO tracking.

Straight Track

Training Goal

1. Teach the puppy to follow the scent from footstep to footstep.
2. Establish the zigzag style of tracking.
3. Prevent the puppy from turning back on the track.
4. Teach him to lay down when he reaches the article.

Preparation

1. Boiled beef heart cut into cubes of 0.5cm, fifty pieces.
2. A small plastic container with a lid about the size of 5cm x 5cm x 5cm. We can also use plastic film canister.
3. An indication flag.
4. A green piece of grassland, the more lush the grass the better, the height of the grass should be about 5cm to 10cm. There should be no visual, audio, or olfactory distraction for the puppy.
5. As when teaching the scent pad, we train on a cool morning with plenty of moisture on the ground without any rain or strong wind. I come to the grassland and find a good spot to lay the track. If there's a light breeze, I make sure it's blowing on my back so the puppy won't track upwind, as oncoming scent blowing into the puppy's face encourages air scenting (high nose). I look far ahead and try

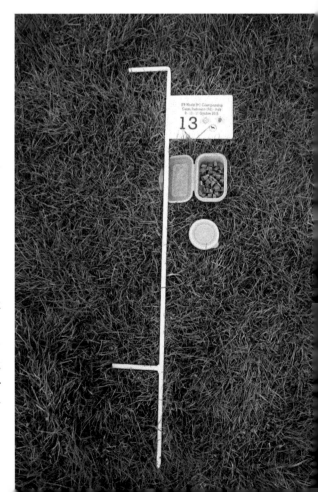

to find two landmarks such as a tree and a house with one directly behind another. I align these two landmarks with myself like the sight of a rifle, so I can walk in a straight line as I'm laying the track. I set the flag into the ground next to my left. After slightly stepping on the starting point a few times, I take a step back so I can put four pieces of beef heart on where I've just stepped. I then start going forward. I take the first step by pointing my toes slightly outward. At the toes of my footprint, I lay down one piece of beef heart. The heel of my first step is connected to the starting point I've stepped before. I then take a second step with my toes pointing slightly outward and put down one piece of beef heart at the toes of my footprint again. The heel of my second step is connected to the toes of my first step. In other words, I'm walking ahead in a zigzag way with the toes of each step touching the toes of the next. Every time I finish printing one step, I pull it back about an inch so I can put down one piece of beef heart at the tip. I keep every step as light as possible instead of stomping my feet or rubbing them too hard against the ground. By leaving just enough of my scent on the ground, I sensitise my puppy's nose. Stomping creates scent bombs and widens the scent picture of the track. Once the puppy has formed a habit of searching on such a heavily laid track, his olfaction is desensitised, which works against our purpose. As I'm stepping forward, I look ahead at the two landmarks to ensure I'm aligning myself with them to form a straight line. I continue to lay the track in this manner until I've printed thirty steps. There I stomp a hole in the ground with my heel so I can push the little plastic container in, which is filled with more beef heart. If the ground is too hard I can also dig up a small piece of the crust to make a space to put the food box. I deliberately put the food box into the ground so its lid is level with the surface, making it difficult for the puppy to find it with his eyes. If necessary I'll grab a handful of grass and spread it on top of the food box to camouflage it.

6. The zigzag style of laying the track teaches the puppy to follow the track layer's scent from side to side. When the track is laid in a normal way in the future (how a person normally walks, left–right–left–right), the puppy has already established a good habit of tracking by sniffing left and right as he's moving forward. This technique prevents him from favouring one side only or just tracking in the middle instead. The left-right sweeping style also increases the accuracy of following corners and article indication. This is an essential foundation for the beginning of straight tracking.

7. After I put down the plastic container, I keep walking forward for another few steps. Then I go back to my car, avoiding walking on my freshly laid track again.
8. A track laid in the direction of the breeze is important for the early stages of tracking. It helps

form the habit of a deep nose. For now we also avoid laying cross-wind tracks. Cross-wind can move the track layer's scent sideways, affecting the puppy's precision in following the track. Up-wind and cross-wind tracking are to be done later on when the puppy has more experience in scent discrimination.

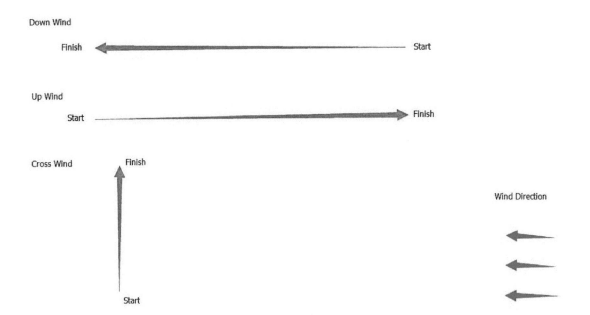

Down Wind

Finish ⟵————————————————————— Start

Up Wind

Start —————————————————————⟶ Finish

Cross Wind   Finish
↑

Start

Wind Direction

⟵
⟵
⟵

As the photos taken on a grass field can't clearly illustrate the footprints, I've duplicated the track on soft soil so you can see how each step is laid down in detail. Please note that this is only for the purpose of showing you how the track is laid exactly. For the early stages of tracking I usually wouldn't train on a surface without vegetation, the reason being that in a clear field it is too obvious for the puppy to see the footsteps, the food, and the food container. This will cause him to form the bad habit of searching with his eyes instead of his nose. Once established, this will be very difficult to change. The two white stakes in the first photo illustrate how I use two points in front of me as a sight to align a straight track.

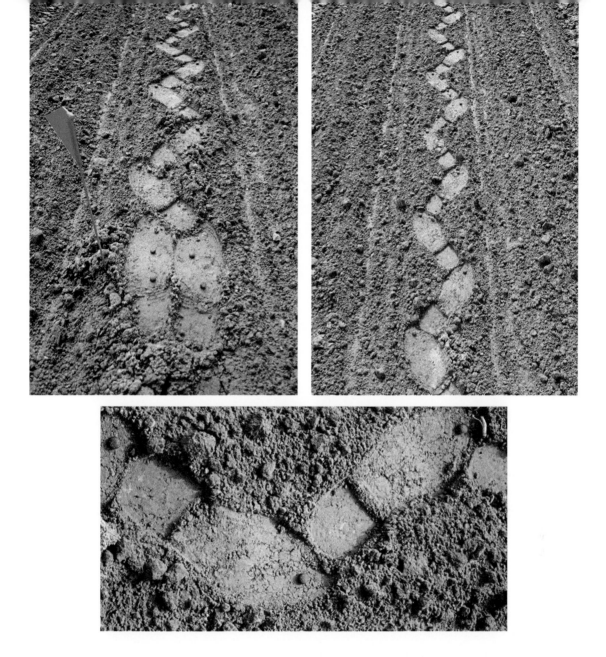

I first walk my puppy on leash around the tracking field for five to ten minutes so he can adapt to the environment and go to the toilet before beginning the track. We then come to the starting flag. As the puppy already has the foundation of scent pad training, he naturally starts sniffing the ground by himself. As soon as he hits the now reduced scent pad, he'll realise my scent isn't spread in a big circle like before, but going forwards instead. I carefully observe his behaviour. For the convenience of more effective control, at this time I'd lean over the puppy with my legs stretched engulfing him so I can guide him directly from above. If I don't have enough control of his movement by holding his leash alone, I'll gently hold his collar with one hand and hold his belly with another. My hand under his belly encourages him to put his nose to the ground and go forwards to follow the track step by step. This also prevents him from going to the sides, going backwards, turning around, lifting his head, and

lying down, as my hand can easily shift his centre of gravity forward to tilt his head down. When the puppy starts following the first step of the track, I'd loosen his collar so he can trace the footprint until he finds the food at the toes. At this moment I make him pause briefly by tugging his collar softly, so he can eat the piece of beef heart he's found (the blocking technique of negative reinforcement). As the puppy eats the food, I loosen his collar again so he can continue to the second step. When he's at the toes, again I tug on his collar softly to let him pause to eat the food. By tugging and loosening his collar, I control the puppy's tracking speed and concentration. If he attempts to go out of the track by one head length, I'd block him from going in the wrong direction further by withholding his collar until he heads off to the correct direction again. If he tries to turn around, I'd block him with my hand under his belly. Sometimes, when a puppy gets distracted and stops tracking, I'll guide him by tracing my hand along the next step if necessary. Once he's on track again, I'll stop tracing the steps to avoid him depending on me to show him where the track is. When the puppy reaches the thirtieth footprint and finds the food container, I'll gently press on his neck and his back while extending his paws forwards so he lies down in front of the container with his paws next to it and his nose pointing at it. I say "Yes" to tell him it's the end of the task, and then I open the container to pour the food out so he can eat it. This is the foundation of the article indication. By reinforcing the puppy for lying down and pointing at the food container (article), I increase the frequency of this behaviour. Once he's finished eating the food, I take him back to my car.

When teaching straight tracks, I train around three to five days a week consecutively or separately depending on what suits a particular puppy best. Once my puppy consistently initiates tracking by

automatically sniffing at the starting point, I link the command "Seek" with the behaviour. When laying the tracks, sometimes I start with my left leg and sometimes with my right. The same applies to the placement of the food container. If the puppy makes continuous progress, usually I'd increase the length of the track by ten steps every time. Normally, after five to ten straight tracks the puppy will show the positive responses below:

1. He begins to follow every footprint from left to right in a zigzag motion.
2. He pauses briefly at the tip of each footstep to eat the food.
3. The behaviour of turning around or lifting the head happens less and less.
4. I don't need to show him to go forward by tracing my hand along the footprints anymore.
5. When he finds the food box at the end of the track, as soon as I press him on the back he responds quickly by laying down.

Serpentine

When the puppy shows the above progress after numerous straight tracks, I can advance his training to the next level. The upgrade of training depends predominantly on the dog's improvement and not on the time of his practice. The same behaviour that takes three sessions for one dog to learn might take another ten sessions for another. A serpentine is a snake-shaped track that bands and curves in various degrees. The deeper the curve, the more difficult it is, as it demands higher concentration from the dog.

Training Goal

1. Gradually increase the length of the track by adding more footsteps
2. Control the puppy's tracking speed
3. Develop the puppy's best tracking rhythm
4. Gradually decrease the food on the track
5. When the puppy has formed a habit of lying down at the food box, add one to three more
6. Accustom tracking on various types of grass fields.

Preparation

1. A starting flag, several small plastic containers, and sufficient beef heart for a track of seventy steps.
2. A 3m leash for tracking. The increased length of the tracking line allows more freedom for the puppy and gives him greater opportunities to develop his scent discrimination skills.
3. At this stage I still prefer cool mornings for tracking but the conditions don't have to be as ideal

as before. Mild wind and a little bit of rain are actually good for the puppy at this level of training, as they desensitise him from working in bad weathers, which he can certainly encounter in future IPO trials. The grass fields I choose would vary from very short and sparse grass to lush grass up to the length of about 15cm. Long grass is still avoided in this period to prevent the puppy tracking with a high nose. I arrive on a grass field and start laying the track with the wind on my back. I continue to put down my footprints in the zigzag style, placing one piece of beef heart per step. I use two landmarks in front of me as references but sometimes I curve slightly to the left and sometimes slightly to the right to produce a serpentine.

4. I've laid seventy steps; I place the food box in a hole in the ground and take my puppy for a walk.

With the previous tracking foundation I've imprinted into the puppy, usually by the time my car arrives at an open field he already knows what we're there for. If I've done my foundation training correctly, as soon as I let him out of the car he should quickly show anticipation to track (the scenario triggers his food drive and exploring drive). He might display his enthusiasm by jumping around or pulling on the leash. This is a good sign and a good working attitude. However, we must be careful not to let him get too excited. Tracking is a discipline that requires a high degree of concentration, composure, and precision. The dog has to learn patience and self-control to excel in tracking. If he gets too eager, his excitement can work against him, affecting his tempo and judgement on the track. From now on, when I take him for his walk before the track, besides giving him the chance to become accustomed to the environment and to empty himself, I also walk and breathe slowly and calmly, using my behaviour and emotional state to bring the puppy into the ideal tracking mode. Once I see that he's also calmed down, I put him back in the car and give him a little bit of water to drink to moisturise his rhinarium (the skin of a dog's nose). A wet rhinarium increases the function of a dog's olfactory system. I keep him in the car for a few minutes. When his breathing and demeanour are calm, I take him out to track.

In the education of my puppies, I begin the training with the end goal in mind, which is achieving IPO3 with the best possible points. In the trial, the dog has to track with or without a line 10m in front of the handler. In IPO3, the track layer is a stranger to the dog and the handler doesn't know the position of each leg, corner, or article of the track. We need to teach our dogs to eventually follow the scent independently without our influence so he'll be able to work out the track on his own in trial conditions. During a trial, there's also no food allowed and the length of an IPO3 track is a minimum of 600 steps. So we have to gradually reduce the food and increase the distance of the track in training.

The handling principle of tracking on the serpentine is the same as tracking on the straight. We begin at the starting flag as usual. With the input of the foundation training before, the puppy has established a good habit of the side-to-side sweeping motion of footstep-to-footstep searching. My job now is to cooperate with him and to guide him when necessary. When he's following the scent correctly and slowly, I give him more freedom by extending the leash (that's why I now use a 3m leash instead of a 1.4m leash). When he loses accuracy or goes too fast, I restrict his freedom by blocking or tugging the line. For every footprint he traces, I slightly tighten and loosen the leash, so he pauses to

eat the food before proceeding to the next step. This is a technique to control the speed to establish the most suitable tracking rhythm for the dog. In the IPO trial regulations, there's no rule to deduct points if a dog is tracking fast as long as he's focused, precise, and maintains the same speed from start to finish. However, a fast tracker is more prone to making mistakes such as overshooting corners or lying on the article with his chest instead of pointing at it with his nose. So I prefer my dogs to track slowly and calmly in a relaxed state of mind. My end goal is to let my dog track on a loose line, so he follows the scent without my help. As I won't know where the track is in an IPO3 competition, I want my dog to be able to work independently so I can count on him to find the track layer's scent. The loosening and tightening of the tracking line teaches the puppy two signals: 1) a loose line represents the correct tracking speed; 2) a jerked line indicates a tracking speed that is too fast. When the puppy goes too quickly on the track, I give the line a tug. When he slows down to my desired tempo, I immediately make the line slack again. This is the same principle as using the reins to slow down a trotting horse, which is a negative reinforcement technique by leading. I train my puppy in serpentine tracking about three to five days a week. How I plan each track depends on how the puppy performs in the previous session. When he continues to develop desired tracking behaviours (searching from footprint to footprint, deep nose, slow tempo, and not turning around), I can start reducing the food I need to put down while laying the track. The procedure is as follows:

1. At the beginning of food reduction on the track, I start by reducing 10% of the beef heart intermittently. The empty steps (footprints without food) should be laid separately. At this stage the empty steps must not be placed together, otherwise you might run the risk of the puppy losing his concentration in the empty section (the segment without food) of the track. When we lay the track, we should alternate between left and right footprints for the empty steps, and not always leave a particular side without food. Usually at the beginning period of food reduction, I'd leave an empty footprint every eleven steps. That means I don't put any beef heart on the 11th, 22nd, 33rd, 44th, 55th, 66th, 77th, 88th, 99th, 110th steps and so on. This way I can easily remember where not to put food.

2. Once the puppy is used to a food reduction of 10%, I'll bring it down to 20% off, at the same time extending the distance of the serpentine. Now I shall leave an empty footprint every nine steps, setting an empty step pattern of 9th, 18th, 27th, 36th, 45th, 54th, 63rd, 72nd, 81st, 90th steps, etc.

3. We continue to reduce the food on the track as the puppy improves his tracking skill. The empty step pattern should be more random as we move on, as a strict formulation for too long a period might cause some dogs to begin counting steps, making them less focused and faster on the steps where they anticipate the absence of food. Dogs of course cannot count numbers like we do, but they can anticipate the approximate distance of the next empty step if they're always prepared with the same formula. Once we can reduce the food by 30%, we can randomly place the empty steps on the left or right footprints. Sometimes we can even leave up to two successive steps without food.

4. As we're reducing the food placed on the footprints, we increase the number of plastic food containers gradually up to small four boxes. The benefits of this include a compensation of less food on the steps, and offering a chance for a short break every time the puppy finds a box (article) before he has to start concentrating on the search again.

5. The left and right curves of the serpentine gradually bend deeper as the puppy progresses in tracking, from some 170° turns at the beginning to down to 120° at a more advanced stage of serpentine. For the teaching of 90° corners, I'll explain it in detail in the tracking strengthening stage.

6. As the puppy's handler and track layer, it's very important we observe and review his progress and response in each tracking lesson. The success of the tracking discipline largely depends on laying the right tracks for the dog in order to keep him motivated, build his confidence, challenge his olfactory function, and sharpen his tracking skills.

Progress until Tracking Strengthening Stage

1. Increase the distance of the track to a minimum of 180 steps.
2. Successfully control the puppy's tracking speed.
3. Effectively establish the puppy's best tracking tempo.
4. Reduce up to 30% of the food on the track.
5. The puppy starts showing an understanding of article indication by lying down at the food box once he's located it. We can then increase the number of food boxes up to four, spread at various spots on a track.
6. The puppy is used to tracking on different grass fields including lush grass, sparse grass, wet grass, dry grass, short grass, and medium-length grass up to 15cm.

Different Types of Serpentines

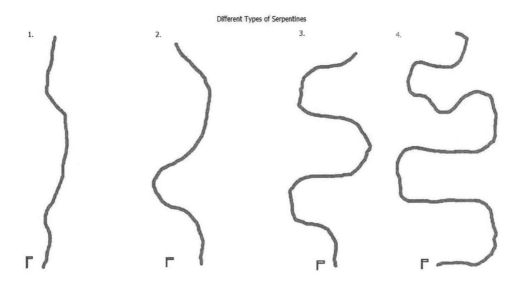

Obedience Learning Stage

Winning Criteria in IPO Obedience

1. The dog is full of life and energy in his work. He's happy and eager, walking with his head up and a high tail.
2. The dog is completely focused and devoted to his handler during the entire obedience routine.
3. Each exercise is executed with speed, style, elegance, and precision.
4. With the exception of the send away, each part of an exercise is done with a single verbal command from the handler, who moves naturally, gracefully, and smoothly, without the slightest awkwardness or extra body movement to support or suppress the dog.
5. The handler and the dog work perfectly in sync like a pair of dancers, two beings with one spirit.

IPO3 Obedience Exercises

Basic Components	Heeling off leash	Heeling in motion	Sit in motion	Down in motion	Stand in motion	Retrieve	Retrieve over hurdle	Retrieve over A-frame	Send away	Down stay
Attention	✓	✓	✓	✓	✓	✓	✓	✓	✓	✓
Look forward						✓	✓	✓		
Sit	✓	✓	✓	✓		✓	✓	✓	✓	✓
Down				✓					✓	✓
Stand					✓					
Front position				✓	✓	✓	✓	✓		
Go ahead						✓	✓	✓	✓	
Basic position	✓	✓	✓	✓	✓	✓	✓	✓	✓	✓
Hold						✓	✓	✓		
Release						✓	✓	✓		
Jump							✓			
Climb								✓		
Additional Components										
Heel right										
Backwards										
Target plates										

The IPO3 obedience routine is composed of the nine exercises in the above table. We break them down into twelve independent basic components. The three additional components act as special aids that make the teaching of certain exercises much more effective. The total fifteen fundamental behaviours are easy for a puppy to learn. We first teach them to the puppy through positive reinforcement in the obedience learning stage, then strengthen them with negative reinforcement, and finally put them all together to develop all the obedience exercises.

Teaching Attention through Free Shaping

Attention to the handler is the foundation of IPO obedience. In my puppy's first week home, I've already established a strong bond and pack relationship with him. I've also taught him coming to me and looking at me. During our daily interaction, he's used to directing his attention towards me because I'm his source of food, fun, and guidance. All I need to do now is to link the "Look" command with him paying attention to me. In an environment without distractions, I walk around casually and let my hungry puppy follow me freely. He can be in front of me or next to me. When he looks at me by chance, I say "Look". As he keeps his eye contact with me, I click and feed him a dry kibble, and repeat this procedure five to ten times, gradually increasing the time of the attention. At the end of the session I give him the jackpot of feeding him a full meal, playing with him, or letting him bite his toy. To refresh your memory, please refer to "Developing Stage: A Puppy's First Week Home: Part 2: Free Shaping".

Teaching Sit, Down, Stand, Heel Left, Heel Right, Backward, Hold, Release, Jump, Climb, Look Forward, Go Ahead, Target Plates through Luring

Training Goal

1. Introduce all of the obedience basic components.
2. Luring is our main method of teaching in this stage, because it is fast, direct, and positive.
3. Build a foundation for the introduction of targeting, blocking, and leading later on.

Sit

I take a clicker in my left hand and some dry dog kibbles in my right. I let the puppy follow my food hand as I lift it just over his head. I turn my palm downwards to encourage him to lift his head in order to eat the food in my hand. I keep my hand at this level while slightly moving it horizontally towards the direction of the puppy's hindquarters, causing him to shift his centre of gravity backwards. The transfer of weight causes the puppy to sit. As soon as his buttocks make contact with the ground, I click and feed him a kibble. I should now keep my food hand stationary above his head to keep him sitting. When he stays sitting, I click and treat again. I continue to reinforce multiple times as long as he stays in the sitting position. When I have only one kibble left in my hand, I say "Yes" and lure him out of sitting before giving him the last kibble. This teaches the puppy to end the practice briefly when I say "Yes". I then take another handful of kibbles and repeat this procedure three to seven times.

When luring a puppy to sit, we should pay attention to the hand that's holding the food above the puppy's head. If this hand is held too high, it entices him to jump up or scratch the hand with his paws. If held too low, the puppy might sit in a slouch or with one leg folded crookedly beneath him. Once he's sitting, we have to keep the food hand steady to maintain a straight sit, otherwise the puppy will move out of his position following the instability of our hand. A puppy sitting with his right paw up indicates his weight is too much on the left. You need to manipulate his centre of gravity by luring him to shift his weight to the right. He'll then put down his right paw in order to support his weight evenly. If the dog doesn't sit or keeps stepping backwards while you attempt to lure him with your hand above his head, you can gently press on his hindquarters with your clicker hand to restrict his movement. The touch and feel of the handler are essential in generating the desired behaviour from the dog. Every dog is different and you must work with your feeling and common sense.

Down

I have some kibbles in one hand and hold it in front of the puppy's nose while bringing my hand straight down. Because he wants the food, he lowers his head to follow my hand. I click and treat with my palm facing down on the ground, at the same time adjusting the position of my hand to try to lure the puppy into putting his elbows down. I click and treat as long as the puppy keeps his head and elbows close to the ground, while pushing my hand forward into the puppy, so his weight shifts backwards, causing his abdomen to make contact with the ground as well. I continue to maintain his down position by keeping him interested, pushing his snout under my palm to get the treats after each time I click.

When I have only one kibble remaining in my hand, I say "Yes" and let him out of lying down by taking my hand off the ground. I give him the last kibble, and then take another handful of dog food to repeat the procedure three to seven times.

When luring the dog to down, it's very important you lower your food hand straight down vertically or even push your hand down in between the dog's two front paws. Don't try to lure him down and forward, as this will teach him to take a few steps forward when going down. This will slow the dog's speed and he'll develop a habit of always crawling a few steps forward in the down in motion exercise, costing you points.

The down position is a little bit trickier than the sit. Some puppies with higher dominance often dislike lying down for someone because it is a sign of submission. When luring the down, we should mark the behaviour as soon as the puppy lowers his head. When an elbow makes contact with the ground we click and treat again. To have his belly touching the ground, sometimes we can press his back or hindquarters with the clicker hand.

Stand

Out of the three positions, sit, down, stand, the standing position is the most difficult to stabilise because it only takes one little step from the dog to cause you a downgrade in the rating of the exercise in an IPO trial. When we teach a puppy to stand, we have to take this into consideration. If we click and treat him like before, he'll most likely step out of the stand by himself to receive the food. Once this has become a habit, he'll keep on stepping forward while standing. That's why the techniques of teaching the stand are a little different from the sit and the down. One approach towards stabilising the stand is to gently hold the puppy's belly with my clicker hand while feeding him with the other as he's standing. My hand under his belly prevents him from stepping forward as I'm clicking and feeding him. This is an example of gentle application of blocking in negative reinforcement.

The second approach is to utilise reverse targeting with luring by bringing the puppy to the edge of a low stair step or a bench. The height should be safe enough so the puppy won't hurt himself if he jumps off. I bring the puppy's front paws to the edge of the step. As he sees there's a drop in front of him, by instinct he'll usually stand stiff at the edge even when I'm feeding him from the front. Every time I see that he's standing sturdily, I click and treat him. After about ten to fifteen times of reinforcing the behaviour, I say "Yes" and carry him off the step.

Heel Left, Heel Right

Heeling is broken down into static heeling and dynamic heeling. Static heeling is when the dog is sitting attentively by his handler's left side with his right shoulder aligned with the handler's left knee. This is also called the basic position in IPO because almost every exercise begins and ends with the dog sitting on his handler's left in a trial. Dynamic heeling is when the dog is following attentively on his handler's left side as he walks. I teach the puppy both forms from the start. As I'm doing this with luring, all the puppy has to learn at this stage is to follow my hand as I walk, and sit by my side as I stop. As long as the position of my food hand is at the right spot, the puppy can learn to heel precisely in a short time. To develop a good habit in heeling, I teach my puppy next to a wall or a fence. I utilise reverse targeting to prevent the puppy from swinging his hindquarters out when he's walking along. (To better illustrate the heeling techniques, in the related photos here I've replaced the wall with portable sticks as the reverse targets.) When teaching the puppy to heel on my left, I hold some dog kibbles in my left hand and the clicker in my right. The puppy sits by my left with the wall on his left (represented by the portable sticks in the photos). Sufficient space should be left between the puppy and the wall, or he might feel crowded and follows behind you or jumps in front of you instead of heeling beside you when you start moving forward. I begin static heeling with luring the puppy to sit by my left leg. As he has already learned the sit by luring, as soon as I hold the kibbles above his head he'll sit automatically. I try getting him to sit so his collar aligns with the seam of my left trouser leg. I click and treat several times when he's sitting correctly before I start walking ahead, slowly leading with my left leg. When I'm training the puppy to heel on my left side, I lure him to follow the movement of my left leg by holding my food hand (left hand) next to my left thigh or left knee depending on the puppy's head height. I position my food hand at a level that can best keep the puppy following with his head up, but not so high that it might entice him to hop. I keep reinforcing him as he follows me correctly by sticking his nose to my left palm. I adjust my walking speed so the puppy can heel by my side correctly. Sometimes I come to a standing stop and lure him into sitting, returning into the basic position in which we began. I teach him to follow me as I walk, and to sit next to me as I stop. When I come to the end of the wall or have only one kibble remaining in my hand, I'd say "Yes" to temporarily stop the heeling before repeating the practice again. In a single session I'd teach the puppy both heeling on my left and heeling on my right alternately. When our practice of left heeling reaches the end of the wall, I'd turn around, hold the food with my right hand and the clicker with my left, and lure the puppy to my right side. Now the wall is on our right. This technique of heeling left and right alternately has the following benefits:

1. The side transport exercise in the IPO protection phase is basically having the dog heeling by the decoy's right side. We start teaching this to the puppy here.
2. Teaching the puppy to heel left and right alternately in the same lesson is beneficial to stimulate his mind and muscle memory, balancing his body awareness on both sides.
3. A dog that learns heeling on the left alone will become one-sided over time just like a footballer that can only kick with his right leg. Before a puppy starts favouring any side, teaching him heeling on both left and right is simple, as there's no difference in their difficulties.
4. When we practise left heeling along the wall, as we reach the end we have to turn around anyway. So why not take this opportunity to teach the puppy something useful?

After a few sessions, the puppy starts to get a feeling of the exercise and we can now teach him to follow both the outside hand and the inside hand. Let's take left heeling as an example. When the puppy is heeling on my left, my left hand is the outside hand and my right hand is the inside hand. I taught him to follow my outside hand (left hand) before. Now I teach him to heel left following my inside hand (right hand). In practice, I hold the food in my right hand and the clicker in my left. I lure the puppy to sit by my left with the kibble in my right hand. The wall is to the puppy's left. As soon as he sits correctly I click and treat. I then start walking ahead leading with my left leg while holding the food against my left thigh or left knee with my right hand. The level of my right hand should be positioned at a height that the puppy can follow comfortably with his head up without bouncing. As he's heeling well, I keep reinforcing. When I stop, I lure him to sit so we're back into basic position.

Why do I have to teach the puppy in such an awkward way and not just let him follow my outside hand alone? This is because our end goal is to have the puppy follow us attentively without a luring hand. In all IPO trials, the handler is expected to walk and move naturally and gracefully without any further body language to cue the dog. To achieve this, the first step is to accustom the puppy to our outside hand (left hand) swinging naturally next to his head as we walk. Because we still need to lure him somehow at this stage, we use both the outside and the inside hand. For heeling on the right, the same principle applies, only now the sides are opposite like a mirror reflection.

Backwards

Although walking backwards is not really a behaviour you see in any exercise in an IPO trial, teaching it to a dog will bring many advantages. It serves as an effective aid in heeling, hold and bark, and back transport, which I'll explain further in the later portions of this book. I teach this behaviour with the puppy facing me. I have food in both of my hands, and I use them to gently push the puppy backwards at his throat level. As he's trying to eat the kibbles out of my hands and finds himself too close, he has to step backwards in order to give himself enough space. With both my hands full, I can't hold a clicker anymore. Instead, I introduce a new signal, "Good", to replace the "click" sound. Every time the puppy steps backwards, I say "Good" and feed him a kibble. I continue to softly push him backwards and reinforce him by saying "Good" and treating him with food. When there's one last kibble remaining in my hand, I say "Yes", give him the food, and repeat the procedure again with more kibbles in my hands.

Hold

The hold component is the integral part of the three dumbbell retrieval exercises. We actually began teaching this in the puppy's first week home during bite development. I encourage the puppy to chase and bite a puppy sleeve. Once he's had a full, firm, and calm bite on the sleeve, I occasionally shake it slightly or hook it downwards with my fingers to maintain the quality of the grip. As the puppy is holding the sleeve the way I want, I link the command "Hold" with his behaviour and gently put my hand under his chin to encourage this. Sometimes I can turn the puppy around so his hindquarters are facing me. I then pretend I want to pry open his mouth with one hand on top and one hand below his jaws to stimulate him to bite harder to keep the sleeve. After a few repetitions I let him win the sleeve as a reward.

Release

There are several ways to teach the release. At this point I prefer to use food as a lure. I first prepare some fresh meat and some dry dog kibbles. After the puppy has won the sleeve, I prevent him from going away by holding his collar. I then hold a handful of dry kibbles in front of his nose and let him sniff it. If he releases the sleeve, I'll link the behaviour with the "Give" command as the sleeve drops onto the ground. I then reward him with a kibble and move my hand away from the sleeve as I feed him some more, keeping his focus on my food hand. When I have one remaining kibble in my hand, I say "Yes" and end the practice by giving him the kibble while putting the sleeve away to prevent him from biting it again. If we're training indoors, I can also throw the kibble on the floor to encourage the puppy to chase it, stimulating his hunt drive and food drive simultaneously. This should be avoided on a grass field though, as food on ground with vegetation will encourage the puppy to search with his nose and shifts his attention to tracking instead of biting. If the puppy isn't willing to give up the sleeve in exchange for the kibbles, we can try fresh meat and see if this will get him interested.

Jump

The introduction of the jump focuses on teaching the puppy to clear the hurdle without touching it with any parts of his body. A height between 10 and 20cm is enough for this purpose, depending on which height is the easiest for the puppy to clear. To keep the puppy more focused on the hurdle rather than on me, I keep the food in my pockets instead of luring him with my hand. I bring the puppy to the front of the hurdle and let him walk freely. I step over the hurdle and call him from the other side, tapping on the hurdle if I feel it would help him jump. If he successfully clears the hurdle without touching it, I say "Yes" and reinforce this with a kibble. If he touches it, I'll just encourage him to jump again by going to the opposite side. Teaching a puppy to jump the hurdle is very similar to teaching a horse to do the same. The hurdle itself is a reverse target for the animals to avoid. Some less confident puppies might try avoiding the jump by going around it. To prevent this, I can attach the puppy to a leash, or put two 1m fences next to the hurdle so he has to jump over it.

Climb

The climbing of the scaling wall focuses on the puppy maintaining contact with the wall as he goes up and comes down. Jumping off from the top of the wall is discouraged as this can easily cause injuries. We lower the height of the wall to about 50cm to have two gentle slopes. This encourages the puppy to maintain contact with the wall throughout the passing. I lure the puppy with food, feeding him as he's climbing and descending.

Look Forward, Go Ahead

For the introduction of these two behaviours, I usually use raw meat to maximise the puppy's food drive. Send away is the last exercise in the obedience routine of an IPO trial (or the down stay, depending on your draw). I normally practise these two components at the end of an obedience training session so the puppy can end his lesson with a jackpot (a full meal of fresh meat). When I'm at the initial stage of teaching the send away exercise, I always let my puppy aim at the same landmark of the training field as his visual target. Most IPO clubs in Europe are located on football fields or similar sporting grounds for ball games, and ball games have goals. I use one of the goals as a visual target so my dog aims at this when I send him. First I place a bowl of fresh meat in the centre of the goal, pairing the reward and the target together. I take the puppy in front of the goal and let him see the bowl of meat. As the puppy has already gone through food drive enhancement earlier on, as soon as he sees the meat he'll instantly kick into drive and want to rush at it. I now hold him by the collar while pointing at the goal with my hand and say "Watch". When I feel he's pulling into the collar with the most intensity, I say "Go" and release him so he can dash at the food bowl like an arrow leaving its bow. I let him take a mouthful or two before pulling him back a few metres by the collar again, all that time keeping his head facing the goal. I repeat the same procedure to teach look forward and go ahead, increasing the distance from the goal gradually every time. After three to five repetitions I let him finish all the meat in the bowl and complete the session on a high note.

Target Plates

Target plates are simple devices that are widely used in the sport of Belgian Ring. They're not very often seen in traditional Schutzhund training. I've adopted these valuable tools and their techniques in training my IPO dogs as they're highly effective in teaching the jumps and the send away. This is an example of cross-training. The introduction of the target plates is as follows:

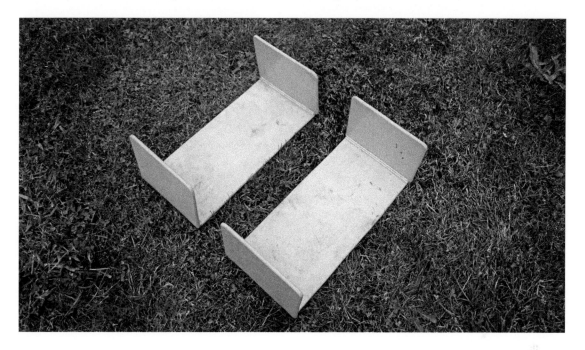

1. I place a pair of target plates on the ground facing each other at a distance of about 1 to 2m apart. I take my puppy by the collar and stand between the plates, facing one of them. I let the puppy see me putting some food on the plate we're facing, stimulating his food drive.
2. With all the food drive enhancement we've gone through, the puppy can't wait to run to the plate; as soon as I let him go, he's on it to eat the food.
3. As he finishes the food on the plate, I take out more food to lure him to turn around and lay down on the plate.
4. Now he's lying on it while facing the second target plate. Now I hold him by the collar and put some food on the second plate.
5. I let him go so he can run to the second plate to eat the food.
6. When he's eaten the food on the second plate, I lure him to turn around and lie down, facing the first target plate again.
7. We repeat this procedure several times, ending on a good note.

Teaching Front Position through Targeting

Targeting is a very effective technique to get the dog following a particular object without having to lure him. Here, I'll explain its introduction and benefits in detail.

For teaching the front position (dog sitting closely in front of the handler attentively), I use a little tool I call the target tag. A target tag is a safety pin name tag used by many companies so their employees can display their names and positions when serving customers or attending meetings. It is a plastic card about the size of 8cm by 4cm with a safety pin and a clip on its back. You can buy this in your local stationery store or search "name tag safety pin" on the internet to purchase online.

The intention of using a target tag in teaching the front position is to get the puppy to pay attention to the centre line of my body without searching for my hands for food. To get the puppy interested during the tag's introduction, I first rub a drop of fish oil on the front surface of the tag. This is a scent that attracts most dogs. You can also achieve the same effect by briefly rubbing a piece of grilled beef liver on the tag. I hold both a clicker and a target tag with my left hand. The clicker is held normally between my thumb and forefinger, and the tag between my forefinger and middle finger. I take a handful of dry dog kibbles with my right hand and place it in my left underarm. I show the puppy the tag. As the fish oil scent attracts him, he'll most likely come closer to investigate, naturally touching the tag with his nose. At this moment I click to mark his behaviour, and then I deliver the food to the puppy in a motion that looks like I'm brushing down my left sleeve with my right hand. After I treat him with a kibble, my right hand returns to my left armpit again. Why do I have to feed my puppy in such a strange way? This is because, from my experience of practising this technique with quite a few dogs, many of them focus on my food hand instead of the target tag initially. Although I show the puppy that he can obtain the food through touching the target first, most likely he'll fix his attention on my food hand after he realises the food comes from it. If I feed him the usual way (right hand taking food out from my right pocket), there's a possibility he'll focus on my right side much more then on my left, and this can become a habit that works against what I'm trying to achieve. I also don't want to compromise this training by holding the target tag and the food with the same hand as this is simply cheating by just luring the dog. Consequently, I keep my right hand (food hand) in my left armpit (target tag arm), so that the target and the food are both on the same side. As the height of the food is higher, hidden in my left underarm, and more difficult for the puppy to get, and the height of the tag is lower and offered to

the puppy invitingly, he won't focus on my food hand anymore and will follow the target tag much more easily.

I alternate between both hands, sometimes holding the tag with my left and sometimes with my right. After two to five lessons, the puppy should develop a lot of interest in touching the target with his nose, following it as it moves, just like the movement in luring. Now I can teach him to come to the front position:

1. First I have some dog kibbles in my training vest's left and right pockets. I hold the tag in my centre line with both hands at the height of the puppy's head.

2. I face the puppy while stepping backwards slowly, letting him follow me. As he focuses on the tag and comes closer, I say "Yes" and then feed him two kibbles simultaneously, one from each hand. Because I want the puppy to come in front of me as close as possible at

this stage, I keep my feet apart to prevent him stepping on them (it's a bad habit when a dog always steps on his handler's feet).

3. I have to teach him to automatically sit closely in front of me as I stop moving. When I come to a stand, I keep my feet spread and pull my pelvis back so the puppy has more room to park in front of me. At this moment, I slightly raise the target tag above his head, simulating the movement of luring him to sit. If he doesn't understand this, I can use some food to lure him to sit at this point.

4. Once he's sitting nicely in front of me, I repeat the practice by stepping backwards and letting him follow again, reinforcing him for sitting straight and tight in front of me when I stop.

After a few repetitions, we end the session on a good note. In a few more lessons, when the puppy can follow me quite well by focusing on the target tag, I'll raise the training level again:

1. I can now attach the target tag to my jacket or vest by its clip or its safety pin on the back. The tag's level should be about the puppy's head height. If it's too high, it'll entice the puppy to hop or jump up on me, which is undesired for what we want to teach him here. The material of my vest should be stiff and thick so the tag can be set on it steadily. If the fabric is too soft and flexible, the target attached to it will swing and bounce around, distracting the puppy as I'm moving backward, making it difficult for him to park in front of me precisely. The purpose of the target tag is to fixate the puppy's focus onto my centre line. This takes his attention away from my hands.

2. Once I've attached the tag at the right spot, I first continue to hold it with both hands like before and get him to follow me backwards. After a few steps I stop to let him sit. I might still need to raise the tag a little bit to cue him to sit straight and close. Once he's in position I say "Yes" and feed him with both hands in front of the tag.

3. I begin stepping backwards again and let him follow. I observe his behaviour and determine if he's now ready to follow the tag without me holding it. If I see that he understands the idea, I'll let go of the tag and keep my hands to my sides, just letting the attached target tag do its job. The puppy can now come into the front position by focusing on the tag without me having to hold it. He should walk closely towards me as I step backwards, and sit tightly in front of me when I come to a stop.

Fetching Toys

Besides food drive, hunt drive/prey drive and pack drive are two very powerful sources of motivation in obedience training. For that reason, in the learning stage of obedience I encourage my puppy to bite and fetch a wide range of toys. The toys I choose have the following features and criteria:

1. Appropriate size, easy for the puppy to pick up but not so small that he can swallow it or choke on it. Harmless to his teeth, made of supple materials that allow him to bite and hold it comfortably. My choice of toys includes a fluffy ball, fluffy bite roll, rubber ball, rubber ball with rope, floating ball, floating dummy, and jute bite roll.

2. At this age, I've already begun training the puppy in bite work. I use different equipment from the above toys to develop a full, firm, and calm grip. The role of the toys is different

from the role of the bite sleeves. The purpose of the toys is to let the dog have fun and release his energy. Although I apply certain rules while I let my dog play with these toys, how he bites them is not important here.

3. Once my puppy has developed enough interest in various toys, I teach him to bring them back to play with me. This is a game and is different from the retrieve exercises in obedience. In the three obedience retrieves, there are many criteria such as the dog must hold the dumbbell firmly without mouthing it; when he returns he must sit precisely facing me in the front position as he's sitting in front of me calmly he must hold the dumbbell up at me without touching me. All these details are not so relevant in our game of fetching. The function of a toy is to satisfy the dog's hunt drive/prey drive and pack drive through the game of biting, bringing it back, and interacting with me. The fetching game has some rules but they're not as strict as a formal exercise. Otherwise the dog would feel suppressed and inhibited by always having to act in such constrained manners. A dog is not a robot. If we want him to work for us in a long, healthy, and happy career, we must consider his needs and feelings. Sometimes, the best reward is to just let a dog be a dog, leaving him to do what he enjoys.

The technique of stimulating the puppy to bite a toy is the same as what I did in bite development. The only difference here is I don't need a full, firm, and calm grip. My goal now is to teach the puppy to bring me back the toy so we can play together. An easy way to teach this is to attach a thin rope to the toy. This prevents the puppy from running away after winning. Every time he tries snatching the toy away, all I need to do is reel him in, just like fishing. I then wrestle or play tug-of-war with him a little bit through the toy and let him win. When he wants to steal the toy away again, I just reel him back in. After a few repetitions, he will learn:

1. It's not possible for him to snatch the toy away as it's attached to a rope held by me.

2. There's nothing for him to gain trying to steal the toy from me. On the other hand, when he wrestles with me, he gets to win every time. This makes him feel strong and victorious, which is very rewarding.

3. It won't be long before the puppy realises the fun of the toy is in playing with me and not in trying to snatch it. He'll start initiating the game by bringing the toy back. When I can throw out a toy in several different environments and my puppy will fetch it every time, I can now remove the rope and link the "Fetch" command with the behaviour.

Before I can throw the toy again for another fetch, the puppy has to release it first. So far I've taught him to release an object with two methods, by prying his mouth open or by luring him with food. I'll now teach him to release with a third method:

Teaching Release through Pressing

1. I let the puppy bite a rubber ball with rope. He has to bite the ball and not the rope.

2. When I want him to release, I take the ball by firmly enclosing it with my fingers. At the same time I look into the puppy's eyes directly, calmly, and determinedly.

3. My intention is not to pull the ball out of the puppy's mouth, because as soon as I start pulling it will stimulate his prey drive, causing him to pull back in resistance. In contrast, I actually push my hand into his mouth while rolling my wrist forward. This is an act of dominance. The puppy can clearly sense my intention is to take the ball. By this time I already have my whole hand around it. As I squeeze and roll my wrist forward, the puppy has no option but to let go because I'm much stronger than he is. To prevent him from pulling back, I can also hold him by the collar with my other hand. The pressing out technique is a utilisation of the dog's opposition reflex, as captured prey

would never try squeezing deeper into the predator's mouth. I link the "Out" command with the release of the ball.

4. Now I have the ball in my hand. The puppy can't bite it even though he wants to. The only thing he can do is to watch the ball with anticipation. At this moment I say "Yes" and let him bite the ball again. This is the reward for him releasing the ball.

5. After several sessions, I gradually fade out the movement of taking the ball with my hand by only doing so when my verbal command alone isn't responded to by an instant release. Once the puppy has outed, I open my hand to give him a chance to snatch the ball. If he tries, I'll immediately close my hand and grunt at him as a sign of disapproval. When he can maintain staring at the ball for five to ten seconds without trying to steal it from me, I say "Yes" and let him bite it again as his reward for outing and guarding.

6. When the puppy can out on command every time, I'll increase my distance from him, progressively extending the distance between us by several metres. So as soon as I say "Out" he'll release the ball and stare at it. When he can keep watching the ball without attempting to bite it or getting distracted, I say "Yes" to let him take the ball again. This is very useful for the guard in the protection phase.

Note: The above pressing technique for the out is only suitable for puppies under six months old. Do not try this on an adult, especially on a strange dog, or you might risk being bitten!

Contents in One Lesson

In the obedience learning stage, we focus on teaching the fifteen fundamental behaviours including attention, sit, down, stand, basic position, heel right, front position, backward, hold, release, jump, climb, look forward, go ahead, and target plates. Because a puppy has a limited attention span, I usually categorise the length of my training sessions into three types: 1) a three-minute short session, 2) a seven-minute medium session, and 3) a ten-minute long session. In the beginning, our lessons should mainly be made up of short sessions. The puppy learns one to three components in a session. Once he's learned all the basic behaviours, we can employ more medium sessions, sometimes focusing on the quality of one to three behaviours, or sometimes doing a brief revision of five to ten behaviours. When the puppy becomes proficient with all fifteen components, occasionally I can give him a long session to run through each behaviour. To avoid getting him too tired mentally or running the risk of his decline in interest, in the learning stage I usually don't give too many long lessons.

For a puppy below twelve weeks of age, I normally feed him three meals a day. During some of his meals I can incorporate a three-minute session of obedience. At this age I try to keep obedience training to no more than ten minutes a day. That means in one day I can choose to do three short sessions, or one short session plus one medium session, or just a single long session. Long sessions can easily drain a puppy's interest in learning if done too much. Normally I do this only once a week with a puppy.

Some components are interrelated. I usually let my puppy practise them in the same session. For example:

- Sit, down, stand
- Heel left, heel right
- Hold, release
- Jump, climb
- Look forward, go ahead.

Some behaviours are either more independent or time consuming to teach; I would let my puppy concentrate on them in one individual session without mixing them with other components. They're the hold, release, and fetching.

Should We Continue Free Shaping when We Are Busy Teaching the Basic Components of the Obedience Exercises?

Because free shaping is the most effective system in stimulating a dog's proactiveness and creativity, besides teaching my puppy the basic components of the IPO obedience exercises I'd still spend two to three sessions a week in free shaping with him to develop behaviours that have nothing to do with the IPO regulations. This is very useful to keep the puppy interested in training, as repeating the same thing over and over again for a long period can sometimes cause boredom.

Developing the Handler/Dog Partnership

When training a dog, we must be quick-thinking and adaptable. Don't act like a robot and be trapped in a box of theories, because every dog is different and there are always exceptions to the rules. Besides using food and toys as training aids, we must focus on using ourselves as a motivation, encouraging our dogs to play, interact, and seek contact with us in and out of training. Dogs are highly intelligent animals. They're able to differentiate our intentions and emotions. We have to be able to influence our dogs with positive emotions, so at the end he's not solely working for his food or his toy, but for us as a pack. When we eventually step into the stadium for competitions, there's no more food or toy or leash allowed. There's only the handler and his dog. The only thing left is the bond of the pack. At competition level, we should be able to throw away all the help and our dogs will still work for us with pleasure. When we take away all the theories and gadgets, dog training only comes down to one thing, "Here's a dog and here's a man. The dog must listen to the man." It's as simple as that. Through utilising all the different training systems and devices in teaching our dogs all these various skills, our ultimate goal is to have an unbreakable connection with our dogs, so two beings can be in one spirit. For me, that's what dog training is all about.

Progress until the Obedience Strengthening Stage

Practice makes perfect. Through daily interaction, if a handler carefully observes his puppy's behaviour, develops his communication, and thinks with logic and common sense, even as a beginner, he can have significant breakthroughs in as little time as two months. Improvement in the handler means improvement for his dog. In every training stage, every day, every lesson, down to every movement, as dog trainers we should always search for room for improvements. First we improve ourselves, and then our dogs, until we can develop their maximum genetic capabilities.

Below I've listed the goals I'd like to achieve in the obedience learning stage. This means the period from an eight- to ten-week-old puppy until the age of about twelve or sixteen weeks. Before progressing to the obedience strengthening stage, I'd like my puppy to have established the following requirements:

1. When I call my puppy's name in an environment without distractions, he always comes to me instantly, quickly and willingly.

2. For sit, down, and stand, as soon as I lure my puppy with food he responds immediately by going into the correct positions. He'll also stay in these positions as I continue to reinforce him with food.

3. During left and right heeling, he follows me with pleasure, lifting his head and wagging his tail along the way.

4. In practising the front position, my puppy can follow me correctly by focusing on the target tag. When I stop, he sits in front of me automatically.

5. For the backwards behaviour, my puppy willingly steps backwards as I push my hand towards him with a handful of dry dog kibbles.

6. If possible, I prefer him to be able to hold the puppy sleeve with a good grip. But, as every puppy develops in his own unique way, I wouldn't be too obsessive with the hold at this age. Some puppies don't have the kind of drive and grip we want until they're more mature. We shouldn't force them to do something that's way ahead of their time. I have another excellent way to achieve a good, solid hold for the dumbbell later on. It's called the table retrieve system. I'll explain it in detail in the obedience strengthening stage.

7. I can make my puppy out by luring him with food, prying his mouth open, or pressing the ball into his mouth.

8. He can correctly jump and climb the hurdle and scaling wall set at low heights.

9. He's focused and driven in the look forward and go ahead components. I can release him at 5m from the football field goal and he runs at it rapidly in a straight line to eat the food in the bowl.

10. The puppy is very interested going onto the target plates. As soon as I release him, he'll go on the one he's facing to eat the food.

When to Introduce Verbal Commands

The sport of Schutzhund emphasises a single verbal command for a single direct response. For example, when I give the "Sit" command my dog should immediately sit, without any extra body language or influence from me. Throughout our training, when is the best time to introduce the verbal command for a behaviour? Well, different trainers have different preferences. Some training sequences are more efficient than others. The following scenarios are the most common sequences for different trainers in teaching their dogs the verbal cues:

1. The first example is at the earliest stage of training when the dog still has no idea what his handler wants. The handler says "Sit" and applies some kind of pressure to make the dog sit. Once the dog is sitting, the pressure stops. In the successful cases, through repetition, some dogs have learnt the quickest way to avoid the pressure is to "beat it" by immediately sitting after hearing the "Sit" command. In some cases, the dog would link the "Sit" command

and the aversive feeling of pressure together, and yields a negative response towards the "Sit" command. The more he goes through the same training, the more he resists sitting. This depends on the level of pressure applied, the natural instincts of the dog, and the timing of the handlers. This is one of the most traditional methods of teaching a dog but probably not the best method. Even in the successful cases where the dogs are taught to sit on command, usually they don't do this with pleasure, because they've associated the command and the behaviour with pressure

2. In the second example, the dog is also unaware of what his handler wants. The handler first applies pressure to make the dog sit. As the dog is halfway from standing to putting his buttocks onto the ground, he instils the verbal command "Sit", and the pressure stops as the dog's buttocks make contact with the ground. This sequence is better than the first, because the "Sit" command happens after the pressure. In the dog's understanding, the "Sit" command and the sit response cause the pressure to stop. At least he doesn't associate a negative feeling towards the "Sit" command, because it appears after the pressure and not before it. If you have difficulties grasping this concept, you can think of how we introduce the clicker. The "click" sound has to come before the food to create the positive anticipation for the dog. If it comes after the food, it doesn't have the same meaning anymore. This is the same as placing the "Sit" command after the pressure.

3. In the third example, the dog is unaware of his handler's intention also. His handler says "Sit" and lures him to sit with some food, feeding him when his buttocks are on the ground. This teaching sequence is fairly good. At least the dog won't generate a negative feeling towards this kind of learning. On the contrary, his feeling is positive because he obtains food from it. The only shortcoming with this practice is as the dog has no previous training experience, after the "Sit" command, he might fidget around or jump onto his handler or throw all sorts of related behaviours before settling into the sit position. This might only take a few seconds, but in this few seconds he does something we don't want, and these unwanted activities will be associated with the "Sit" command along with the sit position.

4. The fourth example is, at the earliest stage of training, the handler first lures the dog into sit without saying anything. He only inserts the "Sit" command when the dog is halfway between standing and putting his buttocks onto the ground, and gives him the food as the dog's buttocks make contact with the ground. In my opinion, this learning sequence is better than the previous three examples, because: 1) the learning is associated with a positive feeling. The dog has made a good connection with the "Sit" command and the sit response; and 2) the handler only introduces the "Sit" command when the dog is in the motion of sitting. This is the key, because now the dog can only associate the verbal cue of "Sit" with sitting in response. There are no other actions of nonsense in between the command and the desired behaviour. Thus the dog is given an opportunity to learn what we want clearly and quickly.

5. However, I prefer the fifth example for the introduction of the verbal commands for most

of the competition exercises. In this sequence of teaching, I first teach the sit response by luring my puppy with food. Although I don't bring in the "Sit" command here yet, I'm in fact giving him a cue through his senses of sight and smell. After several repetitions, he can quickly realise I want him to sit when I hold my food hand above his head. To make his sit response even more solid before I introduce the "Sit" command, I now instil one more way of communication with my puppy through the sense of touch. I attach a leash to my puppy's collar and hold it with my right hand. I take some dry dog kibbles in my left hand. I gently pull the leash upward with my right hand so there's a little bit of tension, just enough for the puppy to feel a very slight discomfort. Immediately I bring my food hand above his head to lure him into sit. As he has done this many times before, he'll gladly respond by sitting. As he's halfway through the motion of putting his buttocks onto the ground, at this very moment I introduce the verbal command "Sit". As soon as his buttocks touch the ground, I release the tension on the leash, say "Good" and reward him with some food.

I prefer the fifth teaching sequence for introducing many of the competition verbal commands. My reason is that before I link the verbal cue with a particular behaviour, my dog and I already share a strong foundation of communication by the sense of smell, the sense of sight, and the sense of touch. On top of that, by this stage he already understands both the positive and negative ways to go into this behaviour with luring and leading. He will grasp the meaning of "Sit" very quickly, but most importantly he'll understand the verbal command in the way I want him to understand it. When I say sit, he knows that by responding by sitting immediately, he can obtain his food and avoid the leash tension without any redundant behaviour in between. The quicker he sits, the quicker he can switch off the leash tension, and the quicker he can get his food.

1. Avoid or achieve
2. Avoid and achieve
3. Avoid to achieve
4. Achieve to avoid.

These are the important lessons we'll teach our dogs in the obedience strengthening stage.

Protection Learning Stage

Winning Criteria in IPO Protection

1. Fast, direct, purposeful searching of the hides (a hide is a tent or vertical planks fixed on the ground, providing cover for the bad guy to hide in)
2. Clear, powerful, and rhythmic barking
3. Absolute focus on the decoy (bad guy) in the guarding phase
4. Fast, confident, unwavering, and courageous attack
5. Full, firm, and calm grip
6. Clear and forceful out
7. In perfect control under the handler's command.

Basic components	IPO3 Protection Exercises									
	Hide search	Hold and bark	Escape	Prevention of the escape	Re-attack	Back transport	Back transport	Attack during back transport	Long attack	Re-attack
Bite			✓		✓		✓		✓	✓
Out			✓		✓		✓		✓	✓
Bark		✓	✓		✓		✓		✓	✓
Run around	✓									
Attention	✓	✓	✓							
Look forward	✓	✓	✓		✓	✓	✓		✓	✓
Sit			✓							
Down			✓							
Front position (Come)	✓	✓								
Go ahead	✓		✓		✓		✓		✓	✓
Basic position	✓	✓	✓		✓	✓	✓		✓	✓

The ✓ symbol in the above table represents the dog having the choice of barking out or silent out after biting.

The protection phase is the most important discipline out of the three phases of Schutzhund. In a trial, when two dogs end up with the same total scores, the dog with the higher protection points will be given the higher ranking. The protection part is what separates Schutzhund and the other dog sports such as obedience and agility, which are great sports, too. The difficulty of protection lies in its necessity for the dog to attack boldly in certain situations without hesitation, but also in perfect control under his handler's command, releasing when he hears "Out", and returning to his handler when he hears "Here". The protection phase is the part that can best display the balance between the dog's wildness and tameness.

In the IPO3 protection routine, from the hide search to the last re-attack, there are eight exercises in total. We split these eight exercises into eleven basic components. When we carefully inspect these eleven foundation behaviours, we can see seven of them, including attention, look forward, sit, down, front position (come), go ahead, and basic position are components that we're already teaching the puppy in the obedience learning phase. Run around is a new obedience component here. All these eight behaviours are related to the control of the dog in the protection phase. The nature of bite, out, and bark are very different from the eight components for control. These are behaviours directly related to the dog's tenacity. In particular, the attack is a behaviour that can best express the dog's power, as many important elements such as stability, hardness, rank, temperament, trainability, physical attributes, and grip can all be assessed in the bite.

Furthermore, although the three retrieval exercises in the obedience phase require the dog to hold and release the dumbbells, they're not the same as the bite and the out in the protection phase, as the dog works in different mindsets in the two disciplines. In obedience, the dumbbell poses no threat to the dog. It's only an object thrown out by me, to be brought back by him. In the protection phase though, the decoy is a man that threatens, confronts, and hits the dog with a stick. He's an opponent to the dog. Biting the dumbbell and biting the protection sleeve worn by the decoy are two completely different tasks and require two completely different mentalities for the dog. The modern systems of dog training have evolved in many brilliant and innovative ways. There's now a wide range of approaches in how to teach a dog to bite the protection sleeve worn by the decoy. Some IPO trainers emphasise the control elements in the sport much more than the value of the dogs' combative spirit. They teach almost everything in the programme as obedience exercises, including tracking and protection. Everything becomes a robotic act about control. A dog trained in such a way treats biting the protection sleeve just like retrieving the dumbbell. If trained well, he has a good chance of obtaining very high points in the sport, but this destroys the very purpose of a protection dog sport.

We must remember all of the working dog breeds existing today are legacies of our predecessors' visions and hard work. The successful preservation of our dogs' working qualities is largely contributed by the traditional values of protection dog sports such as Schutzhund, Belgian Ring, French Ring, and KNPV. Each one of these programmes has at least a hundred years of history. These sports are still here today because their old founders, breeders, and trainers have given their hearts and souls in developing the sports' structures and selectively bred dogs that can excel in these programmes. Protection dog sports and working dog breeds are gifts from our ancestors. It's our responsibility to preserve and continue their legacies. In many ways, protection dog sports are very similar to martial arts. The original purpose of many martial arts was to defend oneself and one's family and defeat one's enemy in combat. Through the time of peace, some martial arts took on an artistic direction and became a demonstration of acrobatic prowess. However, if this so-called evolution is actually making a combative art into an exhibition of somersaults and air spins that are worthless in a real fight, what's the point of practising martial arts? If one wants to strengthen his body and improve his coordination, he has a wide range of sports to choose from. If he chooses to learn martial arts but is not able to even defend himself from some street bully after years of practice, he might as well spend his time in something more productive instead of fooling himself. Winning the world championship is the ultimate goal of many IPO competitors. However, the preservation of the working abilities in the dog breeds and the practicality of the sport must not be forfeited because of this goal. The regulations, judges, breeders, and trainers of working dog sports have direct influence on which way the breeds are going in the future. Our dogs' working quality must not be compromised in the exchange for higher points or for making our sport more appealing to the general public. Schutzhund is not a sport for everybody, just like any other sport. Obedience is obedience, and biting is biting. If the protection phase is treated as just an extension of the obedience phase and the dog is working solely in play mode, he's only good for the trial field. If a burglar can just walk into an IPO dog's home and take everything without a fight, this goes against everything that Schutzhund stands for.

If we categorise all dogs by their ability at biting, then there should be three types of dogs:

1. Dogs that naturally bite
2. Dogs that bite after training
3. Dogs that wouldn't bite after training.

For a working dog, the first type is highly desirable. You basically don't need to teach him to bite. When he sees the sleeve or an intruder in your house, he'll bite directly with conviction. The genes of biting are already in his blood. All you need to show him is when he can bite and when he can't. The second type of dog is acceptable to be a working dog. He might not be such a natural biter as the first one and will need more time to learn how to bite, but he has certain mouldability. With adequate training, he can be very good in his job. The third type of dog has no natural desire or nerve to bite. Whatever the reason for that is, you'll have to spend a lot of time trying to get him to hold a sleeve with his mouth, and the result is still mediocre at best. His performance is never good enough to pay off your investment. When you start to put some control into the bite session, this dog will get so confused and he'll usually fall apart mentally, not knowing when to bite and when to out anymore. This is not a suitable dog for protection work. You should devote your time and energy to a dog that is capable of doing this kind of training.

I usually begin teaching my puppies how to bite with a decoy from the age of eight weeks. Sometimes I might start even earlier, especially when the puppies are bred by me. In the initial stage of bite work, I first develop my puppy's confidence, competitiveness, grip, and "wolfishness" through practising with my decoy. As these qualities are developing, I insert the elements of control into the training. In the protection learning stage, we focus on teaching the puppy the bite, out, and bark.

Decoys

A decoy is a skilled person who lets dogs bite the protected parts of his body. He's also known as the helper, the villain, the apache, the aggressor, the agitator, and the bad guy in different dog training disciplines. In the Schutzhund programme, the decoy usually wears a thick pair of overalls made of leather or synthetic fabric called the "scratch pants" to protect him from the dog's scratching. He wears a specially made sleeve to protect his arm. A right-handed decoy typically carries the padded stick in his right arm and wears the sleeve on his left, like a warrior would carry his sword and his shield. In an IPO trial, the dogs are only allowed to bite the protection sleeve of the decoy. There are two types of decoys: the training decoy and the trial decoy.

Training Decoy	Trial Decoy
The responsibility of the training decoy is to teach the dog the necessary mindset and skills for combat. The role of the training decoy can be compared to a boxing coach. His job is to teach the dog when to bite, how to bite, and how to channel his aggression into barking and guarding while increasing his confidence and fighting spirit at the same time, making him stronger through correct training. The training decoy must have abundant knowledge of canine communication and how to read a dog. He needs to know when to teach the dog what, so the dog becomes proficient in the protection phase. Timing, judgment, reflex, and coordination are also very important criteria for a successful training decoy	The job of the trial decoy is to assist the judge in the protection phase of a trial. By following the trial regulations and the judge's instructions, he acts as the impartial enforcer and scale of the programme, so the judge can assess the dogs' stability, hardness, rank, temperament, trainability, physical attributes, and grip by observing the confrontation between the trial decoy and the dog. The trial decoy must be strong, fit, and agile, with excellent reflexes and endurance. He needs to work in a consistent manner to all the dogs in a trial so they can be judged correctly and fairly

Besides his dog, a handler's most important team member is his training decoy. As I have a great support team in Belgium with two excellent decoys who know exactly what I want, if we ever come across training problems we can always solve them quickly and effectively. The training decoy is the dog's teacher in bite work. The handler should form a habit to always communicate with his decoy before, during, and after a training session so they both know where the dog's at. He should keep the decoy updated about his dog's latest progress in training including tracking and obedience because different disciplines can sometimes affect each other. When training a puppy or a young dog, only a single experienced decoy should be used to develop the dog's basic skills. If the training decoy always changes when the dog is still learning the foundation biting techniques, often it can have more negative effects than positive ones. Every decoy is unique. Even if two decoys are at the same skill level, they usually have their own styles, systems, techniques, and training sequences in teaching a dog. Continuously changing your puppy's decoy can cause confusion because decoys might work differently. A good training decoy should possess the following qualities:

1. He has a lot of experience and has successfully trained a number of dogs.
2. His primary goal is to develop the dog's confidence and skills. He's practical, thoughtful, and down to earth. He takes training seriously and doesn't use it as a personal exhibition.
3. He's loyal to the people he works with. He won't test his training partners' dogs with the intention of undermining their confidence.
4. He has an open mind towards all working dog breeds, and won't hold a prejudice against breeds that he doesn't own.
5. He can communicate effectively with his training partners and is able to take useful advice.

The Role of the Handler in Bite Work Training

Before a bite work session, the handler speaks with the decoy so they can plan what they will do. Usually, the more experienced person of the two suggests how the lesson should proceed and the other person coordinates with the dog's best interests in mind. After the session, they share their observations and thoughts, and briefly discuss the plan for the next session. Sometimes, the team has a third member who has even more experience and can guide both the decoy and the handler along the way. This person is the coach.

During bite work, as the decoy is busy interacting, stimulating, or confronting the dog, the handler is responsible for collaborating with him and controls his dog at the right time, such as holding the leash to secure the dog's position, calming the dog after he's won the sleeve, applying obedience elements, etc. The handler and his training decoy work together. The better their collaboration, the better the dog will perform.

Introducing the Decoy

Training Goal

1. Let my decoy continue to build the puppy's drive and grip in bite work.
2. Accustom the puppy to biting while being held on the leash.
3. Develop the handler and dog's team mentality in bite work.

Preparation

1. An experienced training decoy
2. Puppy sleeve
3. A 2m loopless leash.

Before training begins, I first take my puppy for a walk outside the training field so he can stretch and empty himself. After five to ten minutes we go into the facility. If this is the first time my puppy has been to this place, I'll first let him explore the training area with me so he can familiarise himself with the new environment. My decoy is also present and he observes the behaviour of the puppy with me. If we see the puppy isn't 100% sure of the situation, my decoy will first make friendly contact with the puppy for a few minutes so he's more at ease before we start training. Once the puppy is showing a positive and outgoing attitude, we begin bite work.

As I always let my puppies go through bite development with me in their first week home, by the time they see my decoy I can already let them bite while they're on the leash. When the decoy begins stimulating the puppy to bite, my job as a handler is to let the puppy go in front of me to the end of the leash. The leash should be kept taut for two reasons: 1) so the puppy can feel that I'm supporting him from behind, that we're going against the decoy as a team; 2) so my decoy knows the exact position of the puppy. If the leash is kept slack, the puppy would have too much freedom to do things that we don't want, such as charging in and out or jumping up and down. This prevents the decoy from judging the correct distance between him and the puppy. A miscalculated distance can cause the decoy to come in too far or too close when presenting the sleeve for the puppy to bite, resulting in a bad grip such as a frontal bite (dog biting with the front part of his jaw instead of a full grip), over bite (dog biting on top of the sleeve), under bite (dog biting the bottom of the sleeve), sideways bite (dog biting with one side of his mouth shallower than the other), or an edge bite (dog biting the extremities of the sleeve instead of the centre).

To appear less imposing to the puppy, the decoy can lower his body by bending over or kneeling down on the ground. He moves the sleeve in ways that simulate the movements of a prey animal. In nature, when the prey sees a predator, one of his first responses is to escape. He can either escape directly away from the predator, or keep changing his directions in a zigzag route in order to make the pursuit more difficult. It is less common for the prey to charge at the predator

unless it is a large species protecting its young offspring. The decoy makes the sleeve dance like an escaping prey. For now he can adopt the zigzag movement, swaying the sleeve from side to side in a jerky, vibrating motion. As he stimulates the puppy's hunt drive/prey drive, he also observes his behaviour towards the sleeve.

When the decoy sees that the drive and focus of the puppy are both at the adequate level for a good grip, he either puts his arm into the sleeve or holds it by both ends so he can effectively present it for the puppy to bite. As a prey animal usually doesn't move directly towards its predator, at this beginning level of training, the decoy also avoids such movement. To shorten the distance between the puppy and himself for the bite, he presents the sleeve by moving across the puppy from one side, simulating a prey running across the predator, offering a good chance for the puppy to grip the middle of the sleeve with one smooth action. The decoy's timing and his judgement of

the distance in presenting the sleeve are crucial. Good sleeve presentation promotes good grip. If the puppy doesn't directly get a full grip (the two corners of his mouth are not pushing against the sleeve), the decoy can press the sleeve onto the ground while I loosen the leash to encourage the puppy to bite down deeper in order to fill his mouth. When it's possible, we should try our best to minimise non-full biting, because if it becomes a habit or the dog has to re-grip to fill his mouth every time, it's pretty unlikely for him to receive very high points in the IPO protection phase consistently. Some dogs are born with an excellent grip and some dogs aren't. When a dog lacks the good grip by genetics, even the best decoys would have difficulties making him a good biter. That's why proper selection of a working puppy is so important.

Once the puppy is biting the sleeve, the decoy can keep his arm in it or he can hold it with both hands. He uses the sleeve as an instrument to simulate a captured prey in distress in order to maintain the puppy's drive and grip. In nature, the relationship between the hunter and the hunted is a game of chess. There's only survival, and any dirty trick is a good trick if it can keep you alive. If a predator wants to live, he must successfully catch his prey. If the prey wants to live, he must successfully escape his predator. Both sides need to be crafty and calculating in the game of survival. When the decoy is developing the puppy's prey drive, he uses the same cunning behaviour as prey animals, moving the sleeve as prey would act in front of a predator, so the puppy can learn how to be a successful predator by increasing his hunting wisdom. The prey knows the predator's intention is to capture him and eat him. If a wolf catches a rabbit, when will he eat the rabbit? He eats the rabbit when the rabbit is dead. How does he know when the rabbit is dead? Obviously it's when the rabbit has stopped moving for a while. Once the wolf thinks the rabbit is dead, he will release the rabbit, put his paw on the body so he can tear open his skin to eat his flesh. The rabbit understands this. He knows that once the wolf thinks he's dead, the wolf will put him down on the ground and start ripping him apart. When the wolf first captures the rabbit, by instinct the rabbit would struggle and kick trying to break free, but soon he realises the more he moves, the harder the wolf is biting. When he feels overpowered, he changes his tactics immediately, and one of his tricks is to play dead. A young and inexperienced wolf might fall for this and release the rabbit, so he can have a sniff before he eats him. The slippery rabbit takes this opportunity and escapes. An experienced predator has probably fallen for such a trick in his younger days, and he won't trust the rabbit at all. Besides feeling for the prey's movement, he might also observe his other signs of being alive, such as his breathing and heartbeat. He would only put down the prey when he's absolutely sure that the prey is dead. When the puppy has his grip on the sleeve, the decoy randomly shakes and moves the sleeve to simulate struggling prey. Sometimes he lets the sleeve go totally still to pretend it's dead, and then suddenly rattles it, pretending to escape. This keeps the puppy alert. He learns that, regardless of the sleeve's struggling or playing dead, if he wants to keep it, he only has to bite hard with constant pressure and not relax for a second. We have used the same principle while practising the hold in the obedience learning stage. If the puppy doesn't pay enough attention to holding the sleeve, the decoy will make the sleeve escape out of the puppy's mouth. They'll start the biting game again until the puppy has a firm grip.

After the puppy has a full, firm, and calm grip of the sleeve for half a minute or so, the decoy releases the sleeve and lets the puppy win it. The decoy stays back and gives the puppy space, letting him know that good biting can win him the prey (sleeve) and drive away his opponent (decoy). The sleeve is like the puppy's trophy. Through this training process, we can satisfy the puppy's hunt drive (pursuing the sleeve), protection drive and rank drive (driving away and dominating the decoy), and prey drive (winning the sleeve from the decoy). In bite development, I've already established

control when the puppy had to hold the sleeve. I now apply the same technique here by gently putting one hand under his chin and one hand next to his torso so he can hold the sleeve calmly without trying to run away with it. I can keep him between my legs for better security. Occasionally, I shake the sleeve with my hands to stimulate prey drive, or push it onto the ground so the puppy has to push his grip into the sleeve deeper. I can pretend to pry open his mouth with one hand on top and the other below his jaw to motivate a stronger hold. This increases his possessiveness of the sleeve. When the puppy holds the sleeve calmly for a while, the decoy can put his arm back into it and wrestle with the puppy like before. When the puppy bites well, he gets to win the sleeve again.

In bite work, the dog and I should face the decoy most of the time. This rule also applies when the puppy has won the sleeve. If he's facing me when he has the sleeve in his mouth, he will see me as his competitor for the sleeve especially when I want him to out. This can cause unnecessary conflicts between us and should be avoided. The head of the dog during the protection phase should be treated like a gun. The dog's head is the gun's barrel. His teeth are my weapons. Your weapon is always pointed at your enemy, never at yourself. The minds, bodies, and spirits of the handler and his dog need to face the opponent together. Besides letting the puppy satisfy different drives when he wins the sleeve, this also gives him time to calm down from all the excitement and take a short rest. This way, the puppy learns when to release his energy and when to contain it, instead of going into hyper-excitement throughout the whole bite work session. To be able to learn, a dog needs both motivation and concentration at the right time. When the motivation is too high, it decreases the dog's ability to absorb information. If the puppy is always worked up continuously in bite work without time to cool down, this will reduce his clarity and controllability in the future. We can compare training a working dog with driving a racing car. If we want to win in a car race, the speed of our car is a very important element. But besides speed, our ability to control the car is just as crucial. If the driver always drives his racing car with full throttle at maximum speed, he can excel only on a straight road. If he continues to do this at a sharp bend, he's going to lose control of the car as a result of excessive speed. This is the same as in bite work. Our goal is not only to develop drives in the dog, but also to contain and concentrate them in certain circumstances so the dog is manageable in drive. Once the puppy calms down from holding the sleeve for one or two minutes, I make him out.

A Clean and Explosive Out

A wolfish dog or a sheepish dog? A devil or a fairy? Every Schutzhund trainer has a particular type of dog he prefers and a certain training system he favours. Bite, out, and bark are three behaviours that can best reveal the raw power of a Schutz dog. Biting and releasing are two opposite behaviours. Their quality is half dictated by genetics and half influenced by training. A dog that can bite very well doesn't always out very well. A dog that outs very well doesn't always bite very well. Some dogs don't even bite at all. The most difficult part of the protection phase is that we want a dog that bites forcefully, fully, and calmly, but he must also be able to out quickly, clearly, and furiously. This is a lot harder than teaching a dog just biting with no out or not biting at all. The more a dog loves to bite the less he's willing to out. The more a dog loves to out the less he wants to engage the decoy. This explains why the best out should be clean and explosive.

There are three types of behaviours when a dog releases his bite from the sleeve:

1. Slipping off the sleeve cheerfully. This is a usual behaviour from a fairy type of dog that's trained solely on prey drive in the protection phase. In their mind, biting is just a game and not a confrontation with the decoy. To many of these dogs, biting the decoy is the same as fetching a ball. Their primary intention in bite work is to snatch the sleeve away from the decoy as quickly as possible.
2. Letting go messily and dirtily. This usually occurs with two types of dogs. The first type is a good dog with bad training. The desire to bite and the pressure for the out causes the dog to go into too much conflict. The out becomes unwilling and unclear. The second type is a dog that's not suitable for bite work in the first place. He doesn't have sufficient stability, courage, and will to bite, so his out is as bad as his bite.
3. Outing cleanly with bad intentions and ferocity. This type of dog bites with power and gusto. When his handler commands him to out, he would first dominate the decoy by a forceful gesture such as giving him a good shake or a deep growl from the belly, and then he would shove his grip off the decoy with much strength and anger, like a brave and injured soldier ripping off the bandage from his wound reluctantly and determinedly at the same time with one swift but painful motion. If this dog chooses the barking out in the guarding, he would display his frustration at the decoy by a man-eater growling bark that is full of rage and threat. You'll able to see this dog takes bite work very seriously and doesn't treat it as a game. This outing behaviour is the best display of the perfect balance between wildness and tameness.

Until now, I've taught my puppy to release an object in his mouth by three techniques:

1. Out by prying his mouth open
2. Release by exchange for food
3. Out by pressing the ball into his mouth.

The first and the third techniques can best achieve a clear and powerful out, because I take away something valuable from the puppy by force. This causes conflict. When used correctly, conflict is a very powerful tool in dog training. This produces positive frustration, which can be channelled into the work. In fact, in my puppy's first week home, I've already started using conflicts to develop positive frustration. All food drive enhancement exercises were intended to produce positive frustration by conflicts, same with the technique of pretending to pry open the puppy's mouth to make him bite harder. The key is to set up a controlled situation where the dog can overcome the conflict to prevail. This makes a dog stronger. This gives him fire.

As a puppy sleeve is rectangular in shape, it's easier to use the prying the puppy's mouth open technique for the out. With one hand on top and one hand below his jaws, I pry the puppy's mouth open. I say "Out" as the sleeve leaves his mouth. When it falls onto the ground, I hold my

puppy back by the leash so he can't bite it anymore. I kick the sleeve to the decoy. This movement simulates the rabbit escaping the puppy's grip and bolting away. It stimulates prey drive, which reinforces the out. My decoy immediately collaborates by picking up the sleeve and making it dance. When the puppy is driven and focused, the decoy lets him bite the centre of the sleeve again.

Sometimes, after the puppy has outed, instead of kicking the sleeve to the decoy, I can pull him back by the leash. The decoy approaches us in a timid and sneaky way, pretending to steal the sleeve but ready to resort to flight at any moment. If the puppy has already possessed a degree of protection drive by now, when seeing the decoy trying to steal the sleeve in such a cowardly and devious manner, he's tempted to defend his prey by showing aggression. A typical display is barking, growling, snarling, or charging at the decoy. Even with the slightest protest or excitement from the puppy, the decoy reacts in a dramatic way, pretending the response of the puppy has the power of a knockout punch, driving the decoy backward in a sudden and forceful way. He then tries to sneak in again, all that time looking at the sleeve instead of the puppy. When the puppy objects, the decoy is driven back again. This reinforces the puppy defending his prey and develops protection drive

and rank drive. When the puppy is excited and concentrated, the decoy picks up the sleeve and rewards him with a bite. A full, firm, and calm grip wins the puppy the sleeve.

We follow the above procedures in exciting the puppy, letting him bite, and making him out for three to five times. The decoy observes the puppy's behaviour to decide when to do what, and how much he should do. That's why a knowledgeable decoy is an essential asset of a working dog training team. As in other disciplines, we finish bite work on a good note. When the puppy gives us his best grip in this session, we end it by letting him carry the sleeve back to the car. I let him keep the sleeve in his mouth for a few minutes so he can satisfy his prey drive by having the prey item. I can then take him for a walk, give him some water to drink, and put him back into his kennel in my car. When the weather is not too hot, I can choose to feed him a small meal to simulate the predator being rewarded with food after a successful hunt, but this is not obligatory as a dog should have received his main reward in the work on the training field already.

Before my puppies start changing teeth, I normally let them bite with my decoy for one to four times a week. When they're changing teeth, I reduce the bite sessions to once a week. If I see they are in pain when biting, I'd temporarily put bite work on hold, and start again when their adult teeth have grown.

Introducing the Clatter Stick

A clatter stick is a bamboo stick split vertically in quarters. When rattled it produces a loud clattering noise. It's an accessory used in ring sports to desensitise the dogs so they're not afraid of noises during the engagement with the decoys. As this tool has many benefits in bite work, I've incorporated its use into my Schutzhund training system. This is an example of cross-training.

The clatter stick can be self-made by first obtaining a dry bamboo stick about 60cm long and 3cm thick. The type of bamboo used should be flexible and not rigid nor soft. Wrap one end of the stick with thick sticky tape to make the handle. Split the other end into six to eight even quarters with a knife and a hammer, and there you have it. The supple split bamboo quarters clap against each other when shaken or tapped against the decoy's thigh, producing a "rak-tak-tak" noise. Proper introduction of the clatter stick can desensitise a dog's tolerance to the sound and contact by the stick. It can also enhance the dog's drive in bite work.

Introduction

1. If you've chosen the right puppy and are raising him correctly, he shouldn't have any problem with the movement and the noise of the stick. Usually, my puppies begin bite work readily with my decoy using the clatter stick. However, if you're not sure how your puppy will react, it's always safer to introduce the stick without biting first, so there's no possibility of an unnecessary mistake.

2. The introduction of the clatter stick is the same as the clicker, by using classical conditioning. We link a sound with a reinforcer (reward) to give it a positive meaning. Previously, we introduced the clicker by clicking and offering the puppy food. For the introduction of the clatter stick, we can do the same, or link the sound with hunt drive/prey drive by rattling the stick and moving the sleeve. The choice we make depends on the puppy's stability towards noises.

3. The clatter stick differs from the clicker in certain respects. We need to take these into consideration when deciding how to introduce it to the puppy: 1) the stick is much larger

than the clicker. Some dogs could be wary of it. 2) The stick makes a loud noise when rattled. Its noise is also accompanied by the image of the decoy shaking it. 3) The clatter stick is used as an accessory by the decoy to threaten the dog (once the dog has been desensitised to it). The clicker on the other hand is never used in such a fashion.

4. The handler or the decoy need to know the puppy well enough before deciding to incorporate the clatter stick into the training. If a dog is scared by the stick in his first encounter, he might have many problems in bite work in the future.

5. Our primary intention in introducing the clatter stick is to desensitise the dog so he's not afraid of its presence, its noise, or contact with it. Desensitisation means gradually accustoming the dog to a stimulus that he might be afraid of. It's the diminished emotional responsiveness to a negative or aversive stimulus after repeated exposure to it. A dog can be sensitive to the stick for two reasons. The first one is because of a non-realistic threat, and the second is a realistic threat. A non-realistic threat is the stick being moved or swung near the dog without actually making contact and the dog perceives this as a threat. A realistic threat is the stick actually strikes the dog and causes him pain, so now the dog perceives it as a threat. In an actual confrontation, an intruder or aggressor might strike the dog with his fists or anything he can get a hold of. You don't want your dog to fail you at the time when you need him the most. Getting used to the stick is a minimum criterion for a protection sport dog, police dog, or personal protection dog. This is the same as a boxer's obligation to be familiarised with hard sparring in preparation for a bout.

6. The desensitisation of the dog towards the stick diminishes his fear or anxiety towards the accessories of the decoy. At the beginning, we let the puppy associate the clatter stick with a pleasant feeling by utilising food drive or hunt drive/prey drive. Then we condition him to enjoy contact with the stick. Eventually, when he's a mature adult, he doesn't care even if he's hit by the stick with force.

7. The safest way to introduce the clatter stick is at a distance with a barrier between my puppy and me. I wouldn't do this kind of training in the dog's outdoor enclosure, as this will create excitement that might cause nuisance barking later on. The kennel should be a place for relaxation and rest. I want any excitement in this area to be kept to a minimum. A fenced garden is a good environment for this. I first place my puppy in my garden and I go out of it so the fence is between us. I stand about 1 to 2m from the fence and rattle the clatter stick several times. I then drop the stick onto the ground and go to the fence and feed my puppy a small handful of fresh meat. I repeat this process about ten times and finish by giving my puppy the rest of the meal. The next day, I do the same while standing closer to the fence. After a few days of practice, I should be able to stand right in front of the fence and shake the clatter stick noisily and the puppy would welcome this with excitement by jumping onto the fence. From this point on I can incorporate the stick in bite work with my decoy.

Using the Clatter Stick to Increase Drive and Confidence

Once the puppy is responding positively to the noise and action of the clatter stick, the decoy can utilise it in bite work. He decides when, how, and how much he uses the stick based on the behaviour of the puppy. His goal is to desensitise the puppy and make him more self-assured and driven by adopting the clatter stick into his work. The time needed from the introduction of the stick until the dog's positive response to the trial stick hits depends on genetics and the effectiveness of training. For a dog that possesses the suitable genetic disposition, it can take as little as several weeks. For a dog that doesn't have the proper working quality though, he can train all his life and still can't tolerate the stick. Below is a step-by-step introduction:

1. The decoy is about 2 to 5m from the puppy. He has the sleeve in one hand and the clatter stick in another. As he's rattling the stick, he also moves the sleeve in swinging motions in front of him to stimulate hunt drive/prey drive from the puppy. He's linking the noise of the stick with hunt drive/prey drive through classical conditioning. With enough repetitions through numerous training sessions, whenever the puppy hears the "rak-tak-tak" sound of the stick he'll automatically go into hunt drive/prey drive, even without the presence of the sleeve. When the decoy sees the puppy has sufficient drive and concentration, he goes to him and presents him the sleeve for biting.

2. The decoy needs to pay extra attention to the puppy's grip now. If the puppy tries to move away from the decoy's stick side, or the grip becomes nervous such as mouthing, frontal biting, continuous growling, shaking the grip wildly, or his eyes rolling insecurely, these are indications of anxiety towards the stick. This could be due to too much stimulation, the puppy being too young for this, or the puppl lacking the stability to handle this kind of stimulus. The decoy must immediately ease the noise and movement of the stick.

3. If the puppy responds positively and his grip and body posture remain neutral, the decoy can focus on maintaining a full, firm, and calm grip. He should always watch the puppy's body language and the expression in his eyes to ensure that he's comfortable in the bite.

4. When the puppy maintains a good attitude, the next step is to pick up the stick again and stroke him as he's biting. This is the same as patting the puppy with your hands as you're praising him. This way the puppy associates the contact with the stick as a kind of

encouragement rather than a hit. When the puppy displays positive response, we let him win the sleeve as a reward.

5.   We continue the above procedure for a few sessions. The puppy should start to enjoy the contact with the stick as encouragement from the decoy. He's ready to learn the counter. The counter is also known as the hit back. This is when the dog retaliates with a dominant action against the decoy's hit. It could be a push, a pull, or a shake with bad intentions. This is the dog's answer to the decoy's challenge. When the decoy feels the counter, he reinforces the puppy by giving him the sleeve.

6.   After several more sessions, when the puppy is used to countering after a slight tap with the stick, the decoy can reward him by acting subordinately instead of giving him the sleeve all the time. To act subordinately means the decoy gives the puppy the feeling

that he can dominate and defeat the decoy. When the puppy counters the stick contact by pushing, for example, the decoy can respond by groaning, acting in pain, being weak, afraid, going backwards, going onto his knees, or lying on his back completely and letting the puppy bite him from on top. This develops the dog's competitiveness, making him stronger and more self-assured.

7. When the dog is used to the clatter stick, we can introduce different accessories with the same principle, such as a plastic bottle with a few beans in it (makes a very loud noise when shaken), pom-pom, whip, and the Schutzhund padded stick. The padded stick is much softer than the clatter stick, and it also doesn't make any rattling noise. If the dog responds positively to the clatter stick, he should have no problem with the padded stick.

All decoy accessories should be introduced to the dog from far to near, and from mild to intense. The behaviour of the dog will always let you know if your training method is appropriate or not. When you're uncertain, the stimulation you apply is better too soft rather than too hard, because once a dog has a bad experience with an accessory it'll be difficult to completely diminish the negative association in his head. In addition, the handler and decoy must consider if a particular dog's stability and grip can handle the demand in the protection phase and how much he can handle the cross-training. In the IPO programme, the only accessory of the decoy is the padded stick. During the IPO3 protection routine, the dog only needs to withstand four hits from the padded stick to pass the examination. The purpose of cross-training with the clatter stick and other accessories such as the whip is to enhance and complement the IPO protection phase, making the dog more resilient and versatile in his work without causing unnecessary headaches for us. We insert other elements into our training to desensitise the dog so he can have a wide spectrum of experience and become more streetwise. However, if a dog is limited in his genetic working abilities and is not suitable for the supplementary cross-training, we should refrain from bringing this in. Otherwise the dog might become sensitive even to the most basic padded stick. Unbefitting training is worse than no training. When the dog's not up for it, sometimes it's better to just leave it alone.

Clear, Strong, and Rhythmic Barking

Besides being an obligatory exercise (hold and bark) in the IPO protection phase, barking is also a very practical tactic in a street combat situation. It is a guarding behaviour very useful for both on and off leash. When confronting aggressors, an on leash dog can be commanded to bark at the crowd at the end of the leash to drive them away. Whoever chooses to ignore the warning and comes in range of the leash will be bitten. This is a very practical way for crowd control and riot management. Below are four methods I usually employ to teach my dogs to bark. You can choose the most suitable approach for your dog or adopt all of them into your dog's training at different times.

1. Luring by decoy on leash: During a bite session, the decoy first gets the puppy in drive by vibrating the clatter stick or moving the sleeve. The puppy might start to make noises to express his excitement. As soon as the puppy gives the slightest bark or yelp, the decoy reacts dramatically by jumping backwards like he has been hit by a devastating punch, or bouncing sideways like his feet are being shot at by a machine gun. Every time the puppy gives a little bark, the decoy responds drastically. This usually entertains the puppy greatly

and causes him to bark more, as he soon realises his bark alone has the power to frighten the decoy and drive him into panic. Gradually, the decoy waits for the puppy to bark more before he reacts, building stronger and longer barking. When the puppy's motivation and concentration reach the optimum level, the decoy presents him the sleeve for a bite. After a brief wrestle, the puppy wins the sleeve.

2. Luring by decoy through fence. In bite training, the decoy teases the puppy with a stick and a sleeve through a fence. As there's a fence between them, I only need to use the leash to prevent the puppy from jumping over the fence. Most of the time I keep the leash loose so it doesn't put tension on the puppy's throat, which can affect his breathing and barking. Because the fence prevents the puppy from biting while the decoy is getting him excited, his frustration is very likely to be expressed by barking. For a little yelp, the decoy immediately reacts by rubbing the stick and the sleeve along the fence. When the puppy gives a clear bark, he's rewarded with biting and winning the sleeve.

3. Luring by handler through fence. I set up this training just like the way I introduced the clatter stick for the first time. My puppy is on one side of the fence and I'm on the opposite side. The puppy has already made the association between the rattling of the stick and food. I now excite him by shaking the stick or rubbing its tip along the fence. When all this teasing brings no food, the puppy might protest by barking. At this moment I press the clicker to mark his behaviour and then reward him with some food. In the beginning I click and treat for one bark, and then I click and treat for two to three barks. I repeat this process to develop longer and clearer barking.

4. Luring by handler with play. In our daily interactions, my

puppy is used to chasing me and making a lot of body contact with me. I often invite him to jump onto me during playtime. So now I initiate him to play with me as usual, getting him to chase me around and jump up on me. This time however, as he's about to slam his paws onto me, I dodge so he misses. I then bend over to simulate the puppy bow, encouraging him to keep playing. When he pounces onto me, I dodge to make him miss, and then simulate the puppy bow by bending over again. This soon becomes a great entertainment for the puppy and causes him to bark in excitement. As soon as he barks, I say "Yes" and feed him some food. Gradually I train him to bark louder, multiple times. After a few sessions, when he sees me standing with my hands on my knees, he already takes this as a cue for barking, and will bark to initiate me to play with him or feed him. Step by step, I shape my puppy's behaviour towards the criteria of the hold and bark. First I selectively reinforce clear barking, then multiple barks, then barking without touching me, then barking while sitting and hopping, and then eventually continuous barking in front of me with absolute focus. When he can do all these, I link the verbal command "Bark" with the behaviour. I reinforce by saying "Yes" and offering him food. Next, I tell him to sit about 2m in front of me while I'm holding a bite roll and standing with my back against a fence (to prevent him from going behind me, learning something I don't want). I give him the command "Bark" to let him come in front of me to bark (hold and bark means barking without touching the target). When he offers me the correct behaviour, I say "Yes" and move the bite roll upward in a short and sharp motion to stimulate hunt drive/prey drive, causing him to bite as his reward for barking. When my dog can do this in three consecutive sessions in different environments, the general picture of the hold and bark has been set. In the upcoming lesson, I can ask my decoy to carry on this work.

When I teach one of my dogs to bark, I usually utilise all four of the above methods. This way, the advantages of each method can supplement what the others lack to develop the best barking behaviour. The four teaching techniques for barking compare as follows:

Luring by Decoy On Leash	
Advantages	**Disadvantages**
As the motive of the dog's barking originates from confronting the decoy, it's easier to develop protection drive and rank drive in the barking later on	As this method develops much excitement from the dog, it might affect his precision in the hold and bark later on, such as coming too close to the decoy, touching the decoy, or even becoming "dirty" (sneaking in for a quick bite when he's supposed to bark)
The dog is used to having his handler and leash tension behind him during barking from the start. He'll be less prone to distraction by his handler controlling him from behind	You need two people for this technique
	The dog needs to go through a transitional period from having a leash to no leash in the hold and bark
	Some dogs pull into the collar too vigorously while confronting the decoy and put too much pressure on their throats, preventing breathing and barking. They can wear a harness instead so the leash tension is evenly distributed on their chest, but this decreases control of their head and neck

Luring by Decoy through Fence	
Advantages	**Disadvantages**
Possesses the advantages of the 1st method	The dog has to go through a transitional period from having a fence to no fence. This is done by gradually lowering the height of the fence until it's totally gone
Using a fence as a barrier solves the problem of the dog not being able to bark due to too much leash tension	
The fence can be perceived by the dog as a visible line of his territory. Working with a fence in between the decoy and the dog can make the dog stronger, more territorial, and more confident because he has a piece of land to defend while being protected by the barrier. This method can be further developed to encourage the dog to guard a property, barking at any stranger that comes too close	

Luring by Handler through Fence	
Advantages	**Disadvantages**
The handler can do this alone	Possesses the disadvantages of the second method
The dog can learn in a calmer mindset with food. The decoy brings much excitement, causing some dogs to go into overdrive and lowers their ability to learn	The dog doesn't gain any experience from barking on leash. He's not accustomed to having his handler and leash tension behind him during barking. This might make him more prone to distraction by his handler controlling him from behind
The dog can learn barking out of bite work. He can continue to learn barking even when he's teething	

Luring by Handler with Play	
Advantages	**Disadvantages**
Possesses the advantages of the third method	The dog doesn't gain any experience from barking on leash. He's not accustomed to having his handler and leash tension behind him during barking. This might make him more prone to distraction by his handler controlling him from behind
The dog learns to bark without a leash. He doesn't need to go through the transitional period from having a leash to no leash in the hold and bark	
The dog learns to bark without a fence. He doesn't need to go through the transitional period from having a fence to no fence in the hold and bark	

No matter which of the above methods you choose to teach your dog barking, the progress is always starting from one little spontaneous yelp, then a loud clear bark, and then constant barking. When the dog can continuously offer five to seven barks, you should develop a rhythmic barking pattern by reinforcing with food, moving the sleeve, or biting the sleeve.

Teaching the Dog to Proactively Challenge an Unequipped Decoy

What's the advantage of having a proactive dog over a reactive dog? In the IPO sport, when the dog finds the decoy in his hide the dog has to alert the handler by strong and clear barking without biting. At this point the decoy doesn't move or do anything to stimulate the dog to bark. The dog has to be self-motivated to offer the appropriate behaviour. In a practical scenario, if a kidnapper enters our home and we need our dog to protect us, we can't ask the bad guy to first put on the sleeve and tease our dog a little bit before the dog wants to bite. The dog has to bite on command regardless of what the aggressor is wearing or doing. The bad guy can be standing, sitting, lying down, or assaulting us. When we say "Take him", the dog must get the job done. We therefore need a proactive dog. The presence of the man alone is enough to bring the dog into drive. As our puppy is growing up, we need to educate him as to when he can bite and when he cannot. Besides training for tracking, obedience, and protection, he needs to go through extensive socialisation, so he's reliable and won't bite people indiscriminately. Responsible ownership is an obligation for having a working dog.

Dogs are intelligent animals with a great ability to observe and analyse. They can associate related events to work out the patterns of our daily activities. For example, after having a puppy for several weeks, when he sees us picking up a leash, he knows we're taking him for a walk. When we arrive at an open field with the car, he knows it's time for tracking. When we put on the training vest and grab the clicker, he knows we're playing the free shaping game. When we bring him to the training field with the decoy waiting, he knows it's biting time. We take advantage of our dogs' abilities in observation and association to develop a proactive mentality in the protection phase. Please note that every dog is unique and develops at different rate. If your puppy is not ready for this part of the training, it's better to wait for a few months so he has enough time to mature. The steps are as follows:

1. Once the puppy has had bite work training for five to ten sessions, if he's already made an association between biting and the decoy, as soon as he enters the training field he'll look at the decoy with excitement and anticipation, especially if he's been through the barking training with luring by the decoy on leash.
2. At the beginning of this session, the decoy stands sideways to the puppy. He glances at the puppy laterally. He doesn't move and he wears no sleeve.

3. The puppy usually responds in one of two ways. The first possibility is that he's already associated the decoy with bite work. When he sees the decoy is passive, he wants to initiate action by beginning to bark at him. If he's been through the barking training with luring by the decoy on leash, he'll be more inclined to instigate. For some dogs, it's an instinctual behaviour to bark at the prey in order to flush it out. This is a common tactic when working with hunting dogs. If this is the case, as soon as the puppy starts barking the decoy will react by staggering backwards like he has been hit by a powerful blow. He then recovers and looks at the puppy sideways in a cowardly and sneaky manner again. The puppy sees the decoy has returned to passiveness; he'll bark again to make him move. Once again, the decoy wobbles back and goes still. By now the puppy has realised that as long as he keeps barking he has the ability to drive the decoy into a state of panic. This is great entertainment for the dog. As he continues to bark at the decoy, I link his behaviour with the verbal command "Watch him". This is an alert command. It means the dog can

now charge to the end of the leash and bark at the decoy. If he comes in range, the dog is free to bite. When the puppy is barking with good energy and focus, the decoy puts on the sleeve and gives him a bite to reinforce good barking and being proactive. He then wrestles with the puppy briefly before letting him win the sleeve

4. In the second possibility, the puppy might not initiate at all when he sees that the decoy is passive. He might just stand there and do nothing. When the decoy sees this, he runs behind a hide and pokes his head out to look at the puppy hesitantly. The distance between the hide and the puppy should be at least 5m so the puppy has enough distance to feel at ease. Although the decoy never applies any mental pressure to the puppy in this training, his suspicious behaviour might make some puppies unsure. Every dog has his own critical distance. Critical distance is the space a dog needs as a buffer to an uncertainty. When the object of uncertainty comes within this range, the dog might choose fight or flight. The decoy gives the puppy enough distance while peeking out from the hide. Sometimes he pops his head out for a quick peek and sometimes he ducks his head back into the hide before popping his head out from the other side again. The way he behaves is just like an amateur thief stealing for the first time. His expression is like when a mouse sees a cat. Because the puppy has already had several sessions of good experience with the decoy in bite work, now he sees that the decoy is acting in such a spineless manner he usually gets excited by it and responds by barking. As soon as the puppy gives the slightest yelp,

the decoy can immediately change his role from being the instigator to being the reactor. He's driven out of the hide in a frightened manner. He then looks around hesitantly before rushing back into the hide. He pops his head out again to peek at the puppy. Every time the puppy barks, he's driven in and out of the hide like a chicken that has lost its head. When the puppy is barking at him most excitedly, the decoy rewards him with a bite on the sleeve and lets him win. In this training, the decoy basically acts like a father entertaining his child by playing the silly clumsy clown in a game of hide and seek.

5. The process of developing a dog's proactiveness in bite work is like the decoy and the dog playing tennis against each other. The decoy first serves the ball, and the dog responds by returning the ball. They hit the ball into each other's court. Each hit is an attempt to cause a reaction from the opponent, but this action itself is also a reaction to the opponent's last hit. How they hit the ball back depends on how the ball comes. Once the dog understands the rule of action and reaction, the decoy leaves the ball in the dog's court and waits for him to serve. In a bite session, it gradually progresses to the dog doing more work and becoming the initiator and the decoy doing less work and becoming the reactor. The dog learns that by barking at the decoy he can instigate actions. He thinks he's in control of the decoy, and this makes him strong. As training advances, we increase our demand. At the beginning, the decoy responds immediately to one little bark by a dramatic knock-back motion. He then reacts only when the dog barks three, four, or five times. His reaction also becomes less drastic. He reinforces good proactivity by acting frightened, running in and out of the hide, rattling the clatter stick, moving the sleeve in swinging motions, and giving the dog a bite.

6. Once the dog is rewarded with a bite on the sleeve, the decoy wrestles with him. A full, firm, and calm grip earns him the sleeve. The handler controls the dog to keep him calm and his drive contained. When he's ready, he makes the dog out and kicks out the sleeve to repeat the whole process again. After three to five repetitions, we end the session by letting the dog win the sleeve and carry it back to the car.

Fast, Direct, Purposeful Search of the Hides (Run Around)

The introduction for the searching of the hide is very similar to look forward and go ahead in obedience. There are several additional criteria:

1. The dog needs to go around each hide. He needs to enter from one side and exit on the other side.
2. He needs to take the shortest route to search each hide. When he goes around it, he has to circle around the hide closely, instead of running in a big arc.
3. Once he's on the inside of each hide, he should look to see if the decoy is there.
4. When he's completed the search for one hide, he should return directly to his handler, and wait for his command before searching the next hide.

I typically employ the three methods below to teach the run around:

1. Luring with food in the hide. To teach this, my puppy must have already gone through food drive enhancement and be highly motivated for food. I first place a food bowl on the inside of a hide with a handful of fresh meat in the bowl. The bowl is set on a bowl stand at the height of the puppy's head so when he's in the hide he has to keep his head up to

eat and not search for the bowl on the ground. This simulates the behaviour of the dog looking up in search of the decoy. I put my puppy on leash and we enter the hide from our left side. (The IPO trial regulations don't specify which side a dog has to enter a hide. As a habit, I teach my dogs to enter from the left because most decoys wear the protection sleeve on their left arms. However, you're free to teach your dog to enter from whichever side you prefer.) I hold his line short and show him the bowl of meat. When I see the puppy is keen to run towards the food bowl, I point my hand at it, link the verbal command "Search", and loosen the leash so he can run to the bowl to eat the meat. When he's finished, I run out from the right side of the hide and call

my puppy's name. When he's in front of me, I take out more meat from a container in my pocket and offer it to him. When we're both out of the hide, I repeat the procedure again. Every time after I place a handful of meat into the bowl, I pull the puppy back further, until eventually the bowl isn't within his sight anymore. The puppy still knows the meat is there by previous experience so he'll continue to run into the hide. When he comes out from the other side, I feed him again so he's reinforced for both going out and coming back. We continue to train this way for a few lessons. Very soon, I can start a session from 2m in front of the hide with the food bowl out of sight. I let my puppy run into it to eat the meat I've already prepared, and come out on the other side to return to me. From now on, I put meat in the bowl randomly. Sometimes there's meat and sometimes there isn't. The puppy should still run around the hide happily. When he realises there's no meat in the food bowl, he'll exit the hide on the other side and run back to me to be fed.

2. Luring with toy in the hide. When the puppy is already highly motivated for his toy such as a bite roll, and can reliably fetch it, I place it on a stand or attach it onto a ball hanger. On the exit side of the hide, I place a portable fence on the ground about 50cm away from the hide. This acts as a reverse target (barrier) to keep the puppy tight when he comes out of

the hide instead of throwing a big curve. Once the tight turning becomes a habit, we can remove the fence in the future. I bring my puppy and show him the toy inside the hide, I point at it and say "Search". As I release him, he runs at the toy to bite it; I run out from the other side of the hide and call him so he brings back the toy to play with me. After a few sessions, I can release the puppy about 5m from the hide without him first seeing the toy. Once he's in the hide, he will discover the toy and bring it back to me. As the training advances, we come to a stage that I can randomly place the toy inside the hide. When there's no toy, I call my puppy out on the other side and take out the toy from my pocket to reinforce his correct behaviour.

3.   Luring with decoy in the hide. If my dog already knows the hold and bark with my decoy by this time, I can ask him to go into a hide and show himself on the left side of the hide. He attracts the dog from where he's standing by rattling the clatter stick or tapping the sleeve for a few seconds before I point at the hide and give the command "Search". My dog might not know the word "Search" at this moment, but if he understands the hold and bark already, once he's in the hide he'll start barking at the decoy instead of biting him because the decoy is standing still by the time the dog is in front of him. For better control and to prevent the dog from being "dirty" (getting in with a cheap shot), I can hold him by the leash and run to the hide with him. When the dog barks well a few times,

the decoy reinforces him by letting him bite the sleeve. As the dog is biting, the decoy comes out on the other side of the hide and lets him win the sleeve. A dog that already knows the hold and bark usually has good control by his handler. Thus this method can advance quickly. After a few sessions, the decoy doesn't show himself from the beginning anymore, but the dog knows he's in the hide by previous association. Once the dog is used to not seeing the decoy, we can place him randomly in the hide. When the decoy isn't in a particular hide, I call the dog back to me and then the decoy shows himself from the opposite hide. I release the dog and let him go to the next hide for the hold and bark. When the barking is good, he's rewarded with a bite. If the dog doesn't know the hold and bark yet and we still want to use the decoy to teach the run around, this is possible, too. The decoy teases the dog from the hide as above, and I release him so he enters the hide from the left. As the dog is entering the hide, the decoy runs out on the right side and lets the dog chase him for a bite. Once the dog has a good grip on the sleeve, the decoy brings him back to me and gives him the sleeve. After several sessions, the decoy doesn't show himself anymore. He's then randomly placed in the hide. When he's not in a particular hide, I call my dog back and send him to the opposite hide. This is where the decoy is hiding.

The key of teaching the run around is to link the hide with a motivational object such as food, toy, or decoy, and having a fast and direct recall. Therefore, if we choose to use a toy as the motivation, the dog must first be very reliable in bringing back the toy. We don't want to play hide and seek with the dog trying to get the toy back every time we send him to the hide. With my own dogs, I usually use all three of the above teaching methods. First I use food, then toys, and when my dog has a very good hold and bark my decoy comes into the picture.

Biting Style

The grip is the quality of the bite including its fullness, firmness, calmness, and force. During biting, the dog displays various behaviours according to his genetics and training. These habitual behaviours make up a dog's biting style. We need to observe the instinctual behaviours of our dogs to determine which style of biting would be the most suitable for them to develop their full genetic potential. In Schutzhund trials, it is preferable when dogs demonstrate an active way of biting. Active biting means besides a full, firm, and calm grip, the dog also utilises his weight dynamically to dominate the decoy during their engagement. Most judges favour an active and gung-ho biter over a passive biter only holding to hang on. Active biters typically demonstrate their vivacity by pushing forward or pulling backward. Passive biters are usually perceived as reactive, lazy, and lacking competitiveness. For both active biting and passive biting, we can categorise them into five types of behaviours:

1. Still biting. The dog bites and doesn't move anymore. He hangs on and waits. This is a passive biting behaviour.
2. Re-gripping. The dog bites, and then he adjusts his grip by biting deeper or shallower, shifting his grip from side to side, or re-biting on the same spot.
3. Shaking. The dog bites and shakes his prey vigorously, like a monitor lizard killing a snake.
4. Pulling. The dog bites and jerks his opponent backwards and downwards in order to take him down.
5. Pushing. The dog bites and drives himself forward, generating power from his rear legs and his back. His action is like a bull ramming forward with his horns.

In the five biting styles below, still biting is the only passive way of biting. Re-gripping, shaking, pulling, and pushing are all active biting styles. Pulling and pushing are the two most widely accepted active biting techniques in working dog sports.

In IPO, the pulling grip is more commonly employed. It's an excellent technique to keep the points. Pulling is easy to teach. It's not so demanding for the genetic quality of the grip in comparison to pushing. The only disadvantage of pulling is it encourages the dog to bite the fabric of the bite suit instead of the man in it during practical training. However, if the only purpose of your dog is for IPO competitions, pulling is the way to go.

Biting Style	
Still biting	
Advantages	Disadvantages
If a dog bites full and firm in one grip, even if he doesn't move, he can still effectively control his opponent by just maintaining the same grip	Passive is reactive. A dog that just bites and hangs on is like a wrestler who only grabs his opponent without following through with a takedown. His mindset is reactive and lacks competitiveness. A still biting dog isn't using his full potential
Usually, there are two types of still biters. The first type is a lazy dog without much drive to bite. He's biting now only because a lot of hard work has been contributed by his handler and decoy. The second type is a very stable dog with an excellent grip. He knows he has the strength to immobilise his opponent by simply holding on without doing anything else. He doesn't have to do any more because the force of his bite will eventually kill his prey. All he has to do is just clamp down his jaws and wait. This is a classical bulldozer type of dog. With training he can be a superior pusher or puller	
Re-gripping	
Advantages	Disadvantages
If the dog didn't get a full grip in his initial strike, he can fill his mouth by re-gripping forward to increase the surface area of the bite	A good biter by nature paired with good training is unlikely to have a non-full grip. So there's normally no need for him to re-grip to fill his mouth
	Constant re-gripping is an indication of anxiety and can't bring a firm grip. In an IPO trial, many points are deducted for nervous grips

Shaking	
Advantages	**Disadvantages**
The shaking grip is a natural behaviour often seen in wolves hunting their prey. There are two types of shakers. The first type is rare, but they exist. He's called "the wrestler". The wrestling biter is dominant and brutal. When he's biting, he shakes the grip with his whole body, forcing the decoy to wobble. The wrestling doesn't affect the fullness, firmness, and calmness of his grip. The wrestler can be trained to combine his shaking with a pushing grip. This presents a spectacular image in the protection phase, which is highly favourable on the judge's score sheet. On the streets, one bite from the wrestler can easily stop a thug	The second type of shaker is more common. He's called the wobbler. His biting style is shaking the grip crazily from side to side, causing his jaws to fall shallower and shallower from the target. At the end he's barely holding on with his incisors and canine teeth. This is a seriously erratic biting behaviour. Most IPO judges would heavily penalise this kind of grip
	Wobbling makes the grip weak and unsteady
	It expresses an unstable mindset in the dog
	As the dog is in a wild state when he's wobbling the grip, this usually also affects his out

Pulling	
Advantages	**Disadvantages**
Pulling encourages prey drive. It also develops a firm grip, because a dog can't pull and shift his grip at the same time	Pulling primarily encourages prey drive. When a pack of wolves is hunting large prey such as a deer, they usually attack from behind. When a wolf has a grip on the deer, one of his tactics is to pull the deer down. This technique allows the wolf to avoid the horns of the deer. If pulling is what the decoy chooses to teach a particular dog, he needs to pay attention in balancing rank drive and protection drive also. Otherwise there's a possibility that the dog will become a prey dog. It means he works solely in prey mode in the protection phase. A prey dog's primary goal is to snatch the sleeve from the decoy as soon as possible so he can possess the prey and not to engage the decoy to get his satisfaction from winning the fight. This mindset lacks intensity and the fire needed for practical work. If the dog's possessiveness of the sleeve continues to increase, this can develop into the dog refusing to out, outing slowly, outing with a partial grip, or whining in the grip, all because the dog doesn't want to give up his prey. These issues can affect the dog's clarity and his handler's control. If pressure is applied in such cases, the dog might develop other problems such as automatically outing or outing too soon when the decoy stops moving (instead of outing on the handler's command). This upsets the balance of drives in bite work. On the other hand, if pulling is employed in conjunction with rank drive and protection drive, you don't need to worry about the above possible issues

Pulling is easier to teach than pushing	When the dog pulls in the grip, he's moving backwards. Even though he's biting, his mindset is defensive compared with pushing
Pulling is a fairly effective technique in practical street work. There's not much a thug can do once he's pulled down onto the ground	When a puller practises bite work with a decoy wearing a full body bite suit, the pulling grip often causes the dog to bite only the material of the suit without putting actual pressure on the decoy's body. Once this has become a habit, the dog might do the same in street work, biting the clothing of the thug instead of going for his body
If the dog's natural grip is average, through the development of pulling we can improve the firmness and calmness of his grip	In practical training for combat, if we want to teach the dog to bite the decoy's legs, a puller is usually frowned upon, as constant pulling prevents the decoy keeping his balance and working properly

Pushing	
Advantages	Disadvantages
Besides being a biting style that encourages hunt drive/prey drive, pushing also develops rank drive and protection drive. A pushing grip encourages the dog to dominate the decoy. When a senior wolf disciplines a junior pack member, he usually grabs the younger wolf and pushes him down onto the ground with his jaws. When a dog wants to protect a bone he's chewing, he guards it by pressing his muzzle on the bone while bringing his shoulders forward. A pushing grip is a display of dominance and conquest	The pushing grip is more demanding than the pulling grip. The dog needs to be a born good biter with a natural full, firm, and calm grip to be a proficient pusher
A naturally good biter combined with a pushing style of biting presents an imposing image in a competition, which is highly favoured on the judge's score sheet	

As the dog is used to pressing his body into his opponent's body during biting, I can use the same mindset to increase the speed in his dumbbell retrieves in the obedience phase	
When the dog pushes in the grip, he's moving forward. His mindset is forceful and insistent all the way	
This is one of the most effective ways of biting in real combat. The pushing grip offers the largest surface area of contact with the target. When the dog is pushing into the bite, everything including the clothing and the limb of the aggressor is pressed into the very corners of the dog's mouth. As the grip is going forward into the opponent, it won't slide off as a result of his clothing getting wet and slippery from the dog's saliva. The pushing grip allows the dog excellent control over his opponent while reducing ripping wounds that are more common from re-gripping, shaking, and pulling due to the backward slicing motion of the canine teeth	
In practical training for combat, if we want to teach the dog to bite the decoy's legs a pusher is the most preferable. A pushing dog allows the decoy to work, keeps his balance, and reinforces the dog by stepping backwards simultaneously. Pushing is the preferred biting technique in Belgian Ring	

The pushing grip is more practical and spectacular when the dog has the proper technique for it. Whether the dog is biting a sleeve, a bite suit, or a criminal on the street, pushing makes the grip full and the dog go forward. The only drawback of this style of biting is some dogs have a higher tendency to pump the grip as they're pushing forward. Pumping occurs when a biting dog opens his mouth wider in order to drive his grip deeper into the target. It can be interpreted as re-gripping and it can cost you points in an IPO trial, depending on how the judge perceives the behaviour. As I prefer my dogs to be both competitive on the sporting field and functional on the streets, I'm a bigger fan of the pushing grip.

Regardless of adopting the pulling grip or the pushing grip, the handler and decoy must observe the dog's behaviour in early bite work sessions to consider which biting style will best suit him. Once they have made their decision, they need to stick by it and work diligently towards their goal. Changing from one biting style to another when the dog is already halfway through the programme is usually not recommended because it wastes a lot of time and the end result is typically far from ideal. Pushing and pulling are two behaviours that are totally opposite to each other. When one of these two behaviours has been established in training, changing into the other behaviour can only bring unnecessary conflicts to the dog's mind. When unsure of which biting style to employ, pulling is the safest bet as it's less demanding and easier to teach.

Teaching the Bite and Pull

Before teaching the pulling grip, the dog should have already developed a full grip. We now teach him to shift his centre of gravity backward in order to pull the decoy down. The steps are as follows:

1. Using opposition reflex to encourage pulling. Opposition reflex is an instinctual response possessed by many animals to maintain balance. When a dog's centre of gravity is shifted due to influences from his surroundings, he'll automatically adjust his distribution of mass to keep his balance. For example, when we're standing in a moving bus, we often have to transfer our weight from one leg to another to refrain from losing our balance. When the bus turns and shifts our centre of gravity to the left, we automatically transfer our weight to the right leg to maintain balance. When the bus turns in another direction and shifts our centre of gravity to the right, we directly transfer our centre of mass to our left to avoid

falling. The decoy can adopt the same principle to teach a dog to pull or to push. For pulling, the decoy lets the dog bite, and then lifts the dog up to his chest with the sleeve he's wearing so the dog's two front paws are off the ground. The decoy then relaxes his shoulders to let the sleeve drop without releasing it, causing the dog to fall. The dog's centre of gravity naturally shifts from high to low, from the dog's forequarters to his hindquarters. The decoy repeats this procedure, lifting the sleeve and letting it drop. The dog gradually learns to shift his weight backward through this stimulation.

2. Decoy stepping forward to encourage pulling. As the decoy uses the opposition reflex to introduce pulling, he steps forward while the dog is dropping, the handler collaborates this practice by stepping backward as well to give the dog space to pull and retreat.

3. Leash tension to encourage pulling. As the decoy is stepping forward and dropping the dog, the handler simultaneously tightens the leash, stimulating the dog to pull backwards and downwards by leading.

Teaching the Bite and Push

Before teaching the pushing grip, the dog should have already developed a full, firm, and calm grip. We teach him to shift his centre of gravity forward in order to drive into the decoy. The steps are as follows:

1. Using opposition reflex to encourage pushing. The decoy lets the dog bite the sleeve he's wearing and then lifts up the sleeve to let the dog put his paws onto the decoy's chest. If it's a puppy, the decoy can kneel down on the ground. The decoy keeps his sleeve up in front of his chest parallel to the ground like he's wearing a shield. With his other hand he pushes the dog's lower jaw or chest while pulling the sleeve towards himself. His two arms are working in contrast. His right hand is pushing the dog but his left arm (sleeve arm) is bringing the dog in. The decoy then suddenly relaxes his right hand (pushing hand), so there's no more force

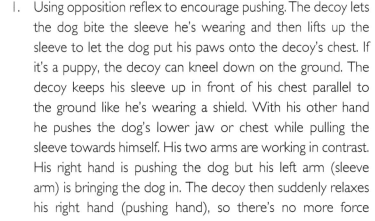

working against his sleeve arm. This causes the dog and the sleeve to push into the decoy because the force that was pushing the dog away has suddenly gone. The decoy repeats this movement, pushing the dog away with one hand while bringing him in with the sleeve arm. Gradually the dog gets the hang of pressing into the grip. The decoy can also work the pushing grip without lifting the dog up. As the dog is biting, he pushes the dog's muzzle, forehead, or lower jaw while pulling the sleeve into himself. This is exactly the same motion as before. Because the dog feels he's being pushed away from the grip, to take a better hold it's natural for him to push back in order to bore into the decoy. As soon as the decoy relaxes his pushing hand, the dog will start driving forwards.

2. Decoy stepping backward to encourage pushing. Once the dog starts to get the feeling of pushing forward, the decoy keeps stepping backwards. The handler should collaborate from behind the dog by giving the leash some slack so the dog has enough leash to go forwards. Every time the decoy pauses before taking another step backwards, the handler tightens the leash so the dog feels tension from behind. This encourages him to maintain the force of the grip, because he feels that if he doesn't bite hard enough he'll get pulled away. When the decoy takes another step backwards, the handler loosens the leash again to let the dog drive in.

3. Leash tension to encourage pushing. Sometimes, when the dog isn't pushing actively enough, the decoy can take the leash and pull it towards himself. By leading the dog forward, the decoy discourages the dog from pulling back or just standing there.

Developing an Active Pulling Grip or Pushing Grip

Like all the other exercises, we encourage a proactive dog in biting. No matter if we're teaching a dog to pull or push, our end goal is to have an active biting dog. When the dog is biting, regardless of the decoy moving or not, the dog should try to actively dominate and defeat him.

The tennis playing principle I've explained in teaching the dog to proactively challenge an unequipped decoy also applies here. For example, when we're developing a pusher, at the beginning it's the decoy's action causing the dog to start pushing. Once the dog has a few sessions of practice, the decoy gets him to push, steps backward, and then waits to give the dog a chance to initiate the push. When the dog feels the decoy isn't moving and starts pushing to initiate, the decoy reinforces this by going backwards. Gradually, the decoy becomes more reactive to the dog's correct behaviour. He lets the dog stimulate his movements. The dog becomes more sure because he believes he's in charge of the decoy and is able to manipulate him. We also extend the time of the dog's proactivity. At the beginning, as soon as the dog pushes, the decoy reacts. Then the dog has to do more work to receive a reinforcement, such as pushing three times before the decoy steps back, and then five times, seven times, and so on. The decoy can reward the dog's pushing by any movement that makes the dog feel good and encourages more pushing. The decoy can go backwards, push back, tap the dog's shoulders with the clatter stick, or lie down on his back so the dog can bite him from on top. This way the dog always feels like he's the conqueror of the decoy.

Teaching the Attack

In foundation bite work training, we usually teach the dog to bite on leash in order to develop his targeting, striking entry, and grip. At the beginning, the decoy goes to the dog on leash and presents him with the sleeve at the right time and the right distance for the bite. Once the dog has established the proper biting techniques, we can start teaching him to leave the handler and run at the decoy for the bite. This is called "the attack". An attack is composed of the three following behaviours:

1. Aiming. The dog's calculation of entering distance, timing, and the attacking target.
2. Entering. Also known as the striking entry, entering is the moment from when the dog opens his mouth to his teeth hitting the target. In the sport of Schutzhund, we require the dog to launch into the decoy during an attack. When the attack distance is 5m or more, the dog needs to take a leap in his entry so he's "flying" into the bite. From the instant all of his four paws leave the ground, this is counted as the entry. For other protection sports such as Belgian Ring, the dogs are allowed to bite the decoy's legs as well as his arms, as the decoys in ring sports wear a full-body bite suit instead of a sleeve. When the dog is a leg biter, his entry would be from the moment he turns his head sideways to align his grip to the decoy's leg until his teeth hit the decoy's suit trousers.
3. Biting. Once the dog has hit the decoy, his grip has to be full, firm, and calm.

All dogs progress at different rates in training. When we're considering if it's time for a particular dog to advance to the next level, the element of concern should primarily be the proficiency of the dog's current skills. In order to increase our demand, the dog must be comfortably capable in his present level of learning. If you want to have a competitive dog with a long working career, everything should be taught methodically according to his abilities. Rushing ahead of the dog's capability often creates problems. When a problem arises, it usually sets the dog back in training and ends up costing us more time than following the plan step by step. Before teaching the attack, the dog should be consistently biting the centre of the sleeve with a full, firm, and calm grip. He should be already accustomed to the clatter stick in bite work. We teach him the attack as follows:

1. I attach my dog to a 5m loopless leash. A longer line gives me control over a longer distance, as now the dog has to go away from me to bite the decoy. The loopless feature prevents the end of the line getting caught when I let it drag on the ground on certain

occasions. We face off the decoy and I give my dog the "Watch him" command so he alerts by barking. The decoy is ready. My dog is about 1 to 2m in front of me at the end of a taut leash.

2. The decoy goes backwards as he's attracting the dog by rattling the clatter stick. He holds the sleeve at about the dog's head height.

3. When the decoy retreats to about 3m away and the dog is in good drive and focus, the decoy indicates me to loosen my grip on the line to launch the attack. I give the verbal command "Take him" as I let the line slip out of my hands with a degree of friction. The friction between the leash and my hands creates resistance as the dog is going out. This enables me to control the speed of launching. At the beginning of teaching the attack, the control of the entry speed is very important. By slowing down

the dog in his striking entry, I give him sufficient time to aim and calculate. Young dogs are inexperienced and often get too excited in bite work. When their drive and motivation are not carefully managed, sometimes they can become too gung-ho and attack wildly with too much speed, causing them to miscalculate and ending up with a less than perfect grip. The decoy watches the dog as he comes; when the dog is about 30 to 50cm from the sleeve, the decoy abruptly pulls back the sleeve by about 30cm before presenting it forward to the dog again. This special trick of the decoy makes the dog enter with a deeper penetration and a greater impact as a result. This is the exact same philosophy taught by one of the greatest martial artists of the twentieth century, Bruce Lee. To develop the most devastating punch or kick, Bruce Lee emphasised hitting through the target. It means that,

when aiming, you focus at an imaginary spot behind the point of impact instead of at the target itself. By aiming behind the actual target, your strike penetrates through it, causing the maximum force. Another great technique demonstrated by Bruce Lee was the one-inch punch. Bruce Lee explained the explosiveness of a strike comes from the last few inches before the collision. By focusing training on the last few inches before the impact, Bruce Lee had developed much faster acceleration, which delivers greater snapping power to the punch. By pulling the sleeve back 30cm before presenting it at the same spot again, the decoy teaches the dog to aim behind the sleeve. Because of the sudden backward movement of the sleeve, the dog has to accelerate in the last 30cm before the strike, creating the one-inch punch effect that develops deeper penetration and greater damage at the moment of impact.

4. Once the dog is biting, I slightly tighten the leash so he can feel I'm supporting him from behind. The tension also encourages him to bite harder due to opposition reflex. The decoy wrestles with the dog as usual to let him push (or pull if the dog is a puller). When the grip is full, firm, and calm, the decoy lets the dog win the sleeve. I secure the dog and let him carry the sleeve calmly for a while before I tell him to out and repeat the above process again.

5. We continue to train for a few sessions following the steps above. Once the dog is used to penetrating through the sleeve in his entries, we can lengthen the distance of the attack to 4 or 5m.

Leg Bite

Over a century of evolution, Schutzhund has developed into the most popular international protection dog sport. Its regulations have also taken a more spectator sport direction compared with its original more functional form. In the modern IPO competitions, the dogs are only allowed to bite the frontal forearm area of the protection sleeve worn by the decoy, without exceptions. This bitable spot on the sleeve is known as the bite bar. When observed from the cross-section of an IPO trial sleeve, the bite bar is a "V"-shaped form that fits perfectly into a dog's mouth. All competitive sports require strict sets of rules and standards to provide even conditions for all players so a fair playing platform is possible. In practical situations however, there are no rules. If we want our Schutz dogs to be functional in actual combats, cross-training in elements other than the rigid IPO rules is a necessity. The amount of cross-training I combine into my Schutzhund training programme depends on the natural capacity of my dogs and their primary functions. Not all dogs can manage both the sportive and practical sides of training and excel in both areas. If competition is your main goal, the cross-training should serve as a complementary aid instead of extra work that can end up costing you points.

When I decide to teach one of my dogs leg biting, he should already be able to bite very well on the arm consistently. If I only want him to have the leg-bite experience to widen his sporting module, three to seven sessions on the legs are enough for a young dog. Good experience of biting other parts of the decoy's body can free up the dog's mind, so he understands his biting target isn't strictly limited to the centre and the frontal area of the forearm. Care must be taken though that the dog knows when he's allowed to bite the other areas of the decoy to avoid accidents happening.

If my puppy has already a very good arm bite before his teeth start to change, I'll let him have a few sessions of leg biting before teething. A dog that knows how to bite the decoy's legs at a young age has the following advantages:

1. Leg biting is one of the most practical tactics on the streets. When we teach a dog to bite the leg, we train him to take the centre of the decoy's shin. Biting this area gives the dog a mechanical advantage by leverage. In real combat, when my dog is biting the aggressor's shin on leash, all I need to do is to keep

the leash low and yank it backward. By doing this, my dog will take down the aggressor by pulling his leg under him, causing him to fall backwards. He's immediately immobilised.

2. No matter how a person is running or standing, he must have one leg on the ground for the dog to bite. Unlike the arms, the legs can't be hidden behind one's back. If the aggressor chooses to hold an obstacle in front of his lower body to block the dog from biting his legs, an IPO dog knows how to bite the arms anyway.

3. Leg biting is a lot more difficult than arm biting. When a person is standing on the ground, his legs are vertical. For the dog to bite one of his legs, the dog must turn his head sideways. A fully-grown working dog has a minimum height of 60cm. This means he must dive down and hold his head lower than his shoulders to bite a  person's leg and continue to push forward in this position. This technique is much more difficult than biting the arm. When a man is standing, his arms are a little higher than the dog's head height. In an IPO trial, the decoy has to hold the sleeve parallel to the ground as a shield between the dog and himself. This always gives the dog a comfortable angle for entry. Dogs are very clever creatures. When they have a choice, they usually take the easiest way to achieve their goals. If a dog has already formed a habit of biting the arm, teaching him to dive his head and turn his neck to bite the leg is a lot more difficult. Some experienced arm biters would simply refuse to bite the legs. Therefore, if we want to teach the leg bite and the dog is ready to learn, it's always better to start when he's as young as possible. When he's not yet fixated with biting the arm, he will absorb the leg biting skills a lot more willingly. Once he's matured enough and knows the whole IPO programme, we can then have the option to do more practical training with him on the bite suit to enhance his fighting ability. This is because he has been imprinted with leg biting at a young age, making this transition is a lot smoother.

Leg bites are practised with a leg sleeve. There are three usual techniques to introduce the leg bite. They're described as follows:

1. The decoy first holds the leg sleeve horizontally and presents it to the dog for a bite. Once the dog has a good grip on it, the decoy puts the sleeve onto his leg and puts his leg onto the ground. He steps backwards to encourage the dog to push in.

2. The decoy puts the sleeve onto his left leg and approaches the dog. He swings his left leg out like he's throwing a roundhouse kick with his shin aiming at the dog's mouth, without letting the dog bite. He does this a few times so the dog can aim well at the centre of the sleeve. When the decoy feels the dog will bite in the middle of his shin, he swings his leg out far enough, so this time the dog can actually catch it. The decoy then puts his leg onto the ground and starts working on the pushing grip.

3. The decoy wears the sleeve with his left leg and puts it onto a block of wood or a step. He can attract the dog's attention onto his leg by tapping the clatter stick on the leg sleeve. When the handler sees that the dog is targeting the leg sleeve, he lets the leash slip out slowly so the dog can bite the decoy's leg at a controlled speed. Once the dog has a good grip, the decoy lands his foot onto the ground and encourages the dog to bore in.

The typical way of leg biting is having the dog's eyes on the outside of the decoy's legs. That means, from the decoy's point of view, when the dog is biting his left leg the dog's eyes are on the decoy's left side. From the dog's point of view, he has to turn his head to his right side. This

technique allows the dog to see what's going on in his surroundings because his view isn't blocked by the decoy's other leg. It also lets the judge (Belgian Ring Sport) and spectators see the eyes and the expression of the dog during the bite.

In most protection dog sports, we emphasise the importance of keeping the dog centred during bite work. If a dog avoids staying in the centre line of the decoy during confrontation it is often a sign of insecurity, especially when he favours the outside in order to move away from the stick or other accessories. For that reason, when we teach leg biting the dog is always kept in the decoy's centre line so he is directly in front of the decoy. If the decoy is standing with his feet parallel to each other during leg biting, from a bird's-eye view the decoy and the dog should form an isosceles triangle. This way, both the decoy and the dog are in a comfortable position as the dog

is pushing forward and the decoy is moving back. To teach the dog to stay in the decoy's centre line, we can use a fence or some kind of obstacle on the dog's outside. Once he's used to biting the left leg, the decoy teaches him to bite the right leg.

The Different Types of Drives Utilised by the Dog during Bite Work		
To the sleeve	Hunt drive/ prey drive	The dog should view the sleeve as his prey as it's the target for chasing and biting. A full, firm, and calm grip is generated by hunt drive/prey drive. To capture the prey, the most effective way is to have as much biting surface area in contact with the prey as possible, which is the full grip
To the decoy	Rank drive, protection drive	The dog should view the decoy as his competitor and opponent. The decoy is not the prey and the dog needs to take him seriously in order to excel in both sport and actual combat
To the handler	Pack drive	The dog should view the handler as his teammate and leader. He has to trust and respect the handler. The two work together to confront and conquer the decoy.

In the protection phase, we employ four drives: hunt drive/prey drive, rank drive, protection drive, and pack drive. The dog's pack drive towards his handler enables obedience and control.

Synopsis of the Learning Stage

The time from the age of seven weeks to sixteen weeks is a crucial period of a puppy's learning. This is when he absorbs the most information. As a habit, I take advantage of this period to teach the basics of tracking, obedience, and bite work to my puppies. When a puppy is carefully selected and his training proceeds without too many major hiccups, by the time he reaches four to six months of age we should be able to advance into the strengthening stage for tracking and obedience. The development of the protection phase usually takes more time than the other two, as when the puppy is changing his teeth training has to slow down or be temporarily put on hold until his new teeth have grown. Furthermore, the dog's protection drive and rank drive usually can't fully develop until he's at least eighteen months old. A dog needs to be physically and mentally mature to go into full gear in bite work. Sometimes we have to wait until the dog is nine months or older for certain instincts, mentality, or behaviour to appear, such as dominance, aggression, and territorial behaviour. A lot of these depend on the breed and genetics of the dog. When maturity is the reason for the speed of learning, we need to be patient instead of pushing the dog into something that he's not ready for.

CHAPTER FOUR

Tracking Strengthening Stage

In the learning stage of tracking, our goal was to develop the puppy's foundation skills in scent discrimination and his interest in utilising the sense of smell. In the strengthening stage, we expand these skills and raise their criteria in order to increase the dog's experience. During this period, we progressively insert and adjust various elements on the track to simulate a wide range of circumstances the dog can encounter in an IPO trial.

From "Zigzag" Steps to Normal Steps

Previously in the tracking learning stage, I used to lay the tracks in continuous zigzag steps to teach my puppy to sweep his nose from left to right as he's following my scent. By now he should have established the desirable IPO searching technique. Henceforth, I can gradually change my zigzag way of laying the track to a more normal way of walking. I shall lay the tracks with my feet apart and pointing forward instead of linking the steps together from heels to toes and pointing

outward. I continue laying the serpentine tracks for a while, so my dog has enough time to adjust to the changes in my steps. When he's accustomed to the longer and wider steps, I'll try laying the tracks with various step lengths, step widths, stepping force, and stepping tempo, so he can gain experience of different styles of track laying. This is necessary because every track layer has a different height, different weight, and different way of walking. The changes should be subtle at the beginning so the dog has the opportunity to adapt.

Right-Angle Corner

The skills developed from zigzag steps and the serpentine are a vital foundation for precisely negotiating corners on a track. Once the groundwork has been set for these two compartments, the dog can quickly adapt to successfully following the 90° corners. The zigzag steps encourage the dog to sweep his nose from side to side while going forward. When we lay a serpentine track, we can make a curve in two different ways. For example, when I want to curve to the right, I can choose to step right with my right foot, or I can choose to step right with my left foot. The principle of the zigzag steps is to teach the dog that, once he's at the toes of one step, all he needs to do is to follow the heel of the next step to find out which direction the track is going. That's why when he can effectively put this technique into practice the error at a corner will be minimised.

When I see my dog is proficient in tracking on serpentines, I'll gradually tighten the curves until I turn in a right angle. To introduce the 90° corner, in the first few sessions I'd ease my steps smoothly at the turn so the corner is rounded like the corner of a pedestrian curb. A raised pavement next to a road is built in a rounded angle so the cars can turn easily. If I want to lay a 90° turn to the right, when I start turning I can first turn my right foot 45° to the right, followed by my left foot turning 45° to the right. I can also first turn my left foot 45° to the right, followed by my right foot turning 45° to the right. 45° + 45° = 90°. By laying the corner smoothly in the initial

teaching, the dog can quickly establish the technique of checking sideways when he realises the next step is not going forward anymore. Once he's formed a good habit of checking at the smooth corners, I start laying sharp 90° turns.

Teaching the Slow Walk with a Pinch Collar

As a puppy is growing up, if his handler has been nurturing him correctly, by now he should be turning into a confident and outgoing juvenile. Sometimes he might be a little bit too confident and outgoing, such as constantly rushing forward when going for a walk. Some puppies as young as four months old can already develop very forceful pulling during a walk. When a dog is pulling too hard into his collar, he puts too much pressure onto his throat. This restricts his breathing and dissipates his energy, resulting in heavy panting. A panting dog breathes with his mouth opened. When he does this in tracking, he loses the degree of sensitivity he needs to precisely follow the scent. To contain the drives of my dogs for good use, I introduce the pinch collar so they can walk calmly on leash. The pinch collar is a piece of equipment commonly used in training working dogs. Its function can be compared with the spurs in equestrian. Both of them are used to applied adequate pressure on the animals so they can give a particular response through negative reinforcement. The pinch collar is often a misunderstood instrument because of its spiky appearance. However, its purpose is not to hurt the dog but to make him uncomfortable enough to either stop an undesirable behaviour or to perform a desirable behaviour. The blunt "teeth" inside a pinch collar imitate a dog's teeth. By applying pressure on the pinch collar through leash tension, you simulate the mother dog disciplining her puppy by gripping the scruff of his neck, which is a natural part of dog language. When training dogs, we must try to think in their world from their point of view. In nature, wolves and wild dogs exist in packs. In a pack there's a clear hierarchy. To maintain order, the alpha sometimes has to discipline his subordinates by force. This is a world where only the strong survive and a show of strength by applying pressure is necessary in certain occasions.

There are two main types of pinch collar, a type that's made of metal and a type that's made of plastic for younger dogs. Both types have flattened prongs that apply pressure when constricted without damaging the skin of the dog. When I first introduce the pinch collar I use the plastic type, which is lighter with rounded teeth. The time of introduction depends on when my dog starts forming a habit of pulling so hard into the collar during his walk that his breathing suffers from it. When I first let my young dog wear the plastic pinch collar, I simply take him for a walk as usual without doing anything different. When he pulls too hard into it, the collar automatically constricts, causing the collar's teeth to put pressure onto his neck. The dog is made uncomfortable by his own behaviour. When he stops pulling too hard and walks normally, the collar automatically loosens, ending the pressure and discomfort on his neck. After three days of walking with the pinch collar on, most of my dogs learn to walk nicely on leash.

Once my young dog has established walking on leash in a relaxed state with the plastic pinch collar, I bring this into tracking. Before I let him track, I take him out from the car and go for a walk so he can warm up as usual. He walks in front of me with the pinch collar on. If for any reason he starts walking too fast or pulls into the leash too hard, I first give the tensed leash some slack ensued by applying a slight jerk towards me, causing the collar to suddenly constrict and give the dog an unpleasant feeling as a result. If once is not enough, I repeat this action until he walks calmly. When he walks nicely again, I link the verbal command "Slow" with his behaviour. From now on, every time before tracking I prepare my dog as above. This teaches him to slow down and relax, which is beneficial for his focus on the track.

Controlling Speed and Precision on the Track with a Pinch Collar

After several sessions of practising the slow walk before tracking, the dog should start to establish a habit of walking slowly and calmly. I can now utilise this technique when he goes too fast on the track. In the IPO trial regulations, there's no rule stating that the dog has to track slowly. The only reference regarding the pace in tracking is that the dog should work the entire track with an even speed. However, when dogs are allowed to track too fast, most of them tend to get too excited, and excessive motivation usually causes a decrease in concentration. By collaborating the slowing technique with the pinch collar, we can control the tempo of the dog during tracking, which is favourable in developing precision. In application, I let my dog follow the scent on the track normally. If he goes too fast, I say "Slow" and then give the line a slight jerk to bring down the speed. Every time he goes too fast, I do this to slow him down. You must pay special attention here, though. The force of the jerk must not be too hard. If you apply too much force in slowing the dog down, you can damage his motivation and confidence. When the correction is too overwhelming, the dog can shut down and stop tracking and then you'll have a problem. The jerk should be given as a slight and quick snap with the leash. Directly after its application, the leash goes slack again, so the dog learns to track on a loose line without influence from his handler. Do not hold back on the leash and put constant tension on the pinch collar in the hope of slowing the dog down like this. It won't. Most dogs will be desensitised by the pinch collar this way and will start to pull stronger and stronger into it, like a racehorse that has learnt to fight the persistently tightened bit.

By correctly using the pinch collar in tracking, we can improve the dog's precision as well. For example, when the dog comes to a corner and overshoots it by more than a 50cm margin, I would stop following him and just stand there. If he continues to go further to the wrong direction, he gives himself a correction by tightening the pinch collar. When he takes the corner correctly and

goes back onto the track, I let the line go slack again. Gradually, the dog learns to track on a loose leash so he can work out the track independently. When I give the line a jerk and release it, it means he's tracking too fast and needs to slow down. When I stop following him and the leash is blocked, it means he's not precisely on track and needs to search for where the scent is. Care must be taken in utilising leash control in tracking. Properly used, it's an excellent technique to establish the right speed and precision, but there's a fine line between shaping the dog gradually so he can track on his own and giving him tactile signals as a habit to make him dependent on them. Too much handler influence in tracking will create a reactive dog that focuses on what the leash is doing behind him instead of working out the scent with his nose in front of him. In such cases, the leash signals become the cue for corners. When the handler doesn't know where the track goes and the dog has to follow the scent independently, he does poorly or gets completely lost. You must be aware of this and try not to interfere in every little detail especially when the dog is still young. Sometimes a dog has to be given a chance to do what's wrong in order to learn what's right. A certain margin of error is important in a dog's learning curve to give him the experience he needs on the competition field. Knowing how much margin for error to give the dog at what age separates the good trainers from the rest.

The Article Indication Box

Besides teaching the article indication with the little food container, I also employ another technique to improve the focus and precision of this behaviour out of tracking. First, I make a simple wood frame to be a training aid. The dimension of the frame is about 100cm long x 60cm wide x 10cm high. At the front of the frame I attach a 90cm PVC pipe with a diameter of 3cm. This works as a food delivery tube. I call the wooden device the "article indication box". The article indication box system has the following advantages:

1. Now I can improve the dog's article indication both in and out of tracking.
2. This system is built for the sole purpose of indicating the article. It allows the dog to learn our criteria faster with a better clarity.
3. This encourages the dog to take the initiative for pointing at the article.
4. The food delivery tube keeps the dog's focus on the article instead of looking at the handler when the food comes from him.
5. This greatly improves the focus and precision in the article indication.

Training Goal

1. Encourage the dog to focus on the article.
2. Encourage him to lie down at the article, with his two front paws beside it.

Preparation

1. Before this training, the dog should be able to down stay for at least one minute.

2. I place the article indication box on a ground with short grass. I drill two holes in a standard-size IPO tracking article. I put two long screws through it so I can anchor it to the ground. This way the dog can't push the article around, which is a behaviour we don't want.

3. I lead my dog to the article indication box and tell him to lie down. In front of him is the food delivery tube. In front of the tube lies the article.

4. When the dog looks at the article by chance, I press the clicker to confirm his behaviour, and then I drop a dry dog kibble into the tube. The food lands in front of the article and the dog eats it. When I construct the article indication box, I attach two pieces of wood and a piece of fabric around the tube. This prevents the food from bouncing around when it lands, causing the dog to turn away from the article to search for the food.

5. I gradually extend the time for focusing on the article. Short sessions that last for about two to three minutes work best. Once or twice a day is sufficient. I train as such for several days. The dog realises that he'll receive food by looking at the article. When his behaviour becomes consistent, I link it with the command "Show me".

6. When the dog can constantly initiate watching the article and he can keep his focus for a minimum of ten seconds, I let him start the exercise by first making him sit out of the article indication box. When I see he's already looking at the article, I say "Show me" and lead him into the box with a leash. When he focuses on the article and lies correctly in front of it, I click and deliver the food.

7. In the following sessions, I prolong the period for the dog to continuously watch the article. I also create

some distractions such as stepping over him and moving around him while he's looking at the article. If the dog loses his attention on the article, I'll give his leash a light jerk to make him focus back on it again. When his attention is back on the article, I click and deliver the food.

8. After a few more sessions, I start a lesson as usual but remove the article indication box after a few reinforcements. Now I let my dog practise the technique on the article alone. When he looks at it, I click. If he keeps his gaze, I click again, and if he continues to keep his gaze, I say "Good" and feed him the food with my hand. The click is a signal that means "Correct, keep looking." The "Good" means "Correct, you don't need to look at the article anymore, but keep staying down." If he looks at me before I say "Good" instead of keeping his focus on the article, I'll give a correction by slightly jerking the leash in the direction of the article until he looks at it again. When his attention is back on the article for at least five seconds, I say "Good" and feed him.

9. We spend several sessions practising the article indication in different environments without the box so the dog can generalise the behaviour and not associate it only with a particular location. I also introduce different types of articles made of materials the dog can encounter in a competition so he will indicate all of them. To make the transition from out of the track to on the track, I place three articles on a short grass track of about forty steps. The first article is on the scent pad, the second article is on about the fifteenth step, and the last one on the fortieth step. The amount of food I leave on the track is a little bit less than usual, but it is not completely without food. When I arrive at the starting point with my

dog, he can see the flag and also the first article on the scent pad. I say "Show me" and he naturally lies down on the article and indicates it. When he stays focused for a few seconds, I say "Good" and feed him. I then take away the article and place a few more kibbles on the scent pad but prohibit him from eating them. He can only look at the food. When his focus on the food is 100%, I say "Seek" and allow him to eat the food and continue to follow my scent on the track. My dog now has the foundation understanding of both tracking and article indication, and I've just linked the two skills in one exercise. As the second and the third articles are in the grass and my dog is in tracking mode now, he'll find them by his olfaction instead of by sight. At the beginning of this practice, I might need to help him a little bit by giving the leash a slight jerk when he finds an article in case he over steps it, but he should pick this up very quickly, as he already knows how to indicate the food container. From the next track on, I don't put any articles on the scent pad anymore. All articles will be placed on the track. When he's consistent in finding the articles, I offer him food randomly and selectively, rewarding him only when he indicates the articles with excellent focus and precision.

Cross Track

When my dog has a solid foundation in tracking, occasionally I'd add a cross track to my existing track. A cross track is a disturbance of scent usually left by other person, animal, or machine rather than the track layer. Because it crosses a section of our track, inexperienced dogs can be distracted by this. A cross track can be laid at a time before or after the track layer lays his track. Sometimes we make cross tracks deliberately, and sometimes they're made without our knowledge, such as farmers working on the field before we arrive or wild animals from the surrounding areas. In all the tracking training so far, we've taught our dog that the scent of the person from the starting point is the target throughout the entire track. We now also teach him that any other scent on the track different from the target is to be ignored.

To intentionally lay a cross track for training purposes, I can ask a friend or a training assistant to walk across my already laid track once. This provides a distraction to my dog. A cross track for an inexperienced dog should be simple. It shouldn't be near the start, the end, the corners, or the articles. It also shouldn't be laid closely along or at a tight angle that's almost parallel with my track. The easiest cross track is laid diagonally across a straight leg of my track at 90°. My training assistant must know exactly where my track and the cross track are. I let my dog begin tracking as usual. When he arrives at the cross track, I observe his behaviour without giving him any clues. If he tries to follow the cross track, I give him a margin of error of 50 to 70cm. If he realises this is the wrong track and goes back onto his track, I let him continue. If he keeps following the cross track over the margin of error, I give him a correction by jerking at his leash twice. I then give him time to work out the scent. When he's back on his track, we continue. Infrequent cross tracks keep the dog focused and alert. It makes his tracking more reliable under distraction.

Sometimes, I choose agricultural lands with deep tyre marks left by tractors. These make excellent cross tracks as they provide both olfactory and visual interruptions to the dog. Again, it's easier to cross the tractor marks diagonally than walking on them at a sharp angle. This kind of training can be done more frequently as the chances of encountering them in a trial are quite high.

Elements to Work on at Tracking Strengthening Stage

In the tracking strengthening stage, our job as a handler is to prepare the dog for situations he can come across in the examinations of IPO 1, 2, and 3. There are many variables to work on, including:

1. Tracks of various ages. The age of a track means how much time has been waited since the track layer left his scent on it. For example, if the track layer puts down the track at 07:00 and the dog starts tracking at 08:00, the age of the track is one hour old. The age of the track has a direct relationship with how much scent is left on the ground. As a general rule, the younger the track, the more concentrated the scent; the older the track, the less concentrated the scent. In addition to this, different weather can affect the scent differently.

Strong wind can blow the scent away. Heavy rain can wash the scent away. When we're training, we need to let the dog follow tracks of various ages. He has to learn that no matter how concentrated the scent is, his job is to find it in the most precise way he can.

2. Tracks of various times of day. The time of day has direct and indirect effects on tracking. In the early morning before the sun is fully up, the lower temperature allows the dog to breathe easier. The dew on the grass holds more scent, and its moisture is beneficial for the dog's sense of smell. The temperature rises when the sun is up at midday. When the dog has to work his nose in the heat, he's tracking and panting at the same time. Additionally, the moisture on the ground is pretty much gone. This is a difficult condition for tracking. When we're training with an inexperienced dog, we should practise more on cool mornings with moist grass until he's ready for the harder afternoon weather.

3. Tracks on various terrains. In a trial, we can come upon many different kinds of terrains, including soft ground, hard ground, dry ground, wet ground, soil, mud, dirt, sand, grass land, bare land, flat ground, mountain slope, farming land, livestock paddock, forest, etc. Terrains that are soft, moist, flat, with plenty of vegetation are usually easier tracking fields than terrains that are hard, dry, sloping, and without any vegetation. We should select the appropriate tracking field according to a dog's training level.

4. Tracks on various vegetation. Besides grass fields, many other sorts of vegetation grounds can be given to us in a trial. There are fields with wild flowers, weeds, domestic plants such as harvested maize, and sometimes even poison ivy, which gives a nasty sting when touched. We need to prepare our dogs to track on all these different types of vegetation so he can gain experience.

5. Tracks of various lengths of grass. At the beginning, dense grass about 3 to 10cm is the optimum length as it encourages the dog to track with a deep nose without him being able to see the food and the articles. Tracking too much on grass longer than 20cm can cause the dog to raise his nose. This should be limited until solid tracking techniques have been established.

6. Tracks in various weathers. Once the dog is comfortable tracking on different terrains, we should let him work under different weathers. They include sunny, rainy, overcast, cold, hot, windy, and snowy days, etc. When we first start to train in various weathers, the challenge shouldn't be too extreme. The dog needs to adapt to different weather gradually.

7. Tracks in various wind directions. For foundational training, we used to always go with the wind (down wind). With experience, the dog can practise in different wind directions, such as cross wind, up wind, and wind blowing in circles.

8. Tracks with various turns. In the serpentines, we've prepared our dog to follow the turns gradually from wide to narrow. Once he's at a level that he can take 90° corners, we still don't limit the turns to right angles alone. The dog should be continuously offered various degrees of curves so he never knows what to expect on a track.

9. Tracks with various stepping styles. Accustoming the dog to zigzag steps, normal steps, longer steps, wider steps, faster steps, crooked steps.

10. Tracks with various track layers. Every person has his own unique scent, weight, height, stride, and way of walking. When my dog consistently works well with me laying the tracks on various terrains, I'll ask several experienced friends to lay my dog's tracks as much as possible so my dog can obtain experience from different track layers. The track layer must remember the entire track clearly, including the straight legs, corners, and articles.

11. Tracks of various amounts of food. The more food on the track the easier it is for the dog to search. However, no food is allowed in an IPO trial. Therefore, we must prepare our dogs to eventually track without food.

12. Tracks with various articles. In a trial, you can be given articles made of wood, rubber, leather, fabric, felt, plastic, etc. The official trial article size is 10cm x 3cm x 1cm. Once my dogs are proficient in finding the articles, I usually put smaller articles on the track, sometimes as small as 3cm x 0.5cm. A friend of mine is able to let his dogs indicate the head of a nail about 0.5cm in diameter with precision and consistency. When it's within the dog's capability, the smaller the article the better it can sharpen the sense of smell because the dog has to search very meticulously for it. The track layer must memorise where the articles are. For articles the size of a nail head, once put in the grass they are impossible to see. That's why in my training I don't use articles smaller than 3cm x 0.5cm.

13. Various ways of placing the articles. In an IPO trial, the articles are usually placed on the track layer's footprints, but sometimes track layers put them in between the steps. In some very windy conditions, lighter articles such as fabric and felt can be blown a few centimetres or further away from their original place. We have to familiarise our dogs with these situations.

14. Tracks with various distractions. Once the dog can track with strong focus and motivation, we gradually add different degrees of distractions in tracking, including distractions by sight, hearing, and smell. For example, we can track next to domestic animals such as cows, horses, sheep, or even the neighbouring barking dog. We can track next to a busy road with a lot of cars passing. We can lay a track on an area with strong animal scents such as a cow paddock, where it's littered with cow dung. If the dog is on competition level and we really want to challenge his nose, we can even lay a track on a football field where a match has just been played (cross tracks everywhere).

15. Various distances between the handler and the dog. In a trial, the handler must stay 10m behind his dog when he's tracking. As the dog progresses in training, we give him more and more line so he's used to working 10m in front of us and follows the scent by himself.

16. Tracks of various lengths. In IPO3, the minimum length of a track is 600 steps. Sometimes it can be longer. In training we need to prepare our dogs for this.

As the dog is still gaining experience, when we increase the criteria of one element in tracking we should ease the difficulties of the other elements. For example, if I'm to lay a track on a hard terrain without any vegetation today, I'll keep the track simple, without too many curves, and I'll step with a rubbing stride so more of my scent can be left on the track by friction. I'll also do this kind of track on a cool and moist day. If this is the first time my dog goes on terrain like this, I'll put more food on the track. I won't make the length of the track too long, and after aging it for thirty minutes, I'll let my dog start.

Memorising the Track

The preparation of the track is one of the major causes for the success or failure of tracking training. The higher the level of a tracking dog, the more complex his track is, and the more straight legs, corners, and articles the track layer has to memorise. The biggest fault a dog trainer can make in tracking is forgetting the details on the track and not knowing where the track is, and the dog doesn't know it either. A handler can't help an off-track dog when he's lost himself. We need an effective system to record the details of every track to ensure we know if the dog is exactly on it. As the dog is tracking, we have to know where the next corner and article are so we can correct him if he loses accuracy. I use the following elements to remember the tracks I lay:

1. Footprints
2. Landmarks
3. Food
4. Articles
5. Steps
6. Indication pins.

Before I start laying the track, I first observe the layout of the terrain and objects I can use as markers

of my track. I visualise an approximate plan and find two aligned points in front of me for laying down the first straight leg. Normally, I use easily identified landmarks that stand out from the field or its surroundings, such as hills, trees, bushes, rocks, flowers, buildings, and power towers. If I lay the track on lush grass, most of the footprints can be quite easily seen. If I put food on the track, I can use the food as references for the positions of turns and articles. For example, in a particular section on the first leg I put food in five consecutive steps; after ten steps without food, I make a left turn. I can use articles as my references, such as putting a wooden article on the second leg, and after twenty steps I make a right corner. When my dog is tracking and he finds the wooden article, I know that twenty steps ahead he has to turn right. If we're training in an area that lacks easily visible landmarks and the ground is too hard to leave any footprints, I'll insert a 20 to 30cm long metal tent nail near a corner or article as a sign. I use nails with a yellow string for articles, and nails with a red string for corners. This method should only be employed when the track is too difficult to remember, as the nails can also be seen by the dog, and relying on them too often will give the dogs extra information about the track. Before, during, and after laying a track I have a habit of writing down the details on paper or drawing them on my smart phone. This way I can keep a comprehensive record of each track and use it for reference as my dog progresses.

Progressing to Trialling Level

1. No food
2. Walking at the end of the 10m line behind the tracking dog
3. Reporting in and out to the judge.

When our dog progresses to a certain level, we should gradually accustom him to trial conditions, such as laying a track with no food and walking 10m behind him at the end of

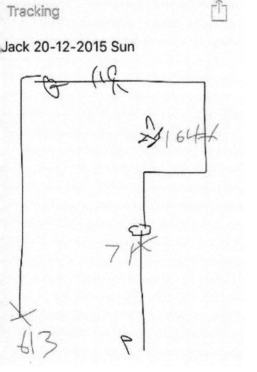

the tracking line. When a friend or training partner is available, I ask him to stand near the starting point so I can simulate a trial scenario when we have to report to the judge at the beginning and the end of the track. When the dog is regularly prepared with situations as closely resembling a trial as possible, we'll minimise errors due to a lack of experience in competitions.

Observing the Dog's Behaviour in Tracking

In IPO2 and 3, the track layer is a stranger instead of the dog's handler. In training we must get our dog used to following a stranger's scent. When the dog becomes a skillful tracker, it's an essential step for the handler to follow him without knowing where the track is (but the track layer knows and he's beside the handler). The track layer's job is to let the handler know where the next corner and article are, but without so much information that the handler becomes too confident and so relaxes in observing his dog. The handler has to develop the ability to read his canine partner by observing his expression, breathing, focus, composure, confidence, motivation, speed, tail carriage, and depth of nose. With experience, he'll recognise when his dog is on target or not solely by reading his behaviour, even without knowing where the track is.

Obedience Strengthening Stage

In the obedience learning stage, our goal was to develop our dog so that he wants to work. In the obedience strengthening stage, our goal is to teach our dog that he has to work. We introduce free shaping, luring, targeting, leading, pressing, and reverse targeting as our communication bridges, with the final goal of having our dog responding to a single verbal command without any additional aids or cues. The purpose of free shaping, luring, and targeting is to build up the dog's willingness for the work. The function of leading, pressing, and reverse targeting is to establish the dog's reliability for the work. These techniques also make up the cornerstone of the electric collar system. When I link the verbal command with a certain behaviour, I prefer to do it at a time when I'm sure the dog won't refuse and can't refuse. Therefore, for most of the basic components, I introduce their verbal commands after I've shown the dog negative reinforcement through leading.

In the obedience strengthening stage, I hope to achieve the following goals:

1. Introduce negative reinforcement into the obedience basic components
2. Introduce targeting
3. Introduce the verbal commands
4. Combine food drive, hunt drive/prey drive, pack drive, and comfort drive to boost the dog's temperament after pressure
5. Familiarise the dog with working under distraction to establish reliability
6. Combine all the basic components to develop the trial exercises
7. Combine all the exercises to develop the IPO3 obedience routine
8. Prepare the dog for his first examination: BH – The Companion Dog Test.

Obedience Strengthening Stage 1st Phase

First, I raise the criteria of the fifteen basic components I've taught in the obedience learning stage by introducing negative reinforcement, targeting, and the verbal commands:

Attention, sit, down, stand, heel left, heel right, front position, backward, hold, release, jump, climb, look forward, go ahead, target plate.

Steps

1. Pressure → discomfort → luring → change of behaviour → pressure stops → reaches comfort → food reward

2. Pressure → discomfort → targeting → verbal command → change of behaviour → pressure stops → reaches comfort → food reward
3. Pressure → discomfort → verbal command → change of behaviour → pressure stops → reaches comfort → food reward
4. Verbal command → change of behaviour → food reward.

Training Goal

1. Introduce negative reinforcement into the basic obedience components (negative reinforcement: blocking, leading, pressing, reverse targeting).
2. When the dog understands negative reinforcement, we introduce targeting.
3. Introduce the verbal command.

Sit: Leading, Targeting, Linking the Command

Leading to Sit

I let my dog wear a normal nylon collar or slip chain and attach it to a leash. I hold the leash with my left hand and some dry kibbles with my right. As the dog is walking or standing, I gently pull the leash upwards to apply tension to the collar so the dog feels a very slight discomfort. I then lure him to sit with the food in my right hand. At the moment his buttocks make contact with the ground, I immediately slacken the leash and then reward him with one or two kibbles. This negative reinforcement method by tightening the leash is known as leading. As my dog has already learnt the foundation of sit by luring, I only need to apply very light pressure in combination with luring to make him understand how to end the discomfort. After I've given him his share of food, I remove my right hand from him. Because I still have food in my hand, it's possible for him to want to follow my hand and leave the sit position. If he does this, I tauten the leash towards the back of his head to prevent him from coming out. When he stays

sitting, I feed him again and relax the line. This negative reinforcement method by tensing the leash to prevent a dog from leaving an already established position is known as blocking. I use leading to make the dog sit, and blocking to make the dog stay. When he can sit straight and attentively for about half a minute, I say "Yes" and let him leave the sit position to come to get a dog kibble. I repeat this procedure for three to five times. The dog learns that by cooperating with me he can stop the discomfort as well as earning some food rewards.

In leading to sit, the handler has to sense how much he has to tighten the leash for the dog to go from not sitting, to sitting. He needs to find the friction point that triggers the change of the dog's behaviour, like a driver knowing when to step on the clutch and release the clutch to change the gears of his car. Every dog is different and you need to develop your touch and feel. Your touch is knowing how much tactile signal to give your dog, and your feel is knowing how your dog is responding. They make a two-way communication bridge.

Targeting to Sit, Linking Verbal Command

After several lessons, the dog should begin to understand the mechanism of leading. He should realise the quicker he sits, the quicker he can switch off the discomfort and the quicker he can obtain his food reward. I can now introduce targeting and use it to replace luring so the dog learns that he has to sit for me even though I'm not holding food in my hand. I hold the leash with my left hand and my right hand is empty. I pull the leash up to create a slight tension on the dog's collar while moving my empty right hand to the top of his head to guide him into sit. The dog has previously learnt sitting by leading and luring, and now the movement of my right hand exactly resembles the movement of luring him into sit. He will naturally go into the sit position. As he's in the motion of sitting, I link his behaviour with the verbal command "Sit". As soon as his buttocks hit the ground, I stop the leash tension and take out some dog kibbles from my pocket to reward him.

I continue the above process for a few sessions. When my dog starts to respond to the leading by automatically going into sit, I'll fade out the targeting and use the verbal command "Sit" alone. When he sits, I release the leash tension and reward him with food.

Gradually, my dog understands the "Sit" command means the sitting action. I'll fade out the leading. If he really knows what "Sit" means, he'll respond by sitting instantly when I give the command. I'll reinforce his behaviour with food. If the dog doesn't respond directly to my verbal command, I'll switch on the leash tension to make him sit, and switch off the tension and offer him food once he's sitting. If he doesn't immediately take action after my verbal command and I have to help him with leading three times in a row, this usually indicates he hasn't linked the word with the behaviour yet. If this is the case, I'll go back to first applying the leash tension before giving the command for a couple of sessions before trying to fade out leading again.

Down: Leading, Pressing, Targeting, Linking the Command

Leading to Down

I take the leash with my left hand and some food with my right. I pull the leash downward under the dog's chin to cause a mild discomfort, while luring him down with the food in my right hand. When his elbows and abdomen touch the ground, I release the leash tension and reward him with food. If the dog wants to follow my hand when I draw it back instead of staying in down, I block him with the leash to keep him in the down position. When he stays in down with attention for about half a minute, I say "Yes", release him, and give him some food. I repeat this practice three to five times.

Pressing to Down

Some dogs tend to keep getting up in the down, and it's a little bit awkward trying to pull him down with the leash all the time. For this I have a second solution. Instead of using the leash to pull him down, I use my thumb and middle finger to apply a slight inward and downward pressure at the base of his skull where it meets the first vertebra. This is a kind of a pressure point for the dog and I combine this with luring him with food in my other hand. When his belly is completely on the ground, I cut the pressure without totally removing my hand in case I need to press him again. I feed him some food and remove my hand. If he tries to leave the down position by following my food hand, I stop him with my pressing hand. When he returns to the correct position, I release my hand again. This technique is called pressing. When the dog stays down with focus for half a minute, I say "Yes", release him, and feed him one or two kibbles. I repeat this three to five times. Some dogs respond to leading better while others respond to pressing more willingly. I stick with whichever technique works best with a particular dog.

Targeting to Down, Linking Verbal Command

When the dog is used to leading and pressing for the down, he knows the faster he goes down the faster the discomfort goes away, and the faster the food comes. Now I'll use targeting instead

of luring. As I gently press the dog's neck downward with my left hand, my empty right hand guides him to lay down like the luring down motion. The dog understands these tactile and visual signals and will lie down on cue. When he's halfway in downing, I insert the "Down" command. I stop the pressure and feed him when he's in the down position.

After a few lessons, when I see the dog will go down when pressed, I'll fade out the targeting by applying pressing and giving the verbal command alone. When he's in the down position, I end the discomfort and feed him.

To test the dog's understanding of the "Down" command, I'll say "Down" and wait for the dog's reaction. If he goes down without the need for pressing, I'll reward him with one or two dry kibbles. If he doesn't down immediately, I'll help him by pressing him as lightly as possible and offer him food after he's in position. If I have to help him with the tactile signal three times in a row, it means he's not clear with the verbal signal yet, and I'll continue the practice as the step before until the dog understands the word "Down".

Stand: Leading, Reverse Targeting, Linking the Command

Leading to Stand

I begin by putting a waistband onto my dog. It should be fitted loosely around his waist. If needed, I'll let him wear it while going for a walk for a few times so he can get used to it. When he's ready to train, I attach a leash to his waistband and let him walk casually near me. As he's walking, I tighten the leash in the direction of the dog's tail to block him from walking forward; this causes him to stand. When he's standing steadily, I slacken the leash. After three to seven seconds, I say "Yes" and invite him to leave the stand position to come to me for food. For now, I avoid offering him food while he's standing as this will tempt the dog into leaving his stance. I repeat this three to five times.

Reverse Targeting to Stand

Besides using the waistband to teach the stand, I can also use my foot or a slight flick with a horse whip at the dog's chest to block him from moving forward. Once he's standing firmly, I remove my foot or the horse whip and wait for three to seven seconds. If he stays standing and his attention to me is good, I say "Yes", release him, and feed him.

Linking Verbal Command

When the dog is used to the blocking stand by reverse targeting, I usually don't need to use the waistband for a while. Now I can insert the "Stand" command as I stop him from moving forward by a light tap with the whip. When this becomes a habit, I can fade out the whip.

Heel Left, Heel Right: Leading, Targeting, Infusing Hunt Drive/ Prey Drive, Reverse Targeting, Linking the Command

Leading to Heel

Once my dog can heel left and right following my outside and inside hands, I'll insert five to ten portable sticks into the ground and use them to replace the wall. The spaces in between the portable sticks allow me and my dog to go through. When we come to the end of the roll, we can do a 180° inside about-turn (with me turning towards the dog) and the dog will still have the portable sticks on his outside to keep his body straight. The portable stick system is a good way to prevent the dog from swinging his hindquarters out in heeling. When it's time to introduce leading in heeling, to have both of my hands free, I'll attach the dog's collar to a double-snap line and a handler leg band strapped onto my thigh. From now on, whenever my dog is not close enough in heeling, he'll immediately feel the tension from the double-snap line and self-correct.

Targeting to Heel, Infusing Hunt Drive/Prey Drive

I first teach my dog to follow a target stick. A target stick is a thin stick with a little ball or a few wraps of adhesive tape at one end, which offers a clear target for the dog to follow. When I introduce the target stick, I first rub a few drops of fish oil at the ball end of the target stick to make it interesting for the dog. The dog is facing me. I hold the clicker and the target stick with my right hand.

There are some dry dog kibbles in my pockets. I move the target stick in front of my dog's nose. When he smells the fish oil on the target, he usually becomes interested and touches it. At this moment I click to confirm his behaviour and treat him to a little bit of food from my pocket. I move the target stick away from him and get him to follow it. Every time he touches the ball end of it, I reinforce his behaviour. As I've already taught my dog the target tag system in the obedience-learning phase, he'll pick up the target stick in just a few minutes.

Before I start using the target stick for heel left, I put a rubber ball with rope in the left back pocket of my training vest without my dog knowing. I have food in both my front left and right pockets. I tell my dog to sit on my left and I attach his collar onto my left thigh with the double-snap line and handler leg band. By my dog's left side, there's a roll of portable sticks. I hold the clicker and target stick in my right hand. I hold the stick's target just above my dog's head. When he lifts his head to look at the target, I click, get some food from my front left pocket, and feed him with my left hand. After several reinforcements, I begin to walk forwards. As I'm walking, I hold the target above his head to keep him looking at it. When he can keep his attention on the target for two to three seconds, I click and treat. After repeating five to ten times, I say "Yes" and unhook his collar from the double-snap line. I take out the rubber ball from my left back pocket and throw it backwards with my left hand to let

my dog retrieve it as his reward. I get him to bring back the ball and play with me. After wrestling briefly, we start the heeling again. The reason I keep the ball in my left back pocket and throw it backwards in left heeling is because this helps to maintain his precision. If I keep the ball in my right pocket and throw the ball forwards, or to my right, after a while the dog will start forging, leaning heavily against me (crowding), or to swing his buttocks out because of anticipation.

In the practice of left heeling, the five to ten portable sticks are always on our left side. Whenever we come to the end of the last stick in the roll, we make a left about-turn, and after the turn the sticks are still on our left. This way, besides keeping the dog's position accurate, we never have to stop when we come to the end of the row. After several successful repetitions, I attach my dog to my right thigh and hold the clicker and target stick with my left hand. I put the ball in my right back pocket and have the portable sticks on our right. We begin right-heeling with the same principle. When the dog is heeling correctly with good attention, I say "Yes" and throw the ball backward with my right hand to reward him.

The advantage of using the target stick in heeling is its ability to keep the dog's head up, focusing on a target without getting him too excited, like using a ball directly as his target. This gives the dog more composure to learn our criteria. By looking up at the target stick, the dog also automatically looks up at me because my face is aligned with the target. This makes the transition from heeling with the target stick to without the target stick a lot smoother.

Reverse Targeting to Heeling, Linking Verbal Command

We continue the above training for three to seven sessions. If I see my dog is ready, I'll start fading out the target stick. I first get him to sit next to my left leg as usual and encourage him to look up with the target stick. I reinforce him several times when he keeps his head high. On some occasions when I see he's looking up at me through the target stick, I slowly remove it and see if he can maintain his focus on my face. If he stops looking at me as I remove the stick, I hold it above his head again to keep his focus. When I can take away the stick and maintain his attention on my face at the same time, I say "Yes" and let him bite the rubber ball. After repeating this fruitfully a few times, I start walking forward to let him follow. Whenever he offers me attention without the need for holding the target stick above his head, I say "Yes" and reinforce him with a bite at the ball. At the start I reinforce him as soon as he looks at me. Gradually I prolong his attention to five seconds. When left heeling is good, we practise right heeling the same way. After gradually fading out the target stick for a few lessons, when the dog is sitting in basic position or heeling next to me, as long as he can keep his focus on me for five to ten seconds I reinforce him with food. If he can persistently sustain his attention after several food rewards, I reinforce him with a bite at the ball and wrestling with me. I'm now using food drive, hunt drive/prey drive, and pack drive together. The dog has also learnt that paying attention to me will get him the rewards. I can now link the verbal command "Heel" with the behaviour. When the dog is in basic position, I say "Heel" and start walking off leading with my left leg. After a few steps I stop. The dog should sit automatically. I give the "Heel" command again and start walking off. After numerous recurrences, the dog grasps the meaning of "Heel". For the command of heel right, I use the word "Right". I can also use "Side transport" as the command for right heeling, as this is the same behaviour in side transport of the protection phase.

When the dog is attentive in both static heeling and dynamic heeling, I can teach him the finish. The finish means getting your dog to come into the basic position from the front position. This is a behaviour required in down in motion, stand in motion, retrieve, retrieve over hurdle, and retrieve over A-frame in the obedience phase, and hold and bark in the protection phase. We can teach the dog the "flip finish" by directly swinging his hindquarters into his handler, or the "go around", in which the dog goes behind his handler and then next to his left side. I prefer the first technique as it's more spectacular.

The Steps of Teaching the Flip Finish:

1. Tucking in sideways. Tucking in sideways is the basic technique of the flip finish and the about-turn. When the dog is sitting next to my left side in the basic position, if I take a sidestep to my right the dog will move parallel into me so he's straight in the basic position again. This is known as "tucking in sideways". As this step requires the dog to swing his hindquarters into me in a small scale, this is the first movement I use to teach him the flip finish. We start by facing a fence (to provide clearer illustrations, here we use portable sticks instead of fences and walls). The fence in front of us prevents the dog from moving forward when I side step. I attach my dog to my left leg and let him sit by my left. I have food in my right hand and a horse whip in my left, I show my dog I have food in my right hand before I take a step to my right, leading with my right leg and followed by my left. The food in my right hand lures him in while the double-snap line leads him in. The problem is

most dogs don't naturally sidestep into a sit in the way we want in IPO. Instead, they usually turn their front without swinging in their hindquarters and they end up facing the handler diagonally and not parking parallel next to him. That's why I use the horse whip in my left hand as a training aid. When the dog comes close to me without tucking in his buttocks, I give him a slight flick with the whip on his left buttock. This causes him discomfort. To avoid it, he naturally swings his hindquarters towards me, which now makes his position perfect. As soon as he's in place, I feed him the food in my right hand. If necessary, I lure him with the food so he sits next to me correctly. I repeat this procedure seven to ten times, and end the session on a high note by giving him the ball as his reward. After a few lessons, when the dog will swing his hindquarters into me without the flick of the whip, we're ready to advance to the next step.

2. Tucking in quarterly. This technique teaches the dog to swing his buttocks 90° into me from the basic position. I turn 90° counter-clockwise and teach the dog to also turn 90° counter-clockwise to park himself next to me. I first stand in a corner of two walls with my dog sitting by my left side. There's a wall on our left and a wall behind us. I turn 90° to my left and flick my dog's left buttock lightly with the horse whip to get him to tuck his

hindquarters towards me until he's in basic position correctly, and then reward him with the rubber ball. I repeat this a few times. After several sessions, we do the same drill on open ground. I only apply the whip flick when it's necessary. When the dog parks himself next to me correctly, I reward him with food. Several correct repetitions earn him a ball reward. By now I can insert the "Return" command. Every time when I finish turning 90° anti-clockwise, I say "Return" and let the dog swing his hindquarters inward so he's in basic position precisely again.

3. Tucking in half circle: This is a movement when the dog follows me in the basic position after I make a 180° turn on the same spot. On open ground, I tell my dog to sit next to me.

I turn 180° counter-clockwise and give the command "Return". If my dog doesn't respond immediately, I tap him slightly on his left hindquarter with the horse whip. When he returns to the basic position accurately, I reinforce him with food. Several consecutive returns gain him a bite of the ball.

4. Flip finish: I let the dog sit in front of me in the front position. To prevent him from anticipating the action (swinging his buttocks in before I give the verbal command), I place the whip next to his right flank without touching him just in case I need to use it to block him. I give the verbal command "Return" and tap him lightly on his left buttock with the whip. As soon as he's moved into the basic position correctly, I say "Yes" and throw him the ball to reward him with hunt drive/prey drive. Once he can respond solely to my verbal cue, I can fade out the whip tapping.

The right finish is the same principle as the left finish. I use the verbal command "Right" for this behaviour.

Front Position: Leading, Linking the Command, From Down to Here

I now continue with the target tag technique I've used in the obedience-learning phase. The first step is to introduce leading in this component. I attach one side of a 60cm double-snap line to the back of my trousers, and the other side goes between my legs and attaches to the dog's collar. I let my dog come closer towards me as I step backwards. Besides the attraction from the target tag, the attached line also leads him in and the tension of the line stops when he's close enough in front of me. I repeat the same drill several times. When my dog comes close to me and has a good habit of sitting in front of me when I stop moving, I reinforce his behaviour by feeding him with both hands simultaneously. I can now link the verbal command "Here" with this exercise.

After a few sessions, when the dog is used to being led into me, I'll make a left or right turn to teach him come in front of me precisely. Every time after I turn, I'll take a few more steps backwards in a straight line before I stand still so my dog has enough distance to straighten up.

When the dog can come straight to my centre line no matter if I swing to the left or right, he's ready to learn the movement from lying down to coming into the basic position. I first attach

a 2m loopless leash to my dog's collar and let him lie down in front of me. I keep my feet apart so they're just on the outside of my dog's front paws. The leash comes out in front of his collar and passes between my legs. I hold it with both hands behind my back. When the dog is focused on me, I give the command "Here" and give the leash a slight tug. He responds promptly as he's familiar with both the verbal and tactile cues. The reason I keep my feet apart is to give him sufficient space to come up close to me. When he's sitting accurately in front of me, I say "Yes" and feed him with both hands. I repeat the above procedure. After several lessons, the dog has made the association between the target tag and my centre line. I can now fade out the tag and increase the distance between us to accustom him to respond to my verbal command alone.

Backward: Reverse Targeting, Linking the Command, Infusing Hunt Drive/Prey Drive

In the obedience learning stage, I've already taught my puppy to walk backwards by pushing my food-holding hands into his chest. Now I apply the same movement with my empty hands. As the dog is familiar with this action, even when I have no food in my hands he'll at least still take a few steps back. When he does this, I immediately say "Yes" and take out some food from my pockets with both hands and feed him. I then repeat the same process. Gradually I increase the distance that my dog steps backwards. At the beginning, I reinforce stepping one or two steps back. Then I increase it to five steps, ten steps, twenty steps, and so on. I can now introduce the "Back" command. I can also diminish the hand-pushing movement. Instead, I'd just walk into my dog after I've given the "Back" command. He should step backwards on cue. To increase his drive for this component, I can insert hunt drive/prey drive into the practice. I hold a 30cm jute bite roll in front of me while facing my dog. I give the verbal command "Back" and step into him to make him go backwards.

When he goes back in a straight line with good attention to me, I say "Yes" and jerk the bite roll towards me to stimulate hunt drive/prey drive. My dog bites the toy as his reward for stepping backwards. I wrestle with him briefly and repeat the drill five to seven times, extending the distance in every repetition.

Hold: The Table Retrieve System

The goal of teaching the hold in obedience is to let our dog take the centre of the wooden dumbbell firmly in his mouth in the retrieve exercises. We don't want him to mouth the dumbbell or treat it like a toy because it will cost us points. Although we've established our dog holding the sleeve calmly in the protection phase, most dogs treat the sleeve and the dumbbell differently. Additionally, the sleeve is made of soft jute, and the dumbbell is made of hard wood. Therefore, I've adopted the following system in training my dogs to hold a given object firmly, calmly, and seriously.

The Retrieving Table

The retrieving table is a solid frame that keeps the dog's head and body secured when we teach him to hold an object calmly in his mouth. The frame limits the dog's movement to prevent him from moving around when we want him to focus solely on holding the dumbbell. The table retrieve system is sometimes mistakenly called the forced retrieve, but this is not its proper name, as we

teach our dogs to hold the dumbbell willingly without any force, and he always has a choice of holding it or not holding it. Making a behaviour reliable has nothing to do with forcing a dog. By force, it means the animal doesn't have a choice. Ingenious dog trainers are always able to give their dogs the choice of complying or not complying. The secret is being able to convince the dog to make the right choice every time without fail. The correct procedure of the table retrieve system is applied as follows.

1st Step: make the dog love the table, get him used to being secured on it, accustom him to accept his handler's touch calmly

As most dogs don't like being restrained without knowing what's going on, the first step of the table retrieve system is to let our dog view the table as a positive place. I connect my dog to a

leash and lead him onto the table. As soon as he goes up on it and turns around I press the clicker to confirm his behaviour, then I reward him with some dry kibbles. When he stays on the table calmly, I click and treat again. I then call him off the table and get him to go up on it again. Every time he goes on it, I click and reinforce. After five to ten repetitions, I feed him a full meal of fresh meat on the table and finish the lesson. I do this for two to five sessions.

When I see my dog eagerly pulls to go on the table, I know he's made a positive connection with it. I can now attach his collar and waistband onto the table. Once he's secured, I sit in front of him. I click and treat when he stays on the table calmly without wiggling around. After about ten reinforcements, I offer him a full meal of fresh meat and release him. I continue this process for another two to five sessions.

When my dog is used to being attached to the table, I touch him slowly and gently on all parts of his body. When he accepts my touch, I click and reinforce with dog kibbles. A dog accepting his handler's touch calmly is a sign of trust and respect. This is also an important step for when we have to visit the vet. After rewarding my dog about ten times with dry food for staying calm to my touch, I give him a full meal and end the session. I repeat this for two to five lessons.

2nd Step: make the dog accept touching of his mouth, get him used to me inserting my thumbs behind his canine teeth, accustom him to open his mouth to gently hold my thumbs

I secure my dog to the retrieve table and sit facing him. I gently hold his head in my hands and stroke the outside and inside of his mouth. If he resists and tries to pull his head away from me, I'll stop him with my voice and hold his head with a firm grip. When he allows me to stroke his

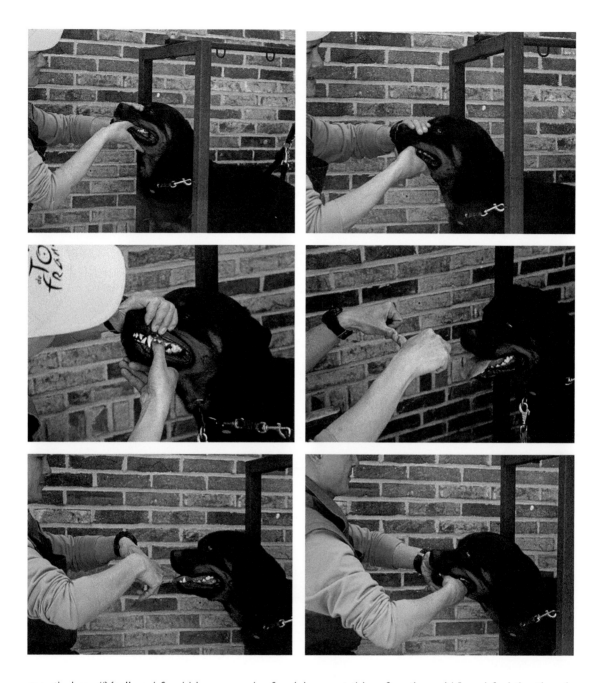

mouth, I say "Yes" and feed him some dry food. I repeat this a few times. When I feel the time is right, I insert my left and right thumbs into both sides of his mouth. My left hand is on top and my right hand is below his jaws. My hands hold the dog's jaw gently to prevent him from spitting out my thumbs, which is his instinctual reaction. If he tries to reject my thumbs, I stop him with my voice and my hands. Once he discontinues struggling and holds my thumbs calmly, I say "Yes" and give him some kibbles. After three to five successful repetitions, I end the session by offering him a full meal. I maintain this practice for two to three lessons. The place I insert my thumbs is always the gap behind the dog's canine teeth. This is the best spot for a dog to hold the dumbbell as this gap offers the ideal space to carry the dumbbell firmly. The canine teeth naturally lock down on the centre bar of the dumbbell and keep it solid in the dog's mouth.

Once the dog will accept me putting my thumbs into his mouth from the sides, I'll connect my thumbs together and insert them into his mouth frontally so he has to open his mouth to take them. If he tries to spit out my thumbs, I'll stop him with my voice and my hands. When he holds them firmly, I say "Yes", remove my thumbs, and reward him with dry food. After three to five repetitions, I complete the session with a full meal. We continue this practice for three to five lessons.

3rd Step: let the dog accept me putting a small wooden stick into his mouth, get him used to holding the stick willingly, teach him to actively open his mouth to take the stick

When the dog willingly holds my thumbs without wanting to adjust his grip or to spit them out, I can replace them with a wooden stick. The stick should have a length of about 20 to 30cm and a diameter of 3 to 4cm. I open the dog's mouth gently and make him hold the wooden stick. His normal response is to spit out any foreign object. I stop this with my voice and my hands gently holding his jaws. When I feel he's stopped refusing, I say "Yes" and feed him some kibbles. After three to five repetitions, I feed him his full meal of fresh meat and end on a good note. I continue this process for three to five sessions.

Up until now, in the whole table retrieve system, I have employed both positive reinforcement and negative reinforcement. The positive is when I reward the dog with food for desired behaviours, and the negative is when I apply slight pressure with my voice or my hands to stop undesired behaviours. We have to keep all discomfort to the dog to the minimum level while teaching the hold, and never try to rush the process by applying too much pressure to force him. This is very important, as once the dog is overwhelmed and loses his trust in his handler, he'll refuse to open his mouth to take the object, and all the time and effort you've spent in earning his confidence up to this point is lost. To repair this takes a long time and a lot of patience, so you must avoid making such mistakes.

4th Step: introduce the constricting collar for leading, use leading as a signal for the dog to take the wooden stick, establish a firm hold, pair verbal command with the behaviour

When the dog can hold the wooden stick without attempting to drop it even when I remove my hands, this is an indication that we're approaching a successful hold. All I need to teach the dog now is an easily understood signal for the action of extending his neck forward to take the stick. I secure my dog onto the table and let him wear a constricting collar. The constricting collar is a very useful tool. By using it gently, we can teach the dog to eagerly take the dumbbell. By using it severely, we can stop an aggressive dog from biting indiscriminately. In the retrieval exercise, we use this collar with a gentle approach. I sit facing my dog. His constricting collar is connected to a 45cm loopless leash, which I have in my right hand. In my left hand I hold some dry dog kibbles. I pull the leash lightly to lead the dog into extending his neck towards me. Immediately I offer him food so his neck extension movement is positively reinforced. As soon as he takes the food, I release the leash tension. This technique has the following essential features:

1. A forwardly constricting collar is a signal for the dog to extend his neck and take something into his mouth (at this point it's dry food).
2. Once the dog has taken the object into his mouth (dry food), the collar relaxes.
3. The dog learns to accept pressure (constriction of the collar) with pleasure (after a very slight discomfort, he receives a reward).

The dog learns that by complying with the cue (extending his neck forward at leash tension) he can switch off the pressure (constriction of the collar) and gain a reward (dry food). After practising this movement for one or two sessions, I bring back the wooden stick again. I hold the leash in my right hand and the stick in my left. I pull the leash gently to lead the dog's head towards me, at the same time offering him the wooden stick. If required, I'll open his mouth with my hand so he can take the stick. As soon as he holds the stick, I loosen the leash, and then I help him close his mouth to keep the stick by gently stroking him under his chin. The whole procedure is best completed within three seconds. The quicker your movement, the shorter the period the dog is in discomfort, and the better it is. When I feel the dog is holding the stick by himself, I'll

slowly remove my hand from his lower jaw, but I'll keep it near him in case he suddenly opens his mouth. We must not allow the wooden stick to drop onto the ground. When the dog can hold the stick for two to five seconds, I say "Yes" to let him release the stick and reward him with some dry food. After three to five repetitions, I end the lesson by feeding my dog his full meal on the table. In the following sessions, I shall lengthen the time so the dog can keep the stick in his mouth for at least ten seconds. If he mouths the stick or perfunctorily lets it sit in his mouth without really holding it, I'll stop it with my voice, constrict the collar briefly, and give him a firm stroke on the chin. When he holds it well, I say "Yes" and reinforce him with food.

I maintain this level of training until my dog automatically extends his neck forward to take the wooden stick when I pull on the leash, and once he takes it, I don't need to help him by putting my hand under his jaw anymore. He should also hold firmly and willingly, with his nose always pointing at me. At this point I can introduce the "Hold" command as he comes forward to take the stick.

5th Step: replace the wooden stick with the dumbbell, let the dog focus on the dumbbell, handler stands beside the dog as he takes the dumbbell, loosen the dog from the table so he can dive down to take the dumbbell

Before I select a dumbbell of a suitable weight, I first consider the age of my dog. Usually I begin the first step of the table retrieve system when my puppy is around five months old. I train about five days a week in this exercise. Each session lasts for about two to five minutes. When we're up to the

fifth step, my dog should be around six and a half to eight months old depending on his progress. I'll choose a dumbbell with a weight that my dog can hold comfortably. If the 650g dumbbell is too heavy at this age, I'll use a lighter one. The technique of letting the dog hold the dumbbell is the same as holding the wooden stick. When the dog can take the dumbbell nicely, I'd stand beside him as he's looking at the dumbbell in front of him. When his focus is on the dumbbell, I'll give him the "Hold" command and the leash signal to take it. Because in the retrieve exercises, the dog always starts in the basic position besides his handler, this step is very important to accustom the dog to looking at the dumbbell before the retrieve instead of focusing on his handler. After a few more lessons, I can unstrap the dog and let him sit on the table. I stand on his right side and hold the dumbbell with my right hand at his chest level to get him to focus on it. I say "Hold" and give the leash a light tug towards the dumbbell so he leaves the table, retrieves the dumbbell, and goes back onto the table. Once he's holding it firmly and sitting on the table, I say "Yes" and reinforce him. We're now ready to retrieve the dumbbell away from the table on to grass.

Release: Luring, Leading

Usually, the more a dog loves to bite, the less he's willing to let go. In the learning stage, I've taught my dog three techniques to release his grip, including:

1. Release by exchange with food
2. Out by prying his mouth open
3. Out by pressing the ball into his mouth.

However, some highly driven dogs might still be slow or reluctant to out. In such cases, I'll wait until they're about nine months old before using other negative reinforcement methods for a faster and more reliable out. We have to be sensible when utilising training techniques with pressure. If the pressure is applied too young or too strongly, it can overwhelm the dog and undermine his desire for biting. I prefer my dogs to have a happy and free puppyhood. Confidence development and drive building should be the priority when raising a puppy. Stricter application for control should wait until after his puberty.

By the time my dog is nine months old, when I let him bite a ball and he doesn't out within three seconds after I've given him the verbal command I'll consider employing the following techniques:

1. Double ball out: I first prepare two identical toys such as rubber balls with rope or jute bite rolls. I let my dog bite one of them, and hide the other identical toy in my pocket. After playing for a while, I hold the rope part of the rubber ball with my left hand while I say "Give". My right hand takes out the other ball from my pocket and I tease the dog to bite it by swinging it near his head. When he releases the first ball and bites the second one, I

put the first ball into my pocket and keep playing with him. After a brief spell of wrestling, I say "Give" again and show him the first ball. I alternate between the two toys to get him to release one and bite the other. After a few sessions, I fade out the showing of the other ball. Sometimes I show it and sometimes I don't. This method has succeeded when the dog can consistently out on command without the need to see the other ball.

2. Out by leash correction: I first let my dog wear a plastic pinch collar. I hold the leash with my left hand and play with my dog with my right. I say "Give" and allow him one second to respond. If he doesn't release the ball in time, I give the leash a sharp jerk sideways to apply enough pressure for him to let go. Once

he's outed, I require him to look at the ball without trying to snatch it again. When he keeps watching it for at least three seconds without taking a dirty nip, I reward him with a bite. I repeat this process several times. After a few sessions, when the dog responds to my verbal command alone without the need for the leash correction, this technique has succeeded.

3. Out by constricting collar: the constricting collar can be used to teach the dog to hold, but also can be used to teach him to out. I let my dog wear the constricting collar. My left hand holds the leash and my right hand plays with the dog. If I say "Give" and he doesn't respond in one second, I lift the leash slowly, calmly, and deliberately to make the collar constrict. The constricting collar gives a choking feeling to the dog. When he's short of breath, he must open his mouth to gasp for air, causing him to drop the ball. I release the leash tension so he can regain his focus and composure. When he watches the ball attentively for about three seconds without attempting a dirty bite, I reward him by letting him play with the ball. After a few seconds of wrestling, I give him the command to out again. When he outs reliably on my verbal cue alone, this technique has succeeded. Out by constricting collar is a highly effective method, especially for stubborn biters. When the collar constricts, all dogs must open their mouths to breathe and have no chance of holding on, without exception.

Target Plates: Leading, Linking the Command

I first put two target plates on the ground. They should align with each other about 2m apart. There's

food on both plates. I attach a 2m loopless leash to my dog and let him sit in the middle facing one of the plates. As he's already made a positive association with the target plates in the obedience learning stage, when he sees the plate in front of him he will have the impulse to go on it. I let him go while I pair his behaviour with the verbal command "Target" and give a slight tug on the leash towards the plate. My dog runs onto the plate and eats the food. When he's finished eating, I lead him over the plate and turn him around so he faces the second target plate. I let him lie down on the first plate by pressing and reinforce him with food. Once he's settled on the first plate and focuses on the second, I say "Target" and lead him to it with a tug on the line. When he's eaten the food on it, I lead him over the plate, turn him around, press him down, and reward him with food. Now I don't put food on the target plates anymore. Every time he looks at the plate ahead, I say "Target" and lead him to it with a tug on the line. Once he's on the plate, I lead him over and around, press him down, and feed him. I let him wait and focus on the opposite plate before I tell him to go on it again. This system is very useful for the hurdle, the A-frame, and the send away.

Jump: Leading, Target Plates, Linking the Command

When the dog shows his understanding of my criteria of the target plates by running onto it, turning around, and lying down immediately when I say "Target" and tug on the leash, I can bring this system into jumping over the hurdle. The principle is the same as before, only now the distance between the two plates is 3 to 4m long and there's a hurdle in the middle. The height of the hurdle is set to about 10 to 20cm. I let my dog put on a 3m loopless leash and tell him to

lie down on the target plate on my left. He's facing the hurdle and the target plate on my right. I stand next to the hurdle. When I see my dog is focusing ahead (looking at the hurdle), I say "Jump" and lead him over it. As he lands on the ground, I say "Target" to command him to go on the plate ahead, turn around, and lie down on it. I say "Good" and reward him with some dry food. I wait until he focuses on the hurdle and command him to jump over it and go on the target plate on my left. I repeat this a few times. When the dog does well, I end the session with a game of fetching the ball.

I gradually increase the hurdle's height. Normally, dogs under one year of age are still growing and their joints are still relatively soft. To avoid injuries, I usually limit the height of the hurdle to below 40cm until they're more mature. The most important things they need to know now are the focus on the hurdle, the correct jumping technique, and going on target to refocus again. As long as they're healthy and mobile, once they can manage the above, jumping 1m is usually accomplished in a few weeks.

Climb: Leading, Target Plates, Linking the Command

Climbing the scaling wall shares the same principle as jumping the hurdle. At the beginning, I set the height of the A-frame at 50cm. On each side of the A-frame I put a target plate. I tell my dog to lie down on the plate on my left and I stand beside the A-frame. When the dog looks at the A-frame with focus, I say "Climb" and give his leash a tug towards it. When he comes down the A-frame, I make sure he comes all the way down to the bottom instead of leaping down from the

top. Once he's landed, I say "Target" to make him go on the plate on my right, turn around, and lie down. I say "Good" and reward him with food. When he's refocused on the A-frame, I tell him to climb over it again.

For dogs under the age of one year, I usually set the height of the A-frame no higher than 1.3m. If the dog comes down too fast, I'd control his speed with the leash to accustom him to keeping contact with the A-frame all the way to the bottom.

Look Forward, Go Ahead: Leading, Infusing Hunt Drive/Prey Drive

In the obedience learning stage, I've taught my puppy to focus on the goal of a football field as his target of look forward and go ahead. Now I let my dog wear a 45cm loopless leash and let him look at one of his toys (e.g. a jute bite roll) in the centre of the goal instead of a bowl of food. As he's looking at the bite roll between the goal posts with a great amount of drive to go and get it, I pull him back for about 5m like I'm loading an arrow on a bow. I point at the goal with my right hand and say "Watch", and then I give the leash a slight tug forward as I say "Go" and release the dog. He charges for the bite roll like an arrow leaving its bow. Once he's taken the toy, I call him back to play with him, and then I tell him to release it so I can place it at the same spot to send him again from a further distance. When he focuses on the goal, I let him go ahead. In every repetition I increase the distance about 2 to 5m. After training for a few weeks, I should be able to send my dog forward 50m from the football goal.

Blending Food Drive, Hunt Drive/Prey Drive, Pack Drive, Comfort Drive Together, Conditioning the Dog to Rebound after Pressure

Up until now in the obedience phase, I mainly utilise four drives:

1. Food drive: reinforce desired behaviours with food
2. Hunt drive/Prey drive: reinforce desired behaviours with biting and fetching a toy
3. Pack drive: reinforce desired behaviours with play or a tug-of-war through a toy
4. Comfort drive: reinforce desired behaviours with switching off pressure.

These four drives all have their own unique advantages, and therefore I employ them all. The amount of applying each drive depends on the dog's genetics, age, and training topic. Below is a table of comparison between these four drives:

Drive	Advantages	Suitable For
Food drive	Easy to use, can keep the dog motivated without winding him up with too much excitement	Teaching the dog a new behaviour, keeping him motivated in lower drive, food can be used to lure the dog into many desired behaviours
Hunt drive/ Prey drive	Bringing the dog into hunting mode, heightened focus, excitement, speed, and pain tolerance. When a dog hunts, his adrenaline increases	To raise the dog's energy level and expression in a behaviour that he's already learnt, this drive is usually employed to sharpen a behaviour and to make it more dynamic and explosive; the adrenaline enables the dog to rebound after pressure
Pack drive	A strong pack bonding between the dog and his master can't be taken away like food or toys. It's invisible but extremely powerful. When every piece of equipment and training aid is taken away, the bond with your dog is the only thing you've got. When the dog has strong pack drive for his handler, he's willing and happy in his work. The presence of his master is sufficient to keep him motivated	This is a drive that's useful at any time, especially when there's interaction between the dog and his handler
Comfort drive	Correct application of negative reinforcement strengthens the dog's behaviours and makes them reliable	I usually adopt this to proof a behaviour after the dog has learnt it via positive reinforcement

When training has reached this level, my dog already has sufficient experience with the four drives above. I'd use dry dog kibbles as little rewards during an exercise, such as reinforcing the dog with food in the middle of heeling and continue to work. When my dogs become twelve weeks old, I start feeding them twice a day instead of three times a day. The size of a meal increases as the dog grows. By the time my dog reaches four months old, he should have a good foundation in drive development and training in the three phases. I no longer need to feed him a meal as a reward at the end of every training session. In most of the lessons, I can end on a good note and play with him or take him for a walk afterwards before giving him a drink and putting him back in his kennel enclosure, in my house, or in the car. I only use a full meal as reinforcement in training such as the table retrieve system. Besides that, I feed his two daily meals at random times depending on my work schedule and preference. By the time my puppy becomes four months old, I don't have a strict timetable for feeding, as in the wild wolves don't eat on time either, and most often they don't even get to eat daily.

I develop my dog's pack drive through bonding and a lot of positive interactions. At the beginning, I link my dog's responses to me with food or with playing through using a toy. For example, when he's heeling well, I say "Good" smilingly and reward him with food. After continuing to heel further, when his focus and expression are at a good level I say "Good" again and give him a pat on his face, and then I say "Yes" and throw him a ball as a reward. With time, my dog responds positively to my voice and my touch, as something good always comes afterwards. Sometimes after I say "Yes" I invite my dog to jump up on me, chase me around, or bump his body into me. After playing with me briefly without any toys, I throw a ball and let him fetch it to reinforce the pack behaviour. Once the dog has linked pack drive with food drive and hunt drive/prey drive, the voice and the touch of his master are as good as food and toys. This is the same classical conditioning as the clicker and the treat. Well-established pack drive ensures the dog's responsiveness on the competition field when no training aids are allowed.

Comfort drive is used to strengthen or correct a learned behaviour. When the dog makes a mistake, pressure is applied to change his behaviour. When he responds correctly, the pressure stops. Therefore, it's very important for the dog to know what we expect of him before we start polishing his behaviour with pressure. As a general rule, the higher the pressure we use, the bigger the reward that comes at his success. Otherwise the dog's working attitude could be damaged, causing him to work with his ears back and his tail down.

Hunt drive/prey drive is a great source of power when it comes to increasing the dog's focus, liveliness, explosiveness, and resilience. When I introduce pressure to establish a behaviour through negative reinforcement at an initial stage, as soon as the dog reaches the desired behaviour I'd boost his hunt drive/prey drive with a bite at a toy, play fetch, or wrestle with him through the toy. Once the dog is used to working in hunt drive/prey drive, he becomes tougher and can overcome pressure with a positive attitude. Using this drive to help the dog bounce back after pressure makes him more dynamic in action.

There's also freedom drive, which I utilise at the end of a session when I let my dog run free or go for a wander in the forest.

Obedience Strengthening Stage 2nd Phase

By the time my puppy has gone through both positive and negative reinforcements for each of the obedience basic components and begins to understand their verbal commands, he should be at least six months old. If I feel his maturity, character, and training level are ready for some simple distraction training, I'll try it for one or two sessions to see how he responds. If I feel he's not ready after these sessions, I'll wait for another month before I try again.

Attention: Practice during Sit, Basic Position, and Front Position. Strengthening Attention under Distraction. Using Hunt Drive/Prey Drive to Rebound the Dog after Pressure

A dog's absolute attention to his handler is one of the winning criteria in Schutzhund obedience. Because the basic position and the front position are two exercises that demand 100% focus to the handler and they both involve the sit position, I'd inject distraction in the training of sit, basic position, and front position and use negative reinforcement to proof them to increase the attention and reliability of the dog. Before I start this process, the dog must be clear on the positive and negative reinforcement of these three components and understand their commands. He should also be a minimum of six months old.

Why do we need to train under distraction?

1. To find out the current limit of the dog's focus and improve it.
2. To let the dog understand that, sometimes even when there are distractions and he's really tempted to leave his work and do something else, once I've given him the command he must complete the task. "Sit" is sit and "Down" is down.
3. Eventually, we want a foolproof dog that can function and be under control in a wide range of environments and circumstances.

Sit under Distraction

I first invite a friend or a training assistant to be the distracter to my dog. His job in this session is to cause sufficient disruption so my dog will look at him while he's supposed to focus on me. The assistant has to observe the dog's behaviour so he doesn't overly distract him. We want the dog to succeed and not to set him up for failure. The goal is to teach the dog to keep his attention back onto me after mild pressure to correct him for looking away. We want to strengthen his focus and his reliability in sit.

I first let my dog sit in front of me with attention as usual. The assistant makes some noise and movement to attract the dog to look at him instead. When my dog looks away, I give his leash a slight tug towards me to make him look at me again. The assistant stops his distraction. When the

dog keeps his attention back onto me for five to ten seconds, I say "Good" and give him some food. The assistant starts his distraction again. My dog loses focus and I correct him. He keeps his focus back onto me again for a few seconds and I reinforce him. We go through this process several times. When the dog doesn't look at the assistant anymore while under the same level of distraction and can maintain his focus on me for three to five seconds, I say "Yes" and let him bite the ball and wrestle with me as a reward. When training under distraction, the handler needs to avoid reinforcing his dog too early. If the dog loses focus and he needs to be corrected to look at the handler again, we should wait at least five seconds before rewarding him. This is because if he looks away and looks back at you again and you reward this immediately, you're actually reinforcing him for looking from side to side.

Basic Position under Distraction

I first hide the rubber ball in my left back pocket and command the dog to sit on my left in the basic position. As he's looking up at me, my assistant disrupts him with noises and movements on

the left. When my dog looks at him, I give him a correction by tugging the leash up towards my face. When he keeps his attention back onto me, I wait five to ten seconds and say "Good" before reinforcing him with food. This is the same as sitting under distraction. Once the dog can maintain his attention in static heeling, we'll practise dynamic heeling under distraction from one or several people. If my dog looks at them, I correct him with the leash. When he can keep

looking at me for five to ten seconds in heeling, I release him and give him a bite of the ball. When left heeling is good, we practise right heeling under distraction.

Front Position under Distraction

I first tie a 50cm cotton rope loosely around my neck and clip a rubber ball onto it with a cloth hanging clip. I wear a training vest over it so my dog can't see the ball. I let him wear a 2m loopless leash, which goes between my legs and is held in my hands behind my back. I tell my dog to come into the front position. My assistant goes about 1.5m behind the dog and starts distracting him with movements and noises. As I'm in front of the dog and the distracter is behind him, it's easier for the dog to keep his focus on me. That's why, besides requiring him

to look at me, I also want his ears facing me before I reward him with food. Once my dog can sit in the front position with focus, I begin stepping backwards to get him to follow me. The assistant distracts him from the side. If he looks away, I correct him by tugging on the leash behind my back. When he keeps his concentration for five seconds or more, I say "Yes" and take out the ball so he can jump up to get it. Please note that the ball

should be attached to the rope on your neck with a normal cloth hanging clip which is not very powerful, so the ball can come off with one slight pull. You don't want the ball to be too securely connected to your neck, as you can be injured if your dog is quicker than you and grabs the ball before you can pull it off.

Warming Up before Training

From the development stage in puppyhood, I've already started accustoming my dog to empty himself before a lesson begins. Now we've progressed to the strengthening stage, he has to learn more skills and the exercises are more demanding. There's a necessity to do a proper warm-up before a training session. Sufficient warming up has the following benefits:

1. It allows the dog time to go to the toilet.
2. It gives him a chance to stretch and prepare his muscles and tendons for exercising, minimising the risks of injuries such as sprains and strains.
3. It offers the handler time to reinforce his leadership and pack relationship with his dog, switching the dog on to working mode.
4. If the dog has any problem physically, mentally, or in the pack order, such as an injury, a female coming in heat, or he's trying to test our leadership, we have an opportunity to recognise any behaviour out of the norm in the warm-up.

When the weather is warm, I spend about ten minutes to warm up my dogs. For colder weather, I spend fifteen to twenty minutes. During the warm-up, I can walk my dog on leash or off leash depending on his training level. I prefer wandering in quiet places near the training field such as in the woods or the meadows. I first let my dog walk in front of me for about five minutes to give him enough time to empty himself. I observe his behaviour to evaluate his physical state, mental state, and our pack relationship. If he runs too far, fixates on certain scents, or pays too much attention to the surrounding people or animals, I recall him and make him perform some obedience exercises such as here, heeling, and down, etc. to enforce my leadership and keep him under control. When I see he's responding positively by being proactive, attentive, and willing, I let him free again. By balancing the dog's control and freedom, I maintain his sensibility and working attitude. When we've wandered long enough and I see my dog is ready by initiating play, I know we're in the same channel and the lesson can begin. I take him onto the training field.

Being in the same "channel" means I'm on the same wavelength as the dog, like tuning the radio and finding the broadcasting station on the exact frequency. The sound is clear and there's no white noise disturbance in the background. When the dog is in the same channel as his master, they're a team and they know what each other is thinking. They're in one spirit. Our goal in training is to develop the one-spirit state with our dogs, so we can summon it in competitions. The warm-up simulates the pre-hunting ritual in a wolf pack in nature. When the alpha decides to hunt, he first assembles all his pack members. Every wolf gathers around and interacts with each other to re-establish their ranks and roles. Besides warming up the body, the pre-hunting ritual is a pre-mission briefing. It clarifies the function and responsibility of each member, just like an army getting ready to go into battle. A good warm-up before training thus increases the chances of a successful session.

Familiarising the Training Field

When I take a puppy under six months old to a new training field, I usually use the first session to familiarise him with the place to establish a positive experience. Once he has a good feeling with the new field, I begin proper obedience training when I go there the second time. I prepare him as follows:

1. After a proper warm-up, I enter the training field with my puppy. If he's reliable with the recall, I can let him off leash. I run away to encourage him to chase me and make body contact with me.
2. I invite him to jump up on me and reinforce the interaction with food.
3. I let my puppy chase me through the entire area of the training field so he can have the opportunity to see the whole environment. After about a minute or two, I take out a toy and let him bite it. We interact through playing tug-of-war with the toy.

4. If my puppy already knows how to fetch, I can throw the toy away and let him bring it back to play with me. After about one or two minutes, I lead him off the field with the toy in his mouth. He's made a positive association with the place. Next time, when we come here, we can do proper training.

Cooling Down after Training

Besides warming up before training, when my dog has entered the obedience strengthening stage, I also spend about five to ten minutes to let him cool down after a session. Giving the dog some time to cool off after vigorous exercise has the following advantages:

1. The dog needs to gradually slow down his heart rate and breathing. It's not healthy to put him directly back into the car when he's still pumped up with excitement.
2. It gives him time to stretch his muscles again after action.
3. It gives me an opportunity to enforce my leadership again after the end of the lesson. This strengthens our bond.

For the cool down, I also walk my dog around the training field. I usually do this with a retractable leash as it gives my dog freedom while I can maintain physical control over him without the need for telling him what to do and what not to do. As we've just finished training, in the cool down I don't require him to pay attention to me anymore. If the training session was good, this should be a time for him to relax. If the training session was bad, whatever correction I needed to make should have been done on the training field and not here. We still have tomorrow to work further on it. The end of a lesson means rest. If a handler still bosses his dog around after a session has completed, this is the same as a little child going to school; the school bell has rung for everyone to go home, he's left the school and is on his way home when he's stopped by his teacher, who demands an additional tutorial on the school bus. This is not fair, and if the handler does this all the time he will cause his dog to develop resentment towards training. Of course, all basic rules are applied for the dog during the cool down, such as not eating rubbish from the ground, not bothering the surrounding people or dogs, etc. But within these basic rules the dog can enjoy his freedom.

Contents in One Lesson

In the obedience strengthening stage first phase, my main goal is to introduce negative reinforcement and the verbal cue to each basic component. During this time, I practise about three to five behaviours with my dog in each lesson. For the table retrieve system, at its initial stage, I'd practise this alone. Once my dog has made a positive connection with the table, I'd let him practise several components before letting him go on the table to practise the hold. The dog is now older than when he was in the learning stage and he also has more experience. I can now spend about seven to twelve minutes in each lesson.

When the dog has entered the obedience-strengthening stage second phase, the elements for practice include the topics in both phase 1 and phase 2, and when he's entered the third phase, everything in phases 1, 2, and 3 will be repeated. The dog has to learn new skills while maintaining old skills. When the dog has a thorough understanding of each obedience component and its verbal command, we can focus on the fourth phase to prepare him for the BH (Companion Dog Test).

When to Introduce the Pinch Collar in Obedience

I've introduced the plastic pinch collar in the tracking strengthening stage. When the puppy is about four months old, he can start wearing this collar in obedience training as well. As he matures and gains more experience in training, his hardness will also develop. When I feel the plastic pinch collar isn't working as efficiently as when he was younger, I'll introduce the normal pinch collar. The application is the same.

In an IPO trial, the only collar a dog is allowed to wear is the metal slip chain. When we've entered the strengthening stage, besides the pinch collar, I also let my dog wear the slip chain in training so he can get used to it. In obedience training, I can replace the nylon flat collar with the slip chain. In some exercises such as send away, where I have to hold the dog's collar and let him pull forward, the chain is better for the dog to pull into than the pinch collar, as it doesn't cause any discomfort to the dog. The chain is harder and narrower than the nylon flat collar, so in bite work I'll still use the nylon collar when necessary for easier breathing for my dog.

Obedience Strengthening Stage 3rd Phase

Once I've linked negative reinforcement and the verbal command with a majority of the obedience basic components, I can start to merge them to form the IPO3 obedience exercises. In the early period of the third phase, I usually go through a session beginning with heeling off leash and end with down stay. Sometimes I'd practise down stay first and heeling off leash second. This is because in an IPO trial the obedience part is conducted by two handlers/dog teams at the same time. The teams with the odd starting numbers (1, 3, 5, 7, 9, 11, etc.) usually begin with heeling off leash, while the teams with the even starting numbers (2, 4, 6, 8, 10, 12, etc.) usually begin with down stay. Once the odd numbered team has completed the send away exercise, the two teams switch around, where the first team now goes for the down stay and the second team begins heeling off leash.

In each lesson, I'd decide which and how many exercises to practise depending on my dog's training progress. For a young dog, I usually select four to seven exercises out of the total nine for practice in a single lesson. I'll start going through the entire routine when my dog is old enough with a more advanced training level.

Basic Components	IPO3 Obedience Exercises								
	Heeling off leash	Sit in motion	Down in motion	Stand in motion	Retrieve	Retrieve over hurdle	Retrieve over A-frame	Send away	Down stay
Attention	✓	✓	✓	✓	✓	✓	✓	✓	✓
Look forward					✓	✓	✓	✓	
Sit	✓	✓	✓	✓	✓	✓	✓	✓	✓
Down								✓	✓
Stand				✓					
Front position		✓	✓		✓	✓	✓		
Go ahead					✓	✓	✓	✓	
Basic position	✓	✓	✓	✓	✓	✓	✓	✓	✓
Hold					✓	✓	✓		
Release					✓	✓	✓		
Jump						✓			
Climb							✓		
Additional Components									
Heel right									
Backwards									
Target plates									

Heeling Off Leash

Heeling off leash is made up of three components including attention, sit, and basic position. In fact, my dog already has plenty of practice in the obedience-strengthening stage phases 1 and 2. All I need to do now is to teach him left turn, right turn, left about turn, the group, figure 8 and heeling in different tempos, and accustom him to gunshots. Although this exercise is supposed to be done without a leash, it doesn't mean I have to remove the leash from my dog at the beginning. If necessary, I'll continue to use the leash and the whip until my dog is 100% precise before I fade them out.

1. Left turn, right turn, left about turn: I wear a training vest. In the front pockets on both sides I have dry dog food. In the left back pocket I have a rubber ball. I hold a horse whip in my left hand and an 80cm loopless leash with my right hand. The leash can be held in front of me or behind me. The dog already knows he should be focusing on my face and staying by my left side when he hears the "Heel" command. He follows me as I walk, and sits as I stop. For the turning, I usually turn more to the left at the beginning, because doing too much right-turn at the initial stage can cause the dog to swing his buttocks out, which decreases his precision. When I practise the left turn, initially I turn slightly to give the dog a chance

to straighten out. After a few times I can do a complete 90° left turn. Previously I've taught my dog to turn 90° and 180° on the same spot with a horse whip. When I do the left turn and left about turn now, I can use the whip to keep his buttocks tucked in. I can also insert several portable sticks into the ground and use them to guide the dog's body and keep him straight after the turns. After a few sessions of practising left turns and left about turns, I can try a few right turns at a slight angle, and do a complete 90° right turn after a few repetitions. I have to keep the dog focusing on me when we're turning. If he doesn't keep his attention on me during the turn, I can correct him by giving him a slight tug on the leash. When he's heeling well, I can praise him with my voice or reward him with food. For an especially nice turn I throw him the ball as a reward. Gradually I decrease the frequency of my rewards and make them more selective to the dog's better performances. I also prolong the period between reinforcements to make the dog work longer. He should eventually be able to continue heeling for three minutes without any reward. I can then give him one jackpot (such as a big piece of meat or playing fetch for two minutes) instead of many little rewards in between.

2. The group and figure 8: in an IPO trial's obedience part, there's a group of four people which I must go through with my dog and perform a figure 8 course. Figure 8 means we have to go around one person on our left and go around one person on our right. After that, we have to go to the centre of the group and stop for about three seconds when my dog sits attentively next to me. In the first few times of entering the group, I'd feed my dog to make a positive association. After several sessions he'll be pumped with drive as we

approach the crowd. The figure 8 is just two extra wide left and right about-turns. If there are not enough people to stand in the group for training, I can place four portable sticks in the ground for practice instead.

3. Heeling in different tempos: in the heeling off leash exercise, the handler has to demonstrate three different tempos, including normal pace, running pace, and slow pace. My dog heels in normal pace most of the time. When we practise running pace, I have to be careful so the dog doesn't get too excited and start to hop with both front paws up like a kangaroo as this will cause a deduction in points. I run with slow and long strides in the beginning. If my dog starts to bounce, I'll give the leash a tug backwards and give his chin a flick with the whip to stop him. In slow heeling, we have to be careful the dog doesn't try to walk and sit at the same time as he's used to sitting when we stop. When I see he anticipates sitting, I'd make longer strides.

4. Gunshots: from IPO I, the obedience phase has four gunshots; two shots in heeling off leash and two shots in down stay. When my dog is about six months old, I start to familiarise him with the sound of firing a starting pistol. Initially, I take him to a forest and ask a friend to fire the gun about 100m away from me and the dog. I sit next to my dog. As soon as the gun is fired, I feed him some food. My friend then comes closer so he's about 90m from us and fires the gun again. I feed my dog again. He then comes to 80m and we repeat the procedure. After three shots, I take my dog for a wander in the forest and we end the session. After a few days, my friend shoots at a distance of 70, 60, and 50m and I feed my dog after each shot. After another few days he fires the gun at 40, 30, and 20m. I observe my dog's behaviour when the gun goes off. Normally he should get used to the sound of a gun quite well, as we start from far away and he's reinforced by food every time, just like

how we use classical conditioning to introduce the clicker. Once my dog is used to hearing the gunshots in the forest, I condition him on the training field the same way, and then in heeling. If a starting pistol is difficult to obtain, you can use firecrackers instead.

5. Fading out the leash and horse whip: dog training equipment is like scaffolding in construction. When a skyscraper is being built, construction workers use scaffolding on its outer walls so they can work on the building. Once the construction is completed, the scaffolding is removed. When maintenance and repairs need to be carried out, the construction workers set up the scaffolding again. The function of the scaffolds isn't to bear the weight of the building or support its structure permanently. Instead, it's a device to help building and repairing. This is the same as us adopting the leash, whip, target stick, rubber ball, etc. into our training. Our intention is to teach the dog all the behaviours of the Schutzhund programme. Eventually, we have to remove all the training aids and the dog has to maintain the same performance standard. Therefore, when the dog is up to a certain training level and I see he can show the same behaviour without the need of regular encouragements or corrections, I'd spend one session without using the leash, the whip, the ball, or food. I let my dog go through three to five exercises without any reward or help and compare his behaviour with the training before to decide which tools need to be continuously utilised and which tools can be faded out. If he can perform the entire heeling pattern under distraction beautifully and precisely without the help of the leash and the whip, I'd stop using these two pieces of equipment for now. When I see there's a need for further adjustment in the future, I'll employ them until the behaviour is consistent again. Regarding food and toys, I keep them in my pockets in most of the training sessions (occasionally I place them somewhere else

instead of on me so the dog can get used to working without me carrying any reward). However, I shall be very selective in my reinforcement, only rewarding excellent behaviour. To keep a young dog motivated in his work, when he's completed a good session, I play with him at the end and take him for a wander in the woods as his reward. Dog training is like body building; there are only periods of peaking but no periods of finishing. A body builder can train his muscles to develop their maximum size and definition to be champion, but if he doesn't return to the gym after that his muscles won't be able to stay in the same peak condition permanently. Perfection can only be achieved with constant maintenance and fine-tuning.

Sit in Motion

The sit in motion exercise requires the dog to sit fast and straight immediately on his handler's verbal command. The handler must continue to walk forward without slowing down or looking back at his dog. He's not allowed to help the dog with any additional gesture.

1. First accustom the dog to respond instantly to the "Sit" command: I connect a 1.4m leash to my dog's pinch collar and walk ahead slowly without giving him any commands. He can walk in front of me, on my left, or on my right. All I want him to do is to hang around and pay attention to me. I keep eye contact with him; when I see he's 100% focused, I say "Sit". If he doesn't respond at once, I tighten the leash upward to apply slight pressure. My dog has already learnt leading to sit and the verbal command. The application of these two cues will surely get the correct response. When his buttocks are on the ground, I reinforce him with food. After he stays in sit for about ten seconds, I say "Yes" to release him before repeating the process again.

2. Accustom the dog to focus on me for thirty seconds in sitting under distraction, prolong our distance to fifteen steps: once my dog can respond to my verbal command alone as I'm walking, I can gradually fade out the leading. When his sit is slow, I can use leading again to increase his speed. If he

can sit quickly without the aid of the leash, I'd reinforce him with fetching the ball. Besides sharpening his reflex for sit, I also raise the criteria of his focus under distraction during sit stay. Its method is the same as what we've done in the second phase. My training assistant makes a disruption while I keep the dog's attention on me. I reinforce good focus

with food and biting a toy. When my dog can sit with focus under distraction for thirty seconds, I'll ease the interruption and extend the distance between us. Eventually he can stay sitting while I leave him for fifteen steps or more. I can pass the leash to my assistant so he holds the dog from behind and corrects him in case he moves.

3. Practise sit in motion like in a trial: when my dog has a solid foundation of sitting with speed and focus, I can practise the exercise like we're in a trial. To prevent him from anticipating my verbal command, I vary the number of steps I take before saying "Sit", such as telling him to sit on the 10th step, 15th step, 20th step, etc. Sometimes I go ahead without telling him to sit at all, then do an about-turn and give the command as we're returning.

Down in Motion

1. First accustom the dog to respond instantly to the "Down" command: I attach a 1.4m leash to my dog's pinch collar and walk forward slowly without saying anything. He can walk in front of me, on my left, or on my right. All I want him to do is to hang around and pay attention to me. I keep eye contact with him; when I see he's 100% focused, I say "Down". If he doesn't respond immediately, I give the leash a downward tug with my right hand while pressing him on the back of his neck with my left hand. My dog has learnt leading and pressing to down and its verbal command previously. Applying all three of these cues will certainly get the correct response. When his elbows and belly contact the ground, I

reinforce him with food. After he stays down for about ten seconds, I say "Yes" to release him before repeating the process again.

2. Accustom the dog to focus on me for thirty seconds in down under distraction, prolong our distance to thirty steps: once my dog can respond to the word "Down" alone as I'm walking, I can gradually fade out the leading and pressing. When his down is slow, I can use pressing again to increase his speed. If he can lie down quickly without pressing, I'd reinforce him with fetching the ball. In addition to sharpening his speed for the down, I also increase the demand of his focus under distraction during down stay with the help of my assistant. I reinforce good focus with food and biting a toy. When my dog can down with focus under distraction for thirty seconds, I'll ease the disturbance and lengthen the distance between us. Eventually he can stay down while I leave him for thirty paces or more. I can pass the leash to my assistant so he holds the dog from behind and corrects him in case he moves.

3. Practise down in motion like in a trial: when my dog has a solid foundation of lying down with speed and focus, I can practise the exercise like we're in a trial. In the obedience phase of IPO3, the handler needs to down his dog in running. In training, I can tell my dog to lie down at different speeds. To prevent him from anticipating my verbal command, I vary the number of steps I take before saying "Down". Sometimes I go ahead without telling him to down at all, then turn around and give the command as we're returning.

4. From down to the front position: I wear a 50cm cotton rope loosely around my neck and clip a rubber ball onto it with a cloth hanging clip. I wear a training vest over it so my dog can't see the ball. My dog is attached to a 3m loopless leash, which is held in both of my hands behind my back. My dog lies down about 2m in front of me and I stand with my feet apart so he can come as close to me as possible. I give the verbal command "Here" and lead him into the front position. When he sits straight before me attentively, I say "Yes" and take out the ball from my collar, and let him jump up to grab it. I can also first detach the ball from the rope and keep it in my hand before dropping it straight down to my dog. This is a safer way to reward him. Please be careful here to prevent injuries. Getting smashed in the mouth by a dog's head butt is not fun at all. Once he's used to coming from down to here, I gradually increase the distance between us to 30m. When my dog is so far away, I can give the leash to my training assistant to prevent the dog from coming before I give the command. The dog should wear a short loopless line now to avoid him stepping onto it when he's running to me and give himself an accidental correction. For this reason, the line should also be attached to a normal collar instead of the pinch collar. When the distance between the dog and me is 10m or longer, I can stand with my feet together as required in a trial. In the IPO obedience phase, the judge wants to see a dog coming fast and close in the front position without touching his handler, so we need to teach our dogs to come in front of us at a range between 1 to 10cm. If my dog is too enthusiastic and likes to body slam me when he comes in, I'll stand with my knees bent forward. When he charges into me too closely, he's going to crash his chest into my

protruding knees. After two or three times he will stop doing it and should sit in front of me without the body slam. If you have a bad knee, it may be safer to wear kneepads. For a fast and correct recall, I reinforce my dog with a bite at the ball.

5. From the front position to the basic position: I've already taught my dog to tuck his hindquarters into me for the flip finish in the first phase. To avoid anticipation for coming to my left when I recall him, I don't ask for the finish all the time. Usually, when my dog comes precisely in front of me after the down, I'd reinforce him with food, or give him the ball, or tell him to sit and I step to his right side before telling him to heel. Once my dog knows

what the finish is, I might ask him for the behaviour one in ten times when I call him to the front position with the command "Return". If I need to make any adjustment to make the finish sharper, I can do it independently away from the down in motion exercise. When he flips quickly and correctly next to me, I reward him with fetching the ball. This principle applies also to stand in motion, retrieve, retrieve over hurdle, and retrieve over A-frame.

Stand in Motion

1. First accustom the dog to respond instantly to the "Stand" command: I first let my dog walk freely in front of me or next to me as I'm holding a horse whip in my right hand. All I need him to do is to hang around and pay attention to me. I keep eye contact with him; when I

see he's 100% focused, I say "Stand". If he doesn't respond directly, I tap him on the chest with the whip. He has learnt reverse targeting to stand and its verbal command previously. Applying both cues will bring the correct response. The force of using the whip is usually no more than a light flick. The lighter it is to get the desired behaviour the better. When he stands stably and has no intention of moving forward, I say "Yes" and reward him with food before repeating the process again.

2. Accustom the dog to focus on me for thirty seconds in stand, the assistant uses the waistband to prevent the dog from stepping forward, prolong our distance to thirty steps: in the three positions of sit, down, and stand, standing is the most unstable position. Just one little step forward in stand in motion in a championship can already lower the rating of the exercise by one category. To develop a solid stand, one of the methods I use is by the waistband as I've previously explained. This time, I let my dog wear the waistband and give the attached 2m loopless leash to my training assistant, who's standing behind the dog. I stand before my dog and show him a moving bite roll to get him a bit excited. When he tries to come forward to get the bite roll, my assistant stops him by tugging on the waistband from behind and loosens the leash again. When my dog stands solidly for at least five seconds, I say "Yes" and the assistant releases the dog so he can come for a bite.

I gradually increase the distance and try to tempt the dog from going out of the stand by constantly tapping the bite roll on my palm. The assistant corrects him if he moves. When the dog is standing well, I go back to about 1 or 2m in front of him and reinforce him with a bite again. I don't let the dog run to me from far away when he's wearing the waistband. This can be dangerous if he steps on the leash. A suddenly tightened waistband can hurt a male dog's penis.

3. Practise stand in motion like in a trial: when my dog has a solid stand, I can practice the exercise like we're in a trial. In the obedience phase of IPO3, the handler needs to command his dog to stand in running. In training, I can tell my dog to stand at different speeds. To prevent him from anticipating my verbal command, I vary the number of steps I take before saying "Stand". Sometimes I go ahead without telling him to stand at all, then turn around and give the command as we're returning. When necessary, I continue to employ the waistband and the help of my training assistant to maintain the reflex and stability of the stand.

4. From stand to the front position: this is exactly the same as in down in motion.
5. From the front position to the basic position: same as in down in motion.

Retrieve

The three retrieval exercises require the most basic components in the IPO obedience phase, but as we've taught our dog each component step by step independently, all we need to do now is to put them together.

1. Accustom the dog to hold the dumbbell in front of me: before starting this step, the dog must have a positive association with the dumbbell and willingly take it in his mouth. The

table retrieve system I've explained in the first phase is an excellent method to teach this. I come to the training field with my dog. He wears a pinch collar connected to a 2m loopless leash, which I hold in both hands behind my back. I tell him to lie down before me and hold a dumbbell in his mouth. I stand with my legs apart and let the leash pass between them. I give the command "Here" and lead my dog into the front position so he's sitting in front of me while holding the dumbbell. As soon as he's in position, I say "Yes" and show him the ball, which was hidden in my collar attached to a rope around my neck. If he's still holding the dumbbell, I say "Give" before letting him have the ball. After playing for half a minute, I repeat the same process. I prolong the distance between us each time. After a few sessions I can call my dog to me from 5m away while holding the dumbbell. I can now use an 8m retractable leash instead. This teaches the dog the quicker he comes into front position with the dumbbell in his mouth, the quicker he can receive the ball as his reward. This training sequence is opposite to the old way of teaching the retrieve. In the traditional method, the handler's first step is throwing the dumbbell away and getting the dog to bring it back in prey drive. Although the dog is motivated to go out for the dumbbell, his common problems with this method are mouthing the dumbbell, returning slowly, and sitting at a distance from the handler in the front position. This is because if the dog hasn't been taught to first hold the dumbbell firmly he usually mouths it and treats it as a toy. When the handler sees this, he typically corrects the dog for mouthing. After a while, the dog becomes reluctant in coming back as he's associated the front position with stress. With the new sequence we employ, we teach the end first, and use back chaining to complete the learning of the whole exercise. This way the dog has a positive association in coming back, and we can make the retrieve fast and firm.

2. Accustom the dog to directly bring back the dumbbell as soon as he takes it in his mouth: when the dog is used to returning with the dumbbell quickly, I can now throw it out for the retrieve. I have my dog in basic position while we're facing a fence about 5m in front of us. I throw the dumbbell towards the fence, and then say "Hold" while I give the leash a slight tug forward. The fence prevents the dog from running over the dumbbell before picking it up. It keeps his return tight and direct. As he takes the dumbbell into his mouth, I say

"Here" and give a light tug at the leash towards me. The dog comes in front of me while holding the dumbbell calmly. This technique keeps the dog fast, straight, and direct in his retrieve. When he's sitting before me correctly and holds the dumbbell firmly, I say "Yes" and reward him with the ball. Once the dog is used to this training, I fade out the leash and increase the distance of retrieve.

3. Increase the retrieving distance: the dog now goes up and comes back quickly while holding the dumbbell. I don't need the leash anymore. The distance is extended to 10m. I can replace the two "Hold" and "Here" commands by one "Bring" command. This is done by classical conditioning. All I need to do is to say "Bring" just before I say "Hold". After a while the "Bring" command will replace the "Hold" command. As the dog has established bringing the dumbbell back as a habit. I no longer need to say "Here".

4. Release: by now, my dog should have a reliable release with all the foundation work in the first phase. Usually, I reinforce the hold behaviour in the retrieval exercises more than the release behaviour, as rewarding the release too often can cause some dogs to chew the dumbbell in anticipation.

5. From the front position to the basic position: same as in the down in motion exercise.

Retrieve Over Hurdle

1. Accustom the dog to come to me over the hurdle while holding the dumbbell: at the beginning, I set the hurdle's height to a level that's easy for the dog to clear. I attach a 5m loopless leash to his collar and tell him to lie down while holding the dumbbell and facing the hurdle. I go to the other side of the hurdle and stand facing him. My training assistant holds the leash for me and stands next to the hurdle. When the dog looks at me, I say "Jump" and "Here" while my assistant leads him over the hurdle and my dog comes to the front position. When he sits precisely and holds the dumbbell calmly before me, I say "Yes" and let him take the ball. After several sessions, my dog is used to returning to me quickly while holding the dumbbell and clearing the hurdle.

2. Accustom the dog to directly bring back the dumbbell as soon as he takes it in his mouth; regardless of where it has landed, the dog must jump out and jump back: I first insert a portable fence into the ground where the dumbbell will land. This prevents the dog from running past it during the retrieve. I stand facing the hurdle with my dog in basic position. My assistant holds the leash. I throw the dumbbell over the hurdle and it lands before the fence. I say "Jump" and my assistant leads the dog over the hurdle. As my dog is jumping over it, I say "Bring". He picks up the dumbbell and the assistant leads him over the hurdle again. When my dog holds the dumbbell firmly in the basic position, I release him and reinforce him with hunt drive/prey drive by giving him the ball. When the dog

has more experience in this exercise, sometimes I deliberately throw the dumbbell out of the centre line to tempt him from going to the dumbbell or returning without jumping over the hurdle. When he tries this, my assistant corrects him with the leash and makes him jump the hurdle like he should. When my dog is proofed in this, I fade out the leash and lengthen the distance for the retrieve.

3. Practise retrieve over hurdle as the trial requires, gradually increase the height of the hurdle to 1m: when the dog has formed a good habit of jumping, we can gradually increase the height of the hurdle to 1m. The release and the finish are the same as retrieving on flat ground.

Retrieve Over A-Frame

The retrieve over A-frame exercise is basically the same as retrieve over hurdle. The only difference is we have to make sure the dog comes all the way down instead of jumping down from the top of the A-frame. At the beginning when I teach the dog to return over the A-frame, I keep our distance very short so I'm standing only about 1m from the A-frame. This way I'm blocking the dog so he has no chance to jump down from the top.

Send Away

1. Associate a landmark as the target for the send away: when I was teaching the look forward and go ahead components, the dog was already learning the foundation of the send away exercise. When he can run the whole length of the training field in the go ahead, I would place a bite roll between the two goal posts before training so the dog doesn't see me preparing it. Before I send him, I'd get him to heel like in the trial. When he's heeling with excellent focus and precision, I send him to the goal to get his bite roll as a reward. Please note I only reward the dog in such a manner in the send away exercise and not in normal heeling and the positions to avoid confusing him.

2. Teach the dog the centre line of the field: as the exercises of heeling, sit, down, and stand are all performed on the centre line of the field, and send away is always after these exercises, when the dog has more and more experience from training in different places he'll realise a requirement of the send away is following the centre line to the end or until I say "Down". When I train my dog on a new field, I let my dog practise the exercises in trial order. By the time we do the send away he's already familiar with the centre line of the new field. All I need to do is to show him the bite roll at the end of the field and send him two

or three times from a short distance. After a few repetitions he can usually run the entire length of the field for the send away.

3. A fast and reliable down: when my dog becomes about one year old and his drives have been well developed, if I feel the time is right, I'll start preparing him for the down in the send away. However, I don't do this on the training field as this might affect his speed and focus for going forward. I'll teach him as follows:

Down Rapidly in the Send Away

1. Teaching a sharp down during a walk: when my dog is used to responding to the "Down" command, I'll tell him to down randomly during a walk. I have him walking in front of me on leash and let him explore the surroundings. I wait until he's not paying attention to me and say "Down" and then give the leash a downward tug to make him lie down. It's essential I teach him to respond to my command when he's not paying any attention to me at all. If he can't do this in a walk, forget about calling him down when he's going in full speed towards the goal when he thinks his bite roll is lying there. As soon as he's in the down position, I say "Yes" and let him come to me for a bite on a bite roll. I do this two to three times in a walk. The idea is to get the dog to lie down immediately on cue when he's not paying attention to me, because in the send away I call him down when he's at a dead run towards the end of the field.

2. Teaching a sharp down while fetching a ball: when my dog can down immediately during a walk without the need for tugging the leash, I now attach his flat collar to an 8m retractable leash and play fetch with him on an open field. I throw a ball forward for about 5m and tell my dog to bring it back; after two or three times, as he's running out for the ball, I say "Down" and give the leash a downward tug. As the leash restricts him from taking the ball, he must lie down. As soon as he's down, I take out a second ball from my pocket and let him come and bite it. This teaches him to turn around in the down during the send away; as he

expects a reward coming from me, he naturally turns to look at me as he goes down. Calling the dog down in fetching teaches him to respond to my command in high drive. It's very important for a working dog to remain functional and controllable when he's in a highly excited state. Otherwise we wouldn't be able to control him and it can be very dangerous in some situations. I keep playing fetch with him and I don't tell him to down anymore in this session. In the next lesson, I tell him to down again after him fetching the ball a few times. Please take note that our goal is to accustom the dog to respond to "Down" when he's not expecting it. Therefore we mustn't overdo it and we should refrain from tugging on the leash too hard, otherwise the dog will pay more attention to us than to going out, and this will affect the speed and focus of the go ahead. When my dog can down immediately on command while chasing a ball, I gradually fade out the leash.

3. Accustoming the dog to run past me in the send away: I stand about 5m in front of the goal and my dog is 5m further away without a leash. When my dog is focusing on the goal, I give the "Go" command so he runs past me to the centre of the goal and picks up his bite roll. I repeat this process several times and for several sessions. When the dog is used to running past me in the send away, I send him in the same way, but this time when he's almost in front of me I give the verbal command "Down" and then I jump in front of him to block him from going further. He has to comply and go down. I take out a second bite roll from my pocket and reinforce him. We end the session. Next time, I do the same, first sending him to the end a few times before calling him down and blocking him.

4. Down the dog in the send away exercise like in a trial: when I feel the time is right, for two sessions I'll send him again from heeling like I would do in a trial. I let him go to the end to pick up the bite roll I've

prepared. In the third session, I send him the same way but this time I don't put any bite roll at the end but by habit the dog thinks it's there. I send him away. When he's about 10m from the goal, I say "Down" in a loud voice as he's now more than 50m away from me. If he lies down, I go to him to reward him with a bite roll from my pocket and finish the session. If he doesn't listen and chooses to keep running to the end, he'll discover the bite roll is not there and he ran for nothing. I now walk towards him and tell him "Down" again. I end the session without giving him anything. The next lesson I do the same. Very soon he'll realise it's more beneficial to respond to my commands than to act on his own. Once he has a fast and reliable down in the send away, I only call him down about one in ten training sessions. When I know in a particular lesson I'll call him down, I don't put any toy at the end so my dog won't be rewarded if he decides to keep going instead of downing.

I can increase the dog's focus, speed, and reliability in the send away by using the target plate, the teletact, and very light negative stimulation on his tail. However, this is a much more advanced technique and will be explained in *The Schutzhund Training Manual 2*.

For the movement of going up into the basic position from down, please see Down Stay.

Down Stay

My dog already has a good foundation in the down in motion exercise. For the down stay, I only need to get him used to staying down for longer periods (five to ten minutes). He'll hear two gunshots in the down stay, which I've familiarised him with previously. There's a quick, easy, and reliable way to stabilise the down stay. I attach two leashes to my dog. One 5m leash is connected to his slip chain and is tied to a fixed object such as a goal post or a fence. Another 10m leash is attached to his pinch collar and held in my hand. I train this in an area with some distractions. If there's one or more dogs training with their handlers in the field, that's even better. At the beginning, when my dog can stay calmly and attentively for one minute, I go to him and reinforce him with dry food. If he moves, looks around too much, and fixates on the other dogs, I give him a leash correction with the long line to keep his focus on me. Gradually I increase the time to ten minutes. I reward him with playing fetch at the end. Besides doing this training in a dog club, when I take him for his daily walk, I can practise this on a street or in the car park of a supermarket. The

different distractions are very good for his experience. Sometimes I go out of sight and watch him from behind a cover, so he gets used to staying in my absence. Once he's reliable in the down stay, I can do this on the training field without a leash.

In a trial, at the end of the down stay I have to go and pick up my dog. This means calling him into the basic position with the "Heel" command from the down. This is simply done by luring him with food with my left hand, and leading him upward with my right hand. By this time my dog has very good obedience; he'll learn this in a few sessions. Afterwards I can fade out the food and the leash and just get him to sit up with the "Heel" command alone.

Obedience Strengthening Stage 4th Phase

Preparing for BH (Companion Dog Examination)

BH Obedience Phase		
Exercise 1:	Heeling on leash	15 points
Exercise 2:	Heeling off leash	15 points
Exercise 3:	Sit in motion	10 points
Exercise 4:	Down in motion	10 points
Exercise 5:	Down stay	10 points
Total		60 points
BH Temperament Test		
Exercise 1:	Encounter with a group of people	
Exercise 2:	Encounter with joggers or inline skaters	
Exercise 3:	Encounter with bicyclist	
Exercise 4:	Encounter with cars	
Exercise 5:	Encounter with other dogs	
Exercise 6:	Behaviour of the tethered dog towards other animals when left alone	
Result	Pass or fail	

If you follow the training sequence I've explained above step by step, by the time your dog is one year old he should have a very solid base for most of the exercises in IPO3 obedience. The minimum trialling age for the BH test is fifteen months old. The criteria in the BH are much easier than IPO. If a dog can perform the whole IPO3 obedience routine, he should have no problem in the BH.

The elements in the BH temperament test are very similar to the things we encounter when we socialise our dogs. As long as a dog has been adequately exposed to different environments, people, and other dogs, he should pass the test without a problem.

To ensure the dog does everything in the BH effortlessly, I'd limit his obedience training to the BH routine alone three weeks prior the test. I'd also walk him in town or markets and let him practise obedience such as heeling and down stay in similar conditions to get him used to performing in a crowd of people.

Protection Strengthening Stage

In the strengthening stage of the protection phase, besides teaching the whole IPO3 protection routine to my dog, my other goal is to develop his practical combative abilities to be a versatile dual-purpose working dog. The main difference between the protection phase and tracking and obedience is the confrontation with the decoy. In addition to the dog's genetic capabilities, his training, experience, physical maturity, and mental maturity are all essential. The dog must have grown to a certain age to handle the decoy's oppression. Therefore, the handler and decoy need to constantly observe and evaluate the dog's behaviour in bite work training to decide when to progress to a more demanding level. For some technical parts for which the decoy is not needed, the handler can teach the dog the proper techniques alone. When the dog is old and experienced enough, we can bring the decoy into the picture to continue with the exercise.

Choosing the Right Sleeve

A dog goes through a range of bite sleeves as he gains experience and maturity. Generally, the younger and greener the dog, the softer the sleeve he bites. The older and more experienced the dog, the harder the sleeve we use. Usually the decoy decides which sleeve suits a dog best based on his observation and feeling. Eventually, when the dog has developed a full, firm, and hard grip consistently, he can bite the trial sleeve. Some specialised European working dog equipment manufacturers have categorised their sleeves based on their firmness and thickness. For example, there are puppy sleeve number 1, number 2, young dog sleeve number 1, number 2, and so on. The decoys have a wide range of choices (see the table opposite).

In the protection learning stage, we've taught the dog the three basic protection behaviours including bite, out, and bark. He's also learnt the run around and the other seven basic obedience components in the protection exercises. This means all I need to do is to maintain control in all the exercises and develop the dog's power as he matures and through working with the decoy. When the dog is old enough, we can combine all the biting and controlling techniques to form the entire IPO3 protection routine while sustaining the balance between the dog's wildness and tameness.

First Step of Introducing Control in Bite Work

When my puppy was developing his skills for biting, barking, and confronting the decoy in the

Common Biting Target in Schutzhund Protection Training	When to Use
Puppy sleeve	For puppies first learning how to bite. The decoy can wear it or hold it in his hands
Young dog sleeve	For a young dog that has developed a full, firm, and calm grip. It's harder and thicker than the puppy sleeve. The dog needs to open his mouth wider to get a full grip. It can be worn or held
Hard bite cushion	For dogs that already have foundational bite work training and are learning the jump attack. Its hardness is the same as the trial sleeve but it's lighter and shorter, and can be worn or held by the decoy at different heights and angles to encourage the dog to jump into the attack. The hard bite cushion is usually employed after a dog has finished teething and has a good grip
Trial sleeve	When the dog has learned all the necessary skills with the other sleeves and bites well on them, he can practise on the trial sleeve, which is worn by the decoy

protection learning stage, my goal was to establish his confidence, dominance, and hunting instincts. Once his grip is consistently full, firm, and calm, and all his adult teeth have emerged, I'll start to insert elements of obedience in bite work to teach him when he can and can't bite. When he responds to me well, his reward is to confront the decoy or get a bite at the sleeve.

1. Making the dog sit when he's alerting on leash: regardless of how well my puppy can bite, to avoid suppressing his wolfishness I usually don't ask for any strict control behaviour such as attention to me during bite work training until he's more mature. After he's six months old, if I feel the employing of control won't interfere with the development of his power, I'd insert a small degree of obedience elements. I begin with holding my dog on a 5m loopless leash and let him alert at the decoy by barking. As he's focusing on the decoy and barking at him actively in front of me, I tell him "Sit" while the decoy temporarily stops his stimulation. My dog usually doesn't respond to my "Sit" command at this point as he's used to being in drive when facing off the decoy. I apply upward tension on his flat collar and press his buttocks down so he has to sit. He might try to struggle free to get to the decoy. I just have to be patient and continue until he sits. Please note that we need time and patience at the initial stage of bringing in control during bite work. To teach a dog not to bite is simple but to teach him to bite is difficult. When a puppy or a young dog shows a lot of eagerness to

engage the decoy, this is a very good sign. It means he has a burning desire. Our job is to nurture this fire so it works in our favour, and not to kill it just because we want to achieve temporary control. The dog won't continue to charge at the decoy wildly forever. As soon as he responds to my command by sitting briefly (one second), I say "Take him" and the decoy starts to stimulate him immediately. I let my dog alert at the decoy on a taut line. When his drive and focus is optimum for biting, the decoy goes backward, and I let my dog run out at him for the attack by releasing the leash slightly, so it slips through my hands with a degree of friction. Once the dog is biting, the decoy maintains the fullness, firmness, and calmness of the grip while encouraging him to push (or pull) actively. If the dog is already familiar with the clatter stick in bite work, the decoy can use it to stimulate the dog's drive. Good biting earns the dog the sleeve. I let him hold the sleeve in his mouth for about a minute so he can satisfy his prey drive and calm down before I tell him to out and start the process again. We continue training as such for several lessons. The dog has learnt that by complying with me, he can go for biting. I gradually extend the time of sitting to up to five seconds. For now he can keep looking at the decoy as he's sitting in front of me.

2. When the dog can respond by sitting during alerting on leash, I make him focus on me in

the basic position: now the dog can sit on command in the alert, I come next to his right side so we're in the basic position. I give the command "Heel". Usually at this point, even though the dog is sitting, in his head he only has the decoy, so most likely he's not going to look up at me just because I say "Heel". The decoy is the biggest attraction to a working dog, but at the same time he's also the biggest distraction. Don't be surprised that your dog can heel next to you with perfect attention in a crowded market but doesn't hear you when he sees the decoy. This is normal at the beginning of putting control in the protection phase. Again, patience is very important. I can just wait without doing anything, or I can tug at his leash upward and whistle slightly to get his attention. I prefer waiting so the dog can learn by self-discovery as he can't look at the decoy forever. After waiting for so long without my release, he'll naturally look up at me to see what's going on. At this

very moment I say "Take him" and the decoy starts his stimulation. I hold the leash until the dog is in good drive and focus, and let the line run through my hands with some friction to control the speed so my dog can enter the bite with correct techniques. His attention to me has been reinforced by biting. We repeat this training for a few sessions until the dog can focus on me in the basic position for up to five seconds.

3. When the dog can focus on me in the presence of the decoy, I make him heel: when I enter the field for bite work now, I require my dog to pay attention to me in the basic position by saying "Heel" before I let him go for the alert. The decoy waits for us on the field and doesn't stimulate the dog at this time. As my dog keeps his focus on me, I start walking forward and make him follow me. When I have taken several steps and the dog can keep looking at me in heeling, I say "Take him" to reward his behaviour. The decoy comes within 5m of the dog. When the dog's motivation and concentration are in balance, I slip the line and let him attack. When I practise heeling and reward the dog with biting, I usually walk away from the decoy or keep the decoy on our left side, so when my dog goes out to alert on the leash the dog goes away from me and not into me. I refrain from having the decoy on my right in this part of the training, because in this situation my dog will form a habit of going to my right side for the alert, and this can cause him to crowd me or swing his hindquarters out while heeling.

The attention and the heeling in the decoy's presence are an essential step in developing the IPO protection routine, as it brings us control over the dog when he's in a highly excited state. When the dog has a good attack and he can heel next to me with very good focus for fifteen seconds with the decoy near us, we can start putting the protection exercises together.

	IPO3 Protection Exercises							
Basic components	Hide search	Hold and bark	Prevention of the escape	Re-attack	Back transport	Attack during back transport	Long attack	Re-attack
Bite			✓	✓		✓	✓	✓
Out			✓	✓		✓	✓	✓
Bark		✓	✓	✓		✓	✓	✓
Run around	✓							
Attention	✓	✓	✓				✓	✓
Look forward	✓	✓	✓	✓	✓	✓	✓	✓
Sit	✓	✓	✓	✓		✓	✓	✓
Down			✓					
Front position (Come)	✓	✓						
Go ahead	✓		✓	✓		✓	✓	✓
Basic position	✓	✓	✓	✓	✓	✓	✓	✓

Searching the Hides

The hide search exercise is made up of seven basic components including run around, attention, look forward, sit, front position (come), go ahead, and basic position. It seems complicated, but it's actually quite simple. All the dog needs to do is to search the hide we direct him to, and come back when we call him. In the protection learning stage, I've already taught the dog three methods of searching the hide, which includes luring with food, luring with a toy, and luring with a decoy. IPO3 requires a dog to search six hides. In the beginning of searching multiple hides, I usually train the dog without the decoy to keep the drive lower and easier to manage.

1. From searching one hide to two hides without a decoy: I've already taught my dog to go around the hide in the learning stage. By now I don't need to reward his correct behaviour all the time. My reinforcement should be selective and random. I use food or a toy as the dog's reward when he demonstrates a particularly good search of a hide. For convenience, I have the food in my pockets most of the time instead of placing it in the hide. With the toy, I can place it on me or on a ball stand in the hide. When I first start to let my dog search two hides, I'd put a ball in the second hide. If I'm using portable hides for training, I'd shorten the distance between them to about 7m so it's easier for the dog to target the hides. I let

my dog wear a short loopless leash and send him around the first hide, which he's familiar with. I call him back as he comes out and reinforce him with a little bit of dry dog food. I take his leash and lead him to face the second hide. I tell him to sit and point at the second hide and wait until he looks at it. I then say "Search" and he goes around it, where he'll find the ball. I call him to me and we have a brief game of tug-of-war. After my dog's outed the ball, I place it back on the ball stand in the second hide and repeat the whole procedure again from the first hide. I do this another two or three times. The fifth time, when my dog is coming to me from the first hide, instead of making him stop to sit in the basic position, I turn my body towards the second hide and send him there directly. If necessary, I take a few steps towards it to better show the dog. When he can search the two hides smoothly without stopping, I end this session or go on practising another exercise. In the following lessons, I continue to train my dog to search the two hides. In every repetition, there are the following possibilities: 1) there's a ball in the first hide. The dog takes it while going around the hide and brings it back to me. 2) There's no ball in either hide. When the dog returns from the first hide, I reinforce him with a ball from my pocket. 3) There's no ball in either hide. When the dog returns from the first hide, I reinforce him with food from my pockets. 4) There's no ball in the first hide. When the dog returns from it, I send him directly to the second hide, where the ball is. 5) There's no ball in either hide. When the

dog returns from the first hide, I send him directly to the second hide. When he returns from it, I reward him with a ball or food from my pockets. Once my dog can search two hides very well, I extend the distance between them gradually until it's close to the trial standard (the width of a football field). After that I can increase the number of the hides in the exercise.

2. From searching two hides to six hides without a decoy: when the dog can search two hides very well, I teach him to search three hides, and then four, five, and six. The principle is the same as searching two hides. When the dog comes back from one hide, I either make him stay by my side or send him directly to the next hide. He's not allowed to go behind my back as if he did he'd be out of sight and the IPO trial regulation also penalises this behaviour. In a trial, the dog has to always go directly to the next hide when he returns from the previous one, so we'd never call him to the front position or basic position on the competition field as the protection phase will be terminated by the judge if we do so. In training, I teach my dog to come to my left or my right depending on my gesture when he returns from the hide. The reasons are: 1) during the hide search exercise, we're allowed to use our dog's name in conjunction with the command "Here". From the very first day I took my puppy home, I've taught him to come and make contact with me when I call his name. I've also taught him to heel by my left and

heel by my right. I now extend these elements into a new behaviour simply by showing a certain body posture. When the dog is returning from my left side, I open my left arm slightly to get him to walk next to my left. He's familiar with this gesture as this is exactly what I do in left heeling (having my left arm slightly away from my body so my left hand won't accidentally brush along my dog's head as I swing my arms naturally while walking). When the dog is returning from the right side, I open my right arm slightly to get him to walk next to my right. He's also familiar with this gesture as this is exactly what I do in right heeling. When I call his name and open one of my arms to get him to come to my side, I don't require him to look at me like in formal heeling, as I don't want him to focus on me but to pay attention to which hide I send him to next. This is an excellent technique to control the dog in the hide search while keeping him focused on the hides. For example, in training, when I tell my dog to go around a hide on my left, as he's going towards it I continue walking on the centre line of the field (like the trial rule requires). When the dog has gone around the hide and is returning from my left side under my command, if I want to tighten the control now, instead of sending him directly to the next hide as I should in a trial, I only have to open my left arm slightly and he'll walk by my left. The next hide is on my right. When my dog follows me to the proper location, I turn my upper body slightly to my right and point my right arm at the next hide and direct my dog to search there. He runs towards the hide and when he returns from my right side on command I only have to open my right arm slightly and he'll walk by my right. This way, I only need one command ("Dog's name" + "Here") to let the dog understand when he should come to my left and when he should come to my right. 2) I can use my dog's name combined with my arm's gesture to make training much simpler, as I don't have to remember when to use the "Heel" command and when to use the "Right" command. Furthermore, these two commands are for formal heeling when the dog must look up at me, which is not necessary and even not desirable in the hide search exercise. I want

him to look at where I'm pointing and where he's going. 3) Once the behaviour has been established, it makes the control in our daily walk so much easier. When I'm walking my dog on a crowded street, I only have to call his name and extend one of my arms and he'll walk next to me calmly while paying attention to his surroundings. This is functional heeling for our day-to-day life, as the IPO competition heeling that requires the dog to focus on his handler is not practical on the streets at all. In the BH temperament test, this is the technique I usually employ when having my dog walk next to my left side in traffic, as he doesn't need to look at me in this situation and there's no need to burn his energy for nothing. When the dog is used to running six hides, I decrease his rewards and become more selective, only offering them when the dog is especially fast going out and coming back or especially tight in the turns.

3. Bring the decoy into the picture, teach the dog he can go to the decoy after searching one hide: the decoy is the biggest reward but also the biggest disruption to a working dog. When searching two hides or more, some dogs are in so much of a rush to engage the decoy that they'll disobey their handlers' command and go directly to the decoy's hide instead of going to the one they're supposed to. For example, when a handler guides his dog to the fourth hide, the dog breaks out and runs to the sixth hide, where the decoy is. If not effectively corrected, this kind of behaviour will become a habit and impact the handler's control and leadership. To solve this problem, some trainers often move the decoy so he's not always in the sixth hide. This method has its benefits but also many weaknesses. As dogs are intelligent animals, regardless of where we place the decoy in training, most trial-experienced dogs know that the decoy is always in the sixth hide in a competition. If we have to spend so much time and effort to move the decoy around in every training session to try tricking the dog, we might as well tackle the problem front on and make the dog understand breaking out is not an option. We need to go to the extreme so that even the decoy is shouting and cracking the whip out of the sixth hide to

try calling the dog to him; the dog must go where we send him. Before we start proofing the hide search, the dog must know the hold and bark (please refer to the next exercise: hold and bark). I let my dog wear a slip chain and a pinch collar, which is connected to a 5m loopless leash. I stand between the 5th and the 6th hides with my dog. I've prepared a portable fence arranged in a "C" shape around the 5th hide to ensure the dog coming back to me after going around the 5th hide (to better illustrate the process, the photos here show portable sticks in the ground instead of a fence). I ask my decoy to come out from the 6th hide to shout and crack the whip to distract my dog. The dog wants to go over there to engage the decoy but I stop him with the leash and take him into the 5th hide. I tell my dog to down with his head facing the exit of the 5th hide and I stand about 2m in front of him holding the leash. I call my dog's name to make him come to me. The fence

and the leash offer him no other options but the correct behaviour. As soon as he comes and makes contact with me, I reward him by sending him to the 6th hide for the hold and bark at the decoy. When his barking is clean (without trying to take a cheap shot by sneaking in for a dirty bite at the sleeve), the decoy reinforces him with a bite and lets him win the sleeve. I repeat this procedure for five to seven times in this session. Every time, I lie my dog down a little bit backwards from the time before, so gradually he's lying down in front of the 5th hide and facing it. I have his leash around the hide so he can only run around it and come to me without any other options. I now point at the 5th hide and tell him "Search". When he's in the hide, I call his name. As soon as he comes out and makes contact with me, I send him to the decoy. Good barking earns him the sleeve and we finish this session. Just like the retrieval exercises in obedience, we're using back chaining here to develop a reliable search. If I start the proofing without the above sequence and the dog has to run towards the 5th hide instead of coming to me first, this is more difficult and the dog might be confused, as he's used to always going to the decoy and not running away from him (the decoy is in the 6th hide; running towards the 5th hide is moving away from the decoy). The dog's instinct and training experience tell him to always face the decoy during a confrontation and never turn his back. Therefore, the first step of the sequence is to reinforce the dog for returning to me from the 5th hide. The moment he makes contact with me, he can engage the decoy. We then reverse the dog backwards so progressively he understands going away from the decoy to search the 5th hide can earn him the reward. The "C" shape fence and the 5m leash are my insurance. Without them, if the dog decides to break out and runs directly to the decoy, or runs past me without making contact, I'm helpless and can do nothing to stop it. Very soon, this will become a frequent and serious problem. Many competitors have lost championships because of this. They were leading on points in both tracking and obedience, and lost all the advantages when the dog broke loose in the hide search and cost them the title. I would train as above for several lessons and gradually increase the distance for sending the dog to the 5th hide. The dog has to understand his job is to search the hide I direct him to, come back to make contact with me, and then go to the next hide I send him to. If he refuses, I make him search the correct hide again and again until he gets it right. When he's reliable searching the 5th and the 6th hides in the full width of a football field, I can replace the 5m leash with a 45cm loopless leash. He's ready to search hides number 4, 5, and 6 with the decoy in 6.

4. Teach the dog that he can go to the decoy after searching two hides: I first set up a fence arranged into a "J" shape in between the 4th hide and the 6th hide to prevent the dog from going directly to the decoy when I send him to number 4. For many dogs, going around the 4th hide correctly is more difficult than the 5th hide, as numbers 4 and 6 are aligned on the same side and it's very tempting for the dog to go directly to 6 on his way to 4, or when he's coming out from 4. When I first begin to proof this, I ask my decoy to stand in front of the 5th hide to shout and crack the whip to stimulate the dog. As my dog already knows he should be searching the 5th and 6th hides diagonally, the technique of searching the 4th and 5th is exactly the same. I let him wear a slip chain and a pinch collar, which is attached to a 45cm loopless leash. I send him to the 4th hide, call him back, and send him to the 5th hide for the hold and bark. When his barking is clean, the decoy rewards him with a bite. I repeat this again, but this time the decoy is attracting the dog in front of the 6th hide when I'm standing in front of the 4th hide and ready to send my dog. The dog has the impulse to go to the decoy directly. I point at the 4th hide and say "Search" while I take a step forward and give the leash a tug to make him go around it. My leash and the "J" shape fence block the dog from going to the 6th hide and he has to go around the 4th and return to me for contact. I then walk him closer to the 5th hide and send him there. As he's used to this from the previous sequence, we should have no problem here. When he comes back to me from the 5th, I send him to the 6th as his reward. He barks at the decoy and gets reinforced.

I gradually extend the distance from which I send my dog to the 4ᵗʰ hide. The emphasis of this sequence is that the dog has to understand he mustn't go to number 6 when he's on his way to 4 or when he's coming out from 4. If necessary in the initial period, I'd make the "J" shape fence longer and use a 5m leash to have adequate control over the dog. Once he's formed a good habit then I can remove them. To further secure the dog's behaviour, when we progress to the stabilising stage, I'll employ the electric collar system into my training. The e-collar is a controversial device that is misunderstood by many people. When being used correctly, not only can it strengthen a dog's reliability; it also enhances his drive and resilience. In Belgium, we call the electric collar "teletact", which means "distant contact". For me this is the best description of this tool, as it's exactly what the name implies – being able to touch your dog over a long distance, just like an invisible hand or an invisible line.

5. Proof the dog so that he understands he must search the hides from 1 to 6 without breaking out directly to the decoy's hide: When the dog can dependably and smoothly search hides number 4, 5, and 6, I can increase the search to four, five, and eventually the entire six hides. Sometimes I send my dog directly to the next hide as he's returning from the previous one. Sometimes I get him to walk next to my left or right to have more control before I send him. If he goes around one of the hides lacking focus, speed, or smoothness, I'd make him do it again until I'm satisfied with his performance before sending him to search the next one.

The Pressure Pot Principle

Once a dog has established the desired behaviours in the learning stage, our goal in the strengthening stage is to make these behaviours reliable. This is called proofing. In addition, we also want to enhance his drive and hardness. Many techniques I've explained in the strengthening stage are based on the "Pressure Pot Principle". In cooking, a pressure pot is used to heat up water or broth when it's sealed to prevent steam from escaping. Pressure is created by boiling the liquid inside the airtight pot. The trapped steam increases the internal pressure of the pot and causes the temperature to rise. We apply this very principle in dog training by using positive reinforcement and negative reinforcement while building up positive frustration at the same time. Just like cooking with a pressure pot, we use fire to heat up the food (positive energy created by attracting the dog with a certain reinforcer, for example biting) while shutting the pot to form pressure (negative energy created by the use of the leash or other training devices). Positive frustration is built up as the dog wants to obtain the reinforcer but is restrained from getting it. When we're proofing the hide search, the decoy cracks the whip to attract the dog (injecting positive energy/heating up the food with fire), but I inhibit the dog from engaging the decoy and apply pressure to send him to another hide (inject negative energy/sealing the pressure pot). When the dog complies and goes to the empty hide, I call him back and send him to the decoy's hide for the hold and bark. The dog expresses and releases the pressurised positive and negative energy by barking while engaging the decoy (dog releasing his frustration/unscrewing the pot's lid in a controlled manner). When he does it well, he's given a bite, which further allows him to channel all his force into the grip. This final step is like hitting the pressurised pot with a speeding bullet. It causes a powerful explosion. We can apply this principle in many exercises, loading the dog and containing him from reaching his goal, putting on pressure to induce him to complete a specific task, and then allowing him to eject his frustration and fulfil his desire by rewarding him with a jackpot. This creates a boost of drive and power in the dog while enhancing his toughness and reliability. What's obtained by a fight and hardship tastes better. Through the utilisation of conflict caused by positive frustration and pressure, we bring out the wolves in our dogs.

Hold and Bark

In the learning stage of the protection phase, I've introduced four techniques to teach the barking. They are:

1. Luring by decoy on leash
2. Luring by decoy through fence
3. Luring by handler through fence
4. Luring by handler with play.

As I usually employ all four of the above methods, besides getting my dog to understand the hold and bark from a young age; as he matures mentally, physically, and technically, I can also increase his intensity and power in the barking.

The name "hold and bark" implies the dog barking at the decoy without touching him. The practical function of this exercise is for the dog to detain an aggressor or intruder with suspended aggression when he's found the person in a search. The dog barks at the stationary suspect to alert his handler of the find while keeping him contained. If the suspect tries to escape or attack the dog, the dog is allowed to bite him immediately. In the learning stage when we reinforced the dog's barking by moving the bite roll or the sleeve, we've taught him that he can bite when the person moves.

Of the four techniques, the luring by handler method is probably the easiest way to establish the dog's habit of barking without touching. Once the handler has taught the dog the hold and bark, all he needs to do is to bring in the decoy to replace him. If the dog is unable to develop the hold and bark with this technique for whatever reason, we can use the leash or the fence to teach him not to touch the sleeve while barking:

1. Keeping the dog clean with two lines: when a dog over six months can alert at the decoy on leash with good focus and continuous barking, I let him wear a slip chain (or a flat collar) and a pinch collar. The slip chain is attached to a black leash and the pinch collar is attached to a red leash. The different colours of the leashes make it easier for me when controlling the dog so I'll use the appropriate leash to either encourage him or correct him. I hold the black leash (slip chain) in my left hand and the red leash (pinch collar) in my right hand. I say "Watch him" and let my dog go in front of me to the end of the black leash (slip chain) to bark at a stationary decoy who's standing with his back against a wall or a fence. We don't directly do this in the hide to prevent the dog associating any undesirable behaviour with the hide when he's still in the learning process. For now I slacken the red leash (pinch

collar). As the dog is barking, I gradually tighten the red leash and loosen the black leash, so he's leaning into the pinch collar instead of the slip chain, causing discomfort. I give the red leash a few jerks towards me to discourage the dog from leaning into the pinch collar. This is a very similar technique to when I was teaching my dog to slow down in tracking. If necessary, the decoy comes towards the dog, keeping a distance of around 20 to 30cm away from him. I can also use the red leash to adjust the dog's position, to keep him centred in front of the decoy and prevent him from getting too close. When he stops lunging into the two collars and I can see both the red and black leashes are relaxed, I link the verbal command "Bark" with the hold and bark behaviour. The decoy reinforces clean barking with a bite and lets the dog win the sleeve after a brief wrestle. After the dog has won the sleeve, I keep him under control and let him calm down before telling him "Out". The decoy puts on the sleeve and stands still in front of the wall again. I repeat the process with the two leashes to ease the dog into the hold and bark. In the following sessions, I progressively replace the handling of the two leashes with letting my dog go to the decoy and give the red leash a jerk when he's about 20 to 30cm from him. The dog has learnt that when I say "Bark" he has to go in front of the decoy, bark at him, and keep him at bay without touching. When the dog is always clean in the hold and bark, we can bring this into the hide and I can use the verbal command "Search" instead of "Bark". The IPO trial regulation requires the command of searching the six hides to be consistent so we can't say "Search" for the first five empty hides and say "Bark" for the decoy's hide. This is not a problem for our dog, as he's already associated a stationery decoy standing in the hide with the hold and bark. When he moves, the dog is allowed to bite.

2. Keeping the dog clean with a fence and a stick: some dogs have problems with barking on the leash because they lunge into the collar to a point that their breathing becomes restricted. Some of them get too excited on leash and express their frustration by jumping around or spinning on the same spot wildly. In such cases, we can use a fence and a loose leash attached to the pinch collar to teach the hold and bark. In the learning stage, I've already taught my dog barking with the fence. Now I use a portable fence arranged into a "C" shape or a "V" shape and place it in front of the decoy while he's standing against a wall. The opening of the "V" shape is facing out so the dog can be contained there for the

barking. I tell my dog "Alert" and let him go into the "V" to bark at the decoy. The fence prevents him biting the sleeve and my leash prevents him from jumping over the fence or going sideways. The "V" shape fence makes it easy for the dog to understand where he has to be and keeps him centred in front of the decoy. If the dog tries to touch the fence, I give his leash a tug to stop him. When he keeps barking at the decoy without touching the fence and the leash is loose, I introduce the "Bark" command and the dog is reinforced with a bite. In the upcoming lessons, we gradually lower the fence. When it's lowered to 50cm and the dog is still clean in the barking, we can remove the fence completely. Eventually, the decoy holds the padded stick in front of his sleeve to remind the dog this is the line he can't cross during the hold and bark. When the dog comes too close, the decoy gives his chest a tap with the stick.

Once the dog understands he has to stay clean in the hold and bark, we prolong the barking period while keeping the barking proactive and intense. Eventually, we want our dog barking with focus and intensity at a totally passive decoy for a minimum of one straight minute. In training, we accustom the dog to the handler and other people moving around him during barking. The dog has to always keep his attention on the decoy in this exercise and not be distracted by any commotion in his environment. Strong continuous barking with absolute focus is reinforced by a bite on the sleeve. The decoy has to be observant and ready. If the dog does anything out of order, such as giving a cheap shot, jumping up too high, swinging to one side, or not being attentive enough, the decoy must act quickly and precisely to keep the dog in line. To encourage the dog's consistent barking, besides letting him bite, the decoy can also give out very subtle movements or expressions to keep him motivated, such as tapping the clatter stick or acting mean, excited, frightened, or feeble, depending what the dog needs at that particular moment. He employs whatever movement, expression, or emotion is needed to bring the dog into the zone.

On top of powerful and suspended barking, the hold and bark requires excellent control. In a trial, at the end of the hold and bark, the handler has to call his dog away from the decoy to the basic position on the judge's signal. To teach this, I employ the following sequence:

1. Calling the dog to basic position during a walk: when my dog can return to the basic position very well by performing the flip finish in the obedience strengthening stage, I'd practise this on an 8m retractable leash when we're going for a wander. The dog wears a pinch collar and is walking in front of me exploring his surroundings. I give the verbal command "Here – return" and allow him two seconds to react. I don't expect him to be immediately next to me but he should at least turn towards my direction within two seconds. If he doesn't, I give the leash several tugs to bring him to the basic position. If I need to lead him to me, when he stays in the basic position with good focus for about five seconds I dismiss him and keep walking before calling him to return to me again after about two minutes. When he responds to my command immediately without the use of the leash, I'd reward him with some food. We train like this for a few days. In a fifteen-minute stroll, I'd call my dog to me for three to five times randomly. When he responds quickly and willingly, I reward him with a ball. When the behaviour is consistent, I do it without a leash.

2. Calling the dog to basic position during fetching: I let my dog wear a pinch collar connected to an 8m retractable leash and let him fetch a ball a few times. I'm careful not to throw the ball too far. If the ball goes further than 8m, when the dog runs to the end of the leash he's

going to receive a correction for nothing and that's not good. After he retrieves the ball several times, I throw it out for him to fetch again but this time, when he's about 50cm from the ball, I say "Here – return" and then push the lock button of the retractable leash briefly so it stops extending. The dog is stopped from going to the ball. When he turns around to me, I release the lock button so the leash retracts as he's coming back. As soon as he's in the basic position, I say "Yes" and give him a second ball from my pocket and play with him to reward his return. I reinforce him regardless of stopping him with the leash or not, as this is a very demanding exercise and the correction from the pinch collar is quite hard. As soon as he's achieved my desired behaviour, I want to boost his drive again so he'll forget about the pressure. After fetching several times, I call him back again. The handler needs to observe his dog carefully in this practice and be sensible about it. Don't do this too frequently and don't give the correction too hard or it can affect the dog's speed and confidence for going to pick up the ball. After some sessions, the dog can return in the middle of fetching by my voice alone. When he can do this consistently, I call him back from fetching without the leash. He's now ready for the final step.

3. Calling the dog to basic position during hold and bark: when I practise this step, my dog must already have an excellent hold and bark at the decoy for at least thirty seconds. He's used to me moving around him and touching him during this exercise and should be at least one year old. I let my dog wear a pinch collar attached to a 5m loopless leash and do a hold and bark at the decoy in the hide. The first time the decoy rewards clean barking by giving the dog a bite as usual. This is to avoid anticipation for the dog to come back before I call him in the future. I then send him in again for the hold and bark. When his focus is perfect on the decoy and the barking is strong, I give the verbal command "Here – return". If he's not in the basic position within three seconds, I correct him by tugging on the leash towards me several times until he's sitting by my left side attentively. At this point, I'll decide my next step depending on my dog's reaction. The possibilities are as follows: 1) if the dog came next to me without the need for using the leash, I'll ask the decoy to step out of the hide. I command my dog to heel next to me for several metres. When the heeling is perfect, I say "Take him" so the dog can go for biting as a reward. 2) When the dog is sitting in the

basic position attentively, regardless of the need for using the leash for his return or not, I can send him back into the hide for another hold and bark. I can choose to let the decoy give him a bite or to call him back again. Once my dog is reliable in the call back without the need for the leash, I practise without it. There should be a mix in the training. Sometimes the dog gets a bite in the hold and bark, sometimes I call him back and send him again; sometimes I call him back and then move on to the next exercise. We need to maintain the balance so that the dog is always focused on the decoy in the barking but responds to me immediately when I call him back. There are a lot

more elements we can play with here to increase the fire, control, and reliability. I'll explain them in further detail in *The Schutzhund Training Manual 2*.

Prevention of the Escape

There are five bites in the IPO3 protection phase. They are:

1. The prevention of the escape
2. Re-attack
3. Attack during back transport
4. Long attack
5. Re-attack.

The prevention of the escape requires the dog to intercept the decoy from running away by biting his protection sleeve. As the striking angle for the dog is 45° on the decoy's hind left (when the decoy is wearing the sleeve on his left arm), some dogs tend to prefer biting the elbow part of the sleeve because it's the nearest striking point at this angle. To ensure the dog is biting the centre of the sleeve and not the elbow position, we teach him to always aim at the middle. This is done as follows:

1. Accustom the dog to attack at the appropriate angle with a portable fence: when my dog has a good foundation in the attack and I can make him sit when he's alerting on leash (please refer to "First Step of Introducing Control in Bite Work"), we can begin teaching the prevention of the escape (escape bite in short). The decoy first stands in a ready to run position. I down my dog about 2m to the decoy's hind left (when he's wearing the sleeve on his left arm). There's a portable fence between the decoy and the dog. The decoy places himself at the front end of the fence, so that he only needs to take one step forward to be clear of the fence and be in the dog's biting range. The decoy and the dog can see each other clearly through the fence. I stand on my dog's hind left holding a 5m loopless leash attached to his slip chain or flat collar to prevent him biting the decoy before he escapes. The decoy holds the sleeve at his waist level and rocks it back and forth like he's rocking a baby to sleep in his arm. The motion stimulates the dog's hunt drive/prey drive and keeps him focused on the sleeve. The bite bar of the sleeve should be facing the dog at a good angle to allow him the optimum entry and grip. If the bite bar is turned too much upward or downward, the dog will end up biting the top or the bottom of the sleeve and get a bad grip. When the decoy sees the dog is focused and ready to come, he runs forwards. The running decoy triggers the dog's hunt drive/prey drive and he chases him instinctually. I link this behaviour with "Take him" and slip out the line with some friction in my hands

to control the speed. The decoy just moves out of the fence as the dog arrives, giving him the best opportunity to bite the middle of the sleeve. When the dog has a full, firm, and calm grip, the decoy slows down his running and he slightly pushes the dog's lower jaw with his right hand while pulling the dog in with the sleeve, creating two oppositional forces (left arm pulling, right hand pushing). When he feels the dog wants to bore in deeper, he releases his right hand. Without the pushing of his right hand, the sleeve on his left arm comes pressing into his body and simultaneously encourages the dog to push forward. Meanwhile, I'm holding the leash behind the dog. As the dog pushes, I slacken the line, and as he's holding I tighten the line so he can feel my support. When the dog pushes well, the decoy rewards him with the sleeve. The portable fence's function is to prevent the dog from biting the elbow of the sleeve, which is not a desired behaviour in Schutzhund. With the restriction of the fence, the dog can only bite the centre of the sleeve as the decoy runs out. We continue to train as such for several sessions, gradually increasing the distance between the decoy and the dog to about 5m. When the dog has entered well and got a good hold on the sleeve, the decoy keeps running for about 20m and then encourages the dog to push. If the dog is a puller, the decoy encourages him to pull (please refer to "Teaching the Bite and Pull").

2. Accustom the dog to attack at the appropriate angle with a leash: when the dog can consistently bite the centre of the sleeve with the presence of the fence, we remove it for one session and see if he bites the same. If he does, we've succeeded using the first method. If he bites the elbow two times or more, I'll get him to bite correctly with the guidance of a 5 or 10m leash. The decoy stands ready and I down my dog 5m from his

hind left. I stand on my dog's hind left. As the decoy starts to run and my dog launches at him, I pull the leash to the left so the dog is dragged away from the striking line and must curve his entry into the decoy in an anti-clockwise path. This teaches the dog to run a little further before coming in for the bite, which causes him to strike a little bit more forward, ending up holding the centre of the sleeve. We continue to guide the dog with the long line until this becomes a habit.

3. Heeling from the hide to the escape bite: when the dog has a good habit of striking in the escape bite, we familiarise him with the first parts of the protection routine. After the dog returns to his handler from the hold and bark, the decoy goes to the spot to prepare for the escape, and the handler has to heel his dog from the hind to a designated place which is 5m on the decoy's hind left. This is a matter of putting the pieces of behaviour together so the dog gets used to the order of the exercises. We start from the hide with the dog in the basic position and I call the decoy out. I say "Heel" and walk towards the spot I need to down my dog for the escape bite. The dog wears a pinch collar connected to a short loopless leash. When the dog can heel next to me with excellent attention, I say "Take him" and the decoy shouts to attract the dog. The dog gets a bite as his reward for good heeling. We gradually lengthen the distance so the dog can heel all the way from the hide to the spot for the down. By then I can choose when the dog can bite: 1) when we're heeling from the hide to the spot for the down. 2) When we've arrived at the spot for the down. I'm standing and my dog is sitting next to me attentively. 3) When we've arrived at the spot for the down. I've downed my dog and walked away. My dog is focusing on the decoy while lying down. We make variations in training, so sometimes the dog can bite when he's following me, or sometimes he can bite when he's down and watching the decoy. This practice keeps the dog balanced in his wildness and tameness.

4. Out: I've already explained how to make a good out, and by now the dog should out on command reliably. The only thing we have to decide now is whether to ask the dog to out and guard the decoy actively (barking out), or out and guard the decoy quietly (silent out). Both techniques are allowed in a Schutzhund trial and the handler is free to teach the technique he prefers. In the table below, I've highlighted the pros and cons of the two techniques:

Outing Style	
Barking out	
Advantages	Disadvantages
Easier to maintain the dog's focus in guarding	If the dog lacks stability, the barking out might affect his grip's fullness, firmness, and calmness in the re-attack
More spectacular as it's more dynamic	The barking out requires very good endurance, breathing, and high drive from the dog. Otherwise he might bark intermittently or keep trying to bark but nothing comes out. When the weather is hot and humid, it gets more difficult
Easier to evaluate the dog's power and dominance by listening to the sound of his barking	
Most dogs with barking out tend to take bite work more seriously	
Silent out	
Advantages	Disadvantages
Easier to maintain the dog's composure in the guard	The dogs tend to lose their focus on the decoy more easily due to pressure or distraction
Easier to teach	Some dogs with the silent out tend to take bite work less seriously and treat it like a game. When the decoy stops moving, they just slip off the sleeve and sit there without any intensity
In the re-attack, the dog has a better chance to aim and strike, which is beneficial for the fullness, firmness, and calmness of the grip	

Throughout the upbringing and education of my dogs, I observe their genetic capability and trainability. The barking out is more demanding than the silent out. Therefore, I'd only employ this technique in competitions with a dog that is highly driven, very stable and with excellent reflex and grip. When I feel a dog is better off using the silent out, I'd adopt this technique for competitions. In training, I teach them both techniques so I can choose which one will suit them best when they're old enough.

If you've been reading this book from the start up to here, you would realise my dogs are actually taught both styles of guarding. They've learnt the barking guard in the clean and explosive out, and in the hold and bark. They've learnt the silent guard in release through pressing, and release through luring and leading. To bring these techniques into the out on the sleeve, all we have to do is to let the dog practise with the decoy. I'll wait until the dog has a consistently good grip and good attack. He should have a clean out with a toy. I can start training the out on a decoy as early as after the dog has got his adult teeth.

1. The barking out: in the prevention of the escape, when the dog has bitten the sleeve and the decoy has run with the dog for some distance, he stands still and lets the dog push (pulling if the dog is a puller). The decoy goes into the locking stance. In the locking stance, the decoy stands with his feet apart and his knees bent slightly. He keeps his back erect to maintain balance while locking his sleeve arm close to his abdomen to prevent the dog from pushing him backwards or pulling him forwards. He holds the padded stick closely beside or behind his right thigh to brace himself. In a trial, this is the position the decoy must adopt at the end of every bite. His job here is to stand firmly and keep his balance to wait for the dog to out without giving him any stimulation. When my decoy has stood still, I say "Bark, out". The dog has previously learnt both commands, but as he hasn't done the exercise this way before, he might not out immediately or he outs but doesn't bark. If necessary, I tug on the leash that is attached to his pinch collar to make him out. If he doesn't go into the hold and bark immediately after the out, the decoy encourages him by making some noise or a facial expression just as he would in the hide. I keep the leash loose

but I stay put in case the dog takes a cheap shot at the sleeve. When he can give a clean hold and bark for a few seconds after the out, the decoy reinforces him with a bite and gives him the sleeve. After numerous training sessions, when the dog is biting and he hears my command "Bark", he understands he has to out and go into barking. I use the command "Bark" for the barking out and the command "Out" for the silent out so I give myself an option with both techniques. The two commands are two stimulus control signals for two different behaviours. If I decide to change the outing style in the future for whatever reason, all I need to do is to give the other command.

2. The silent out: I let my dog wear a constricting collar that is connected to a leash. When the dog is biting and the decoy has gone into the locking stance, I say "Out" and wait for his response. If he's slow in the out or tries to bark after the out, I constrict the collar upward to make him out cleanly and quietly. When the collar tightens up it restricts air, which encourages a clean out and discourages barking. I've already introduced this technique in the release exercise of the obedience strengthening stage, so the dog will immediately

understand it. When the dog has outed cleanly and silently and is guarding with focus, the decoy lets him bite to reward his behaviour. After a few lessons, when I say "Out", my dog knows he has to out and stay quiet.

Re-Attack during Guarding

The re-attack is done after the out when the decoy threatens the dog and hits him twice with the padded stick, attempting to drive him away by force and intimidation. The dog is required to directly counter the aggression by biting the sleeve. The motion of the decoy chasing the dog with the stick during biting is known as the drive. The dog has to show self-assurance, determination, and courage with a full, firm, and calm grip during the drive. When the handler tells him to out at the end of the bite, he has to respond immediately.

In training, we progressively familiarise the dog with the drive. In the protection learning phase, we've already introduced the clatter stick with positive approaches. The dog is used to the sound and the touch of the clatter stick. The padded stick is a lot easier as it doesn't make any noise and is much softer. When the dog has a positive response towards the clatter stick, we can introduce the padded stick into bite work. The padded stick is a lightweight soft stick about 60cm long. It is usually made of a thin and flexible fibreglass interior with a piece of foam wrapped around it and a leather outer layer. It serves as a mentally threatening tool to the dog rather than a physical one, as the light weight of the stick and its soft cover prevent the dog from getting hurt when being hit on the shoulders by it. In the protection phase of a Schutzhund trial, it's employed to test the courage and hardness of the dog. Below are the steps of teaching the re-attack:

1. Accustom the dog to the drive, from short to long, and from mild to vigorous: we introduce the padded stick when the dog consistently bites well under the use of the clatter stick. (Note: for dogs that aren't stable enough to handle the clatter stick, we skip the clatter

stick step and introduce the padded stick just the same way as we introduce the clatter stick before teaching the drive.) The decoy wears the sleeve on his left arm and holds the padded stick in his right hand (for a left-handed decoy it is the reverse). I let my dog wear a flat nylon collar connected to a 2m loopless leash. If the dog has trouble breathing wearing a normal collar, he can wear a harness instead. The decoy lets my dog bite while I have the leash on tension. The dog can feel my support behind him through the taut line, which also serves to strengthen the grip as he has to bite with force to keep his grip from being pulled off by me. The decoy gently strokes the dog with the stick like he's patting him with his hand so the dog doesn't see it as a threat. He encourages the dog to push (or to pull, for a puller). When the dog is used to being stroked gently by the stick, the decoy swings

it in bigger and faster motions, but when the stick makes contact with the dog it remains a gentle stroke. When the decoy sees the dog react positively, he hits the tightened leash with force and lets the dog win the sleeve. The dog could feel the force of the stick on the leash but he didn't have the sensation of being hit. After one or two sessions like this, the decoy can slightly tap the dog's shoulders with the stick. When the grip maintains its fullness, firmness, and calmness, the decoy lets the dog push. As the dog gets older and advances in training, he gets to win the sleeve less and less. With maturity, his rank drive and protection drive develop, and we gradually use these drives more than hunt drive/prey drive, so the dog takes the protection phase more seriously. The decoy progressively rewards the dog more with letting him push (or pull) or letting the dog dominate him during their confrontation, so the reinforcement comes from the fight and overwhelming the decoy instead of winning the sleeve and holding it. The decoy taps the dog and lets him push. The pushing becomes the dog's counter to the tapping, and the tapping becomes the decoy's counter to the pushing. The force of the stick-hits steadily increases. When the dog is used to being hit by the stick and counters with active biting, the decoy can teach him the movement of the drive. During the drive in a trial, the decoy places the sleeve and the dog close to his torso while leaning over him with his upper body. He rushes into the dog at a 45° angle for about fifteen steps while continuously threatening him by swinging the stick above him. All of the stick-swinging is done without contact except for the two stick-hits. In IPO3, there are two re-attacks, one after the prevention of the escape and one after the long attack. So in total there are four stick hits. In all five bites, every bite has the drive, with the exception of the escape bite when the decoy has to run away from the dog. During the drive, it's very important for the dog to stay in the centre line of the decoy. He mustn't swing to the sides – especially to the decoy's left side – to avoid the stick. In training, the decoy familiarises the dog with the drive from short to long, from slow to fast, and from mild to vigorous. Initially, the leash tension I apply from behind the dog also serves to keep him in the middle. If the dog tries to go to the sides, I stop him and bring him back to the decoy's centre line with the leash.

2. Biting when the sleeve moves: in major Schutzhund championships, to clearly distinguish the working quality of the participating dogs, most judges request the decoys to go into the re-attack without any prey stimulation by keeping the sleeve stationary and only swinging the stick up in attacking the dogs. To prepare for this, besides using the sleeve movement as

a signal for biting, we also teach our dog that the raising of the stick is also a signal for biting. No matter whether we teach the dog the barking out or the silent out, for better learning, we begin teaching the re-attack when the dog is sitting quietly in front of the decoy. This way it is easier to maintain the dog's composure, which is better for the strike and the grip. I let my dog sit about 30cm in front of the decoy on leash. When his focus is good, the decoy moves the sleeve upwards in a quick jerking motion. The dog has already seen this movement hundreds of times in training and he bites on cue. The decoy drives the dog and then lets him push. After a while I tell him to out.

3. Biting when the stick raises and the sleeve moves: we now pair the raising of the stick with the movement of the sleeve so the dog can associate that this is also a signal for biting. The decoy simply moves the sleeve upward while raising the stick at the same time to attract the dog to bite. We do this for several sessions.

4. Biting when the stick raises: when the dog is used to biting as the stick comes up and the sleeve moves, the decoy now doesn't move the sleeve anymore and raises the stick alone as the signal. If the dog is slow to respond to this, all the decoy has to do is to raise the

stick first and then move the sleeve directly after it; the dog will learn this very quickly by classical conditioning. After a while, the decoy won't need to move the sleeve anymore. We can practise the routine simulating a trial. If my dog outs by barking, I can now let him bark before the re-attack.

Back Transport

The back transport requires the dog to heel next to his handler while watching the decoy about 5m in front of him. The difficulty of this exercise is its demand of the perfect balance between the dog's drive and control. If the dog is too motivated to bite, he'll keep lunging forward and lose precision in the heeling. If the dog is too attentive to his handler he'll lose the guard on the decoy, which costs a lot of points. The basic component of making my dog go backwards in obedience was taught to prepare for this exercise. In the strengthening stage, I've taught my dog to walk backwards looking at a bite roll. I now continue further in this sequence with the following steps:

1. Teach the dog to watch a ball while heeling backwards: I let my dog sit or stand next to my left. On the dog's left there's a fence or a wall. He wears a pinch collar connected to an 80cm loopless leash, which is held by my left hand. I throw a ball in front of us. The dog wants to take the ball but I prevent him from going so he can only watch eagerly, hoping that I'll let him go. I point at the ball and tell him "Watch". Meanwhile, I'm holding a horse whip in my right hand and I carry it across my dog's chest. I say "Back" and start walking backwards while keeping the dog next to my left thigh by tapping him slightly on the chest with the whip and guiding him backwards with the leash. As long as he can maintain his

focus on the ball and follow me backwards for a few steps, I say "Yes" and release him so he can fetch the ball. I repeat this process for several sessions and gradually lengthen the distance of walking backwards until I don't need to use the whip and the leash anymore to maintain the same behaviour.

2. Teach the dog to watch a ball while side stepping into me: once my dog can heel backwards next to me while watching the ball in front of us without the help of the whip and the leash, we can practise the sidestep away from the fence. We stand in the open and I throw the ball forward. I hold the leash with my right hand and the whip with my left. I use the ball as a centre point while moving around it anti-clockwise to the right. I tap my dog on his left shoulder slightly with the whip and tug the leash towards me as I'm sidestepping to keep him moving into me. All this time I require him to look at the ball. When he can

stick by my left leg and keep focusing on the ball, I say "Yes" so he can fetch it. We keep on training as such for a few lessons. At the beginning I reinforce my dog when he can successfully watch the ball for a few steps. When he can maintain his focus and precision staying by my left for about ten steps, I fade out the use of the whip and the leash. When his behaviour is still correct, I link it with the verbal command "Transport". We're now ready to practise this with a decoy.

Note: by teaching the back transport exercise with a ball instead of the decoy, we can keep the dog at a lower drive so he can concentrate better and understand our criteria faster. I can also teach this with a bowl of fresh meat or another item, just motivating him enough to keep his focus without making him crazy or sending him into overdrive. If we start straight away with the decoy, the drive of the dog will become too high and we'll have to give him very

hard corrections to teach him the exercise. The progress will be very slow and the dog will become confused, which undermines his confidence and frustrates him in a bad way. The idea is to keep the dog watching a target while always staying by his handler, no matter how he moves. The dog has to learn using his sense of touch to maintain the contact with his handler's left leg. Be careful not to use the whip or the leash too harshly here, or you might make the dog nervous and he'll start leaning all his weight into your leg at every step you take. This is called crowding and you'll lose points in a trial because of this.

One of the most common problems in the back transport is forging. The dog is so eager to get to the decoy that he keeps moving ahead too far. Sometimes you see dogs doing the back transport heeling with their hindquarters next to the handler instead of their shoulders. In the worst cases, they leave their handler completely. By first teaching the dog to go backwards, and then sideways, and reinforcing these two behaviours many times, we can greatly reduce the probability of forging.

Attack during Back Transport

1. Replace the ball with the decoy, teach the dog to leap into the attack (the flying tackle): when my dog can focus on a ball while always staying by my left leg, when he's got his adult teeth, when he's a minimum of seven months old, and when he's always biting with a full, firm, and calm grip, we'll start teaching him the flying tackle. My dog wears a slip chain or a flat collar connected to a 2m loopless leash. If necessary, I also use a horse whip to prevent the dog from forging. The decoy stands about 3 to 5m before us. Initially, we limit the distance so the dog can learn the proper technique of the tackle at a lower speed. When an inexperienced dog is allowed to fly at the decoy like crazy, he risks injuring himself as his timing might be off and he can slip off the sleeve because he doesn't get a good hold of it. The decoy doesn't

move to try stimulating the dog. I say "Transport" to have my dog sitting by my left leg while watching the decoy. I take one step back and make my dog follow me backwards. If he's too focused on the decoy and doesn't respond in time, I correct him with the leash and the whip. The moment the dog can come next to me and keep watching the decoy without my help, I reward him by saying "Take him" and hold on to the leash so my dog goes into alert. The decoy starts attracting the dog immediately. To teach the dog the jump attack, the decoy bends forward and swings the sleeve in front of him slowly from left to right at knee height, like the motion of an old pendulum clock. As he's swinging the sleeve, he gives a few shouts to stimulate the dog's hunt drive/prey drive. When he sees the dog's motivation and concentration are in balance, he signals to me and I release the dog for the attack. The decoy observes the dog's approach and his speed. As they're only about 3 to 5m apart, the dog can't pick up too much velocity. When the dog is I or 2m in front of the decoy, the decoy swiftly pulls up the sleeve to his chest level and turns the bite bar towards the dog for the optimum

angle of the bite. As the dog was running towards the decoy, the sleeve was swaying at knee height but now all of a sudden it is raised when the dog is about to enter into the attack, like a panicking pheasant escaping in full flight. As a predator, the dog has excellent reflexes and highly developed fast-twitch muscles. When he sees the sleeve is trying to flee, he naturally accelerates and leaps into the attack in order to catch it. As soon as the dog has hit the sleeve, the decoy follows his momentum and pivots his feet and body to the side like a martial artist deflecting a blow. When the dog is biting fully, firmly, and calmly, the decoy lets him win the sleeve. We continue this process for several sessions, progressively increasing the distance for the dog to follow me backwards while watching the decoy. When the following backwards is very good, I make the dog sidestep into me before I send him for the attack. For the first couple of weeks, I hold the dog after I give him the command for biting so he has enough time to aim and target the sleeve. When he's very good at catching the fleeing sleeve, we steadily increase the attack distance to about 10m.

2. Going through the back transport routine and using the attack as a reinforcement for the correct behaviour: when my dog can follow me backwards and sideways correctly while watching the decoy, and his tackle technique is very good, we can begin to practise back transport following the trial routine. We start by outing the dog after the re-attack. I come to the right side of my dog, tell him to sit, and send the decoy a few metres back for the back transport. The decoy walks ahead about 5m in front of us with his back facing us. When the dog is walking by my side correctly and watching the decoy with excellent attention, the decoy turns around at us for the attack. This is a cue for the dog to bite. At the beginning I can say "Take him" right after the decoy turns around. After a while the dog will learn by classical conditioning that he can bite as soon as the decoy turns. Because the decoy

can't see what's going on behind him as he's walking ahead to reinforce the dog's correct behaviour, I use two methods of communication to let him know when to turn around: 1) I keep the decoy informed during the back transport. When the dog is walking next to me precisely and looking at the decoy with focus, I tell the decoy he can turn around now for the attack. To prevent my verbal signal to the decoy becoming a cue for the dog, most of the time I'd tell the decoy to come for the attack after several more metres. I can also give my dog a command for the attack when he's walking properly. When the decoy hears my command, he turns around to take the dog. 2) When I have my assistant on the field, he can walk on the left side just a little ahead of the decoy while watching my dog and me. When the dog is doing an excellent back transport, the assistant gives the decoy the thumbs up and the decoy turns around for the attack.

3. The decoy uses a bite roll to reinforce the side transport: Traditionally, many trainers teach the dog to walk next to the decoy by reinforcing him with biting on the sleeve. This method causes a lot of dogs to forge in front of the decoy in anticipation of the bite. The right heeling we've taught our dogs solves this problem as he's used to heeling precisely by our right. All we have to do is to get the dog doing the same on the right side of the decoy. To start this, the decoy first puts away his sleeve and takes out a long bite roll with a length of about 60cm. He gives the dog a few bites on this bite roll and then I make the dog sit next to the decoy's right side while he's holding the bite roll above the dog's head. When the dog sits calmly by the decoy and focuses on the bite roll, he gets a bite as his reward.

After several repetitions, the decoy walks forward and I guide the dog with a leash so he can follow the decoy. Precise heeling is reinforced by biting the jute roll. When the dog is used to this, the decoy inserts a small part of the bite roll into the right side of his scratch pants so he doesn't need to hold it anymore but the dog can still see it. As my dog is next to the decoy, I stay beside or behind him with the leash to prevent him from taking the bite roll by himself. Sometimes the dog is rewarded when sitting attentively and sometimes he's rewarded when following the decoy. I can now insert the "Side transport" command. After a few sessions, the decoy removes the bite roll and puts the sleeve back on. As we never reinforce the dog in side transport by letting him bite the sleeve, this keeps him clean and heeling correctly without forging.

4. Reinforce a correct side transport by heel and bite: we can now link the side transport into the protection routine. After the attack during back transport, the decoy drives the dog for some distance before stopping. I tell my dog to out and I come next to him. I tell him to heel and we come to the right side of the decoy. I disarm the decoy by taking away his padded stick (a traditional gesture required by the trial rules). I say "Side transport" and

my dog walks between us while watching the decoy attentively. After some distance, we stop and I give the heel command again so my dog has to put his focus back onto me. I walk away with him; when he's heeling perfectly, I say "Take him" and my dog can go for a bite as the reward for a correct side transport. Once the dog can do this, I don't need to reinforce his side transport very often, as the behaviour of watching the decoy itself is already a reinforcer for him. Sometimes I ask an assistant to stand on the field so we can do the back transport towards him and stop in front of him to simulate reporting to the judge after the back transport and handing him the stick from the decoy.

Long Attack

The long attack requires the dog to perform a flying tackle at the decoy at full speed when the decoy is charging at the dog, shouting and threatening with the stick. The two start at each end of

the football field and the impact occurs near the centre circle. This is the climax of the Schutzhund protection phase and it is one of the most iconic images of the sport.

We've already taught the dog the foundation of the long attack in the tackle during the back transport. Now we only need to gradually extend the distance. When the dog can be sent from 10m away and he can consistently tackle the decoy with a long leaping entry, the decoy no longer needs to swing the sleeve from low to high to help the dog to aim. Before I release my dog for the attack, the decoy can shout and make threatening gestures briefly to familiarise the dog with aggressive behaviours. As soon as I send the dog, the decoy stops the hostility and receives the dog as he comes. The decoy progressively enhances the length, frequency, and intensity of his hostility. After a while, the dog is used to the decoy's aggressiveness and will take his shouting and threatening as an attraction because he always gets to overcome and dominate the decoy in the protection phase. When my dog always jumps well in the long attack and his grip maintains its quality, I can also increase the demand in control, requiring him to heel next to me with attention and letting him bite when he's following me perfectly. At the end, my dog can sit next to me calmly while the decoy is charging at us from the other side of the football field. Good control is rewarded by the long attack. When the dog has entered well and the grip is good, the decoy drives him for some distance, stops in the locking stance, and waits for me to tell the dog "Out".

Re-Attack during Guarding

The last exercise in the IPO3 protection is the re-attack, which is almost the same as the re-attack after the prevention of the escape. The only difference is there's one last side transport after it. The handler has his dog side transporting the decoy to the judge, presents him the stick from the decoy, and reports out, indicating the completion of the protection phase.

In the protection strengthening phase, we teach the dog the biting techniques and the requirement for control step by step. When the dog has a strong foundation, we put everything together to develop the whole programme. The dog trains with one main decoy until he can execute every protection exercise with him smoothly and confidently. We then train with other decoys so the dog can broaden his experience with decoys of various styles. When working with a new decoy, we do this over a few sessions and we go back to basics so the dog has sufficient time to adapt and continues to build his confidence.

The training of a working dog is a constant adjustment between his wildness and tameness. When a dog is too tame, he doesn't want to bite. When a dog is too wild, he doesn't want to out. The dog trainer's job is to understand when he should let his dog be wild, and when he should let his dog be tame. He has to know when, how, and how much. This comes with experience from training many dogs and observing them vigilantly.

Increasing the Dog's Practical Protective Abilities

When my dog can competently perform the entire IPO3 protection routine with about ten different decoys and he's reached physical and mental maturity, I'd consider adding some elements of cross-training in bite work in order to increase his experience, competitiveness, and practicality. When and what elements I choose depend on the genetic capability of the dog, his training level, and my primary goal with him. These elements can include:

1. Full bite suit training
2. Hidden sleeve training
3. Muzzle boxing with a civil decoy (no sleeve, no suit)
4. Bite work in a forest
5. Building search
6. Guarding the house
7. Practical scenario training (simulating specific situations)
8. Combining elements from other protection dog sports (defence of the handler, object guarding, calling the dog back during an attack, etc.).

In my next book, *The Schutzhund Training Manual 2,* I'll explain these training methods in detail. I'll also continue to illustrate the stabilising stage and perfecting stage of tracking, obedience, and protection, physical conditioning, preparing the dog for championships, mental preparation for the competitor, the training of the decoy, and, last but not least, the entire system of using the teletact.

Food for Thought

Every dog is an individual being with his own genetic make-up, personality, and history. I took this into consideration as I was writing this book, so I tried to offer multiple approaches for teaching each Schutzhund exercise to give you a wider range of options to train your dog successfully. In animal training, it's quite common for us to encounter problems. The faster we can find a solution, the faster we put our dogs back onto the right path. We should always strive to find the source of a problem. There's a list of questions you can ask yourself which might be able to help you find that source:

1. Have you chosen the appropriate training system or method for your dog?
2. Are you applying the training technique properly?
3. Have you or your decoy applied too much pressure on the dog?
4. Do you have a strong pack bonding with your dog? Does he trust you and respect you?
5. Have you chosen the right conditions: weather, ground, distractions, etc?
6. Are you using suitable equipment?
7. Did you have adequate preparation before the training?
8. Did you over-train? Does your dog have enough rest? Is he bored by constant repetitions of the same behaviour?
9. Does the dog have any negative experience previously in his day-to-day life or in training?
10. Before your dog began this stage of training, was he physically and mentally ready? Did his experience meet the basic criteria before starting this sequence?
11. Is your dog going through any physiological changes: teething, puberty, heat, nursing, too full, too tired, injury, illness, etc?
12. Is your dog genetically capable of being a working dog?
13. Are your goals realistic?

All roads lead to Rome. I hope you can apply what you've learnt to your dog effectively, and be flexible so you can adapt to training many different types of dogs. Although the training philosophy remains unchanged, there's no one single training system that is universal for all dogs. Even in one system, there are so many variables and you can re-arrange the sequences in it in many different orders. A training system is like a tradesman's toolbox. It's up to the trainer to select the most appropriate tool to solve a certain problem. Sometimes, the simplest and the most obvious method is the most effective solution. Dog training isn't all that complicated. If we need to sum it up in two sentences: "Here's a dog and here's a man. The dog must listen to the man." Every time we're confronted with whatever freaky and bizarre behavioural problem we haven't seen before, take a minute and think about these two sentences. The solution might just appear like a light bulb switching on in front of you. A working dog trainer should modify a dog's behaviour depending on his ability and character. Besides trying to bring out his genetic working capacity to its fullness, his goal should also be providing his dog with a splendid and fulfilling life.

In dog training, our best teachers are in fact our dogs. If we're willing to spend the time and effort to observe and evaluate our dogs' daily behaviours, and frequently reflect how we've interacted with them, we can gradually accumulate the eyes and the fingers that are essential in training animals. When we've reached a stage at which we truly know our dogs, whatever they do we understand at once, and whatever we want they deliver at once, two minds become one spirit.

Felix Ho, 31st December 2016, Belgium

Special Thanks

In my competitive career and during the time of writing this book, I've received much support from my family and friends. I would like to express my gratitude to them here. To my wife, Maggie, thank you for all these years of loving and supporting me. As a man who's fanatical with his work and passion, I know I've neglected you sometimes and I know I'm difficult to live with. Thank you for accepting me the way I am. To my best friend and my colleague Christoph Joris, besides teaching me a lot of valuable knowledge in training and breeding working dogs, you've also taught me many lessons in life. You're like a big brother to me. As a professional dog trainer, you're my role model. Thank you for all these years of helping and encouraging me, and being that person I can always count on. To my good friend and decoy Pieter Goossens, thank you for all your time and help in the protection phase of my training. Your work and dedication in our club, HV Roosdaal, is greatly appreciated. To the president of our club, Danny Goossens, thank you for giving your time generously in managing our club, keeping the field green and clean, and keeping everything functional. Thank you to my first coaches in dog sport, Kris Kotsopoulos and Jim Tokis; you've taught me to train my first Schutz dog and achieve IPO3 with him. Special thanks to my good friend, the president of FMBB and the owner of the Duvetorre Kennel, Johan Weckhuyzen. It was because of your help and because you took me under your wing when I first came to Belgium that I could make something of myself in this beautiful country. Thank you to my friend and photographer Natalie Hill for shooting the cover and the later parts of this book. Thank you to my friend and IPO world championship judge José Buggenhout for your very nice foreword for my book.

I dedicate this book to my mom, my dad, and my mentor and best friend, Julien Steenbeke. To my parents, thank you very much for devoting your lives to me and loving me unconditionally, so I can choose my passion as my occupation. To Julien, *Meester*, I thank you and salute you for everything you've taught me all these years, and being with me in all the good and bad weather on and off the training field. With this book, I hope to continue your legacy, so more people can benefit from the knowledge and skills you've passed on to me so generously.

About the Author

Felix is a canine behaviourist, professional dog trainer, and world championship competitor in IPO. He was born in 1977 in British Hong Kong. At the age of sixteen years, his parents sent him to Melbourne, Australia, to continue his education. He received his Bachelor of Science (Biology) at La Trobe University, Melbourne. During his undergraduate years, Felix began keeping and training working dogs. His hobby became such a fanatical passion that after his graduation he became a professional dog trainer.

In 2005, to further his Schutzhund competition career, Felix immigrated to Belgium. He entered his first world championships in FMBB 2006 Hungary and FCI 2006 Slovenia. In 2008, Felix started with his new canine partner Eclipse van de Duvetorre in FMBB as the youngest dog in the championship and moved up in the world ranking to 25th. The following year was very successful for the team, as they were ranked 16th in FMBB Czech Republic and 19th in FCI Austria, and became winners of the Belgian CAC Special Selection Trial. In 2015, Felix competed with his first Rottweiler in the IFR world championship in Italy and ranked number 9 in the world.

At the time of publication, Felix has competed in nine different world championships with dogs he's raised and trained from puppyhood. He's titled a total of seven dogs in Schutzhund/IPO and Mondio Ring, including Malinois, German Shepherd, and Rottweiler. He travels the world on a yearly basis to conduct seminars and workshops for the training of working dogs. He resides in Belgium where he continues with his training and research of the working breeds. To further understand his philosophies, you can contact Felix through the following links.

Website: www.FelixHo.be
Email: felix@felixho.be
Working-Dog: www.working-dog.eu/user/Felix-Ho-9612
Facebook: www.facebook.com/sacraalhart
Instagram: sacraalhart
Twitter: sacraalhart